1,000,000 Books

are available to read at

www.ForgottenBooks.com

Read online
Download PDF
Purchase in print

ISBN 978-1-332-23128-7
PIBN 10301704

This book is a reproduction of an important historical work. Forgotten Books uses state-of-the-art technology to digitally reconstruct the work, preserving the original format whilst repairing imperfections present in the aged copy. In rare cases, an imperfection in the original, such as a blemish or missing page, may be replicated in our edition. We do, however, repair the vast majority of imperfections successfully; any imperfections that remain are intentionally left to preserve the state of such historical works.

Forgotten Books is a registered trademark of FB &c Ltd.
Copyright © 2018 FB &c Ltd.
FB &c Ltd, Dalton House, 60 Windsor Avenue, London, SW19 2RR.
Company number 08720141. Registered in England and Wales.

For support please visit www.forgottenbooks.com

1 MONTH OF FREE READING

at

www.ForgottenBooks.com

By purchasing this book you are eligible for one month membership to ForgottenBooks.com, giving you unlimited access to our entire collection of over 1,000,000 titles via our web site and mobile apps.

To claim your free month visit:
www.forgottenbooks.com/free301704

* Offer is valid for 45 days from date of purchase. Terms and conditions apply.

English
Français
Deutsche
Italiano
Español
Português

www.forgottenbooks.com

Mythology Photography **Fiction** Fishing Christianity **Art** Cooking Essays Buddhism Freemasonry Medicine **Biology** Music **Ancient Egypt** Evolution Carpentry Physics Dance Geology **Mathematics** Fitness Shakespeare **Folklore** Yoga Marketing **Confidence** Immortality Biographies Poetry **Psychology** Witchcraft Electronics Chemistry History **Law** Accounting **Philosophy** Anthropology Alchemy Drama Quantum Mechanics Atheism Sexual Health **Ancient History** **Entrepreneurship** Languages Sport Paleontology Needlework Islam **Metaphysics** Investment Archaeology Parenting Statistics Criminology **Motivational**

THE
SUGAR BEET:

INCLUDING A

HISTORY OF THE BEET SUGAR INDUSTRY IN EUROPE,

VARIETIES OF THE SUGAR BEET, EXAMINATION, SOILS, TILLAGE,
SEEDS AND SOWING, YIELD AND COST OF CULTIVATION,
HARVESTING, TRANSPORTATION, CONSERVATION,
FEEDING QUALITIES OF THE BEET
AND OF THE PULP, ETC.

BY

LEWIS S. WARE, C.E., M.E.,

FELLOW OF L'ÉCOLE CENTRALE DES ARTS, AGRICULTURE, ET MANUFACTURES,
PARIS; MEMBER OF THE AMERICAN CHEMICAL SOCIETY.

ILLUSTRATED BY NINETY ENGRAVINGS.

PHILADELPHIA:
HENRY CAREY BAIRD & CO.,
INDUSTRIAL PUBLISHERS, BOOKSELLERS AND IMPORTERS,
810 WALNUT STREET.
1880.

Copyright by
LEWIS S. WARE,
1879.
Right of translation reserved.

COLLINS, PRINTER.

PREFACE.

A VERY ample Introduction leaves but little to be said by the author of this treatise by way of Preface. Suffice it to say, that the work of studying this subject, and preparing this book, has throughout been a pure labor of love, and has been undertaken with a view to contribute his portion towards a vast and vital measure for the wealth and industrial independence of his country.

The United States pays an annual tribute of $80,000,000 to foreign countries and foreign labor for sugar, and it is at once the most costly, and the most bulky single article which we import from abroad. There is no country in the world, and there never has been one, in which all of its people are or have been as thoroughly and completely employed as they should be, or would desire to be, and hence the supreme importance, by means of discrimination in that taxation which is necessary in every land, of naturalizing every possible industry, and thus adding to the employments of the people.

The beet would form a new and valuable addition to a proper rotation of crops in this country—a measure which must be practiced if our soil is to be rescued from that exhaustion which has steadily progressed since the settlement of America —and with its accompanying sugar industry would aid in that diversification of employments which must be established if the migratory tendencies of our people are to be arrested, and our civilization, wealth, and power are to be built up and carried to a high level. Beet sugar can, the author has no hesitation in saying, be here produced as cheaply as cane sugar is now furnished to us, and even if for a time it should cost more, it would be a most enlightened measure of statesmanship and national economy to add this one to our industries, at any cost.

There is nothing more delusive than mere prices as expressed in money of account. It may, for instance, be economical to buy an article at a high price, when the circumstances attending the production of that article are such as to produce a market for one's own labor, while it is dear to buy it at a low price when the production of the article makes no demand for that labor. Things produced abroad, which entirely destroy the power of our own unemployed people to produce an equal quantity of the same articles, are dear at any price, because the power to labor—almost the only capital possessed by the great body of the people—is the most perishable of all commodities, and, if not utilized upon the instant of production, is lost and gone forever. Further, price is no accurate or necessary measure of the human effort involved in the production of a thing—cheap things often being produced by means of the enslavement of man.

That the beet sugar industry will, ere many years, be established upon a firm and enduring foundation in this country, the author has not the shadow of a doubt. That it will finally become a magnificent one, like those of France and Germany, he is equally certain. If the publication of this book should result, in even a moderate degree, in opening the eyes of the American people to the magnitude of the interests involved, and in pointing out to them the true, necessary, and fundamental principles upon which success depends—*the proper selection and cultivation of the beet*—the writer will not feel that he has labored in vain.

L. S. W.

PHILADELPHIA, Nov. 25, 1879.

CONTENTS.

	PAGE
INTRODUCTION	xi

PART I.

CHAPTER I.

HISTORY OF THE FLUCTUATIONS IN THE BEET SUGAR INDUSTRY IN EUROPE.

Production of beet sugar in France, 1826–78	32
Germany	35
System of taxation in Germany	36
Production of the beet sugar in Zollverein, 1836–65; Austria	37
Average annual production, etc., of beet sugar in Austria, 1834–67; system of taxation in Austria; Belgium; system of taxation in Belgium	38
Holland; system of taxation in Holland; Russia; system of taxation in Russia; general production of beet sugar in Europe, 1877–78	39

CHAPTER II.

SYNOPSIS OF THE ATTEMPTS MADE IN THE UNITED STATES TO INTRODUCE THE BEET SUGAR INDUSTRY.

Production in California, 1870–73	43

CHAPTER III.

THE PRESENT CONDITION OF THE SUGAR INDUSTRY IN THE UNITED STATES.

Consumption of sugar in the United States, 1860–76; consumption in 1874	46
Countries from which imported, and quantities, 1877; sugar produced in the United States	47
Louisiana, Texas, Florida, etc.	48
Duties and sugar frauds	50
Polarization	51

CHAPTER IV.

PROBABLE RESULTS WHICH WOULD BE PRODUCED BY THE INTRODUCTION OF THE BEET SUGAR INDUSTRY IN THE UNITED STATES.

American yield of agricultural produce in 1876	56
French yield of agricultural produce in the arrondissement of Valenciennes	61

PART II.

CHAPTER I.
Varieties of the Beet.

	PAGE
Classification; Red Beet, or Red Castelnaudary; Yellow Beet, or Yellow Castelnaudary	63
German Red Mangel Wurzel; Long, White, Green-top Mangel Wurzel	64
Long, White, Red-top Mangel Wurzel; Yellow Globe Mangel Wurzel; Red Globe Mangel Wurzel	65
White Silesian; Magdeburg; Imperiale	67
Breslau, Electorale	68
White Silesian Green-top	69
White Silesian Rose-top; White Sugar Grayish-top; Improved Vilmorin	70
Improved Deprez	72
Simon Legrand; Tollet and Improved Carter	73

CHAPTER II.
Examination of the Beet.

With the microscope	74
Chemical examination	80
Sugar in the beet (various theories)	84
External qualities; shape of the beet	87

CHAPTER III.
Leaves of the Sugar Beet.

Analysis of roots	92
Analysis of leaves	93
Effect of stripping the leaves	94
Total elements taken up by the beets and leaves in one hectare of land	95
Author's experience in New Jersey	96
Loss of sugar by stripping	99

PART III.

CHAPTER I.
Soils. General Considerations.

Analysis of Prussian soils	103
Analysis of French soils	104

CHAPTER II.
Preparation of the Soil, or Tillage.

Cultivation in drills	111
Cultivation in hills	117

CHAPTER III.

Various Manures.

	PAGE
George Ville's investigations	125
Elements of which plants are composed	126
Organic; barnyard manures	127
Green manures; oil cake	129
Guano	130
Mineral fertilizers; nitric fertilizer	131
Nitrate of soda	133
Sulphate of ammonia; phosphoric fertilizers	135
Potassic fertilizers	137
Calcareous fertilizers	138
Comparative results obtained with chemical fertilizers and ordinary barnyard manure—beets	140
Champignon and Pellet's experiments; experiments of Corenwinder	144
Choice of a manure; experiments of Deherain	145
Experiments of Pagnoul	148
Vivien's views; George Ville's complete fertilizer	149
Corenwinder's experiments; Coignet's views	150
Joulie's experiments	151

CHAPTER IV.

Seeds and Sowing.

Generalities; analysis of Champignon and Pellet	152
Germination	155
Humidity	156
Heat; air	157
Light; treatment of the seed before sowing	158
Time for sowing	161
Depth of planting	163
Distance most favorable for the roots	165
Sowing broadcast	169
Transplanting	170
Mechanical devices for sowing	171
Changes during vegetation	173
Rain; experiments of Walkhoff	174
Heat; experiments of Champigon and Pellet	175

CHAPTER V.

Production and Improvement of the Seed of the Sugar Beet.

Hereditary principles	176
Characteristic points of beets rich in sugar; choosing of the mothers to be planted	177
Knauer's machine for dividing the roots according to their weight	178

CONTENTS.

	PAGE
Vilmorin's method	179
Mehay's experiments; Dervaux's idea	180
Mr. Walkhoff's views: selection of roots by Deprez & Co.; Viollette's views and tests	181
Simon Legrand's idea; Walkhoff's views	183
Saccharine changes in the roots; the flowers	185
The fruit	186

CHAPTER VI.

HARVESTING.

Time for harvesting	189
Methods of harvesting, machine, hand pulling	191

CHAPTER VII.

YIELD AND COST OF CULTIVATION.

Estimates of Payen	198
Farms in the arrondissement of Cambrai	199
German estimates	200
Walkhoff's figures of cost in Russia; the author's experience in New Jersey and Pennsylvania	201
Value of beets	202

CHAPTER VIII.

ROTATION OF CROPS.

Importance of a rational rotation of crops	207
Experience the best guide for the rotation of crops	211
Rotation practiced in France	212

PART IV.

CHAPTER I.

GENERAL CONSIDERATIONS ON ECONOMICAL TRANSPORTATION—DECAUVILLE, PROVIN, LINARD, ETC.

Duffriné Brothers' road locomotives	215
Corbin's idea	216
Decauville's idea	218
Porteur Decauville	220
Civieres for transportation of beets	221
Building of a silo near the main tract—System Decauville	223
Linard's idea	224
Aerial transportation; Hodgson's idea	225

	PAGE
Provin's idea	226
Support for the wire, Provin's idea	227
Gathering the beets upon the field	228
Starting	229
Arrival of the beets	230
Underground pipes, Linard's idea	232
Conclusions	235

CHAPTER II.

CONSERVATION OF THE SUGAR BEET.

History; general considerations	237
Causes of the loss of sugar; second growth	239
Heat; cold; want of ventilation; prevention of this loss	240
Causes of loss of weight	242
Silos	243
Chaptal's idea of a silo	244
Roots to be utilized shortly, piled on the ground with a slight covering of straw	245
System adopted in the Palatinate	246
Conical silo	247
Silos permitting gases to make their escape	248
Silo on a slant, preventing a deposit of water; Pailly's idea of facilitating the drainage	249
Walls of earth preventing disease from spreading; type of silo permitting the water resulting from evaporation to settle	250
Type of silo employed in Saxony	251
Economical type of silo	252
Good type of silo, ventilation being well understood	253
Type of mode of conservation where charcoal is placed between the layers and the bottom	255
Type of an underground house suitable for conservation in America	256
Preservation of the sugar beet; freezing; desiccation	258
Preservation of the juice; preservation of the leaves	259
Silo for preservation of leaves	260

PART V.

ENEMIES OF THE SUGAR BEET.

Insects and diseases	263
Insects; habits of Melolontha vulgaris	264
Destruction of the Melolontha vulgaris	267
Uses of the Melolontha vulgaris	268
Atomaria	270

	PAGE
Atomaria lineris	271
Curculilo	272
Silpha	273
Altica oleraca; Cassida; Agriote	276
Noctua segetum; habits	278
Destruction	279
Hadena bassicæ	280
Diptera	281
Diseases; Dr. Montague's theory	282
Root attacked by the "brown penetration"	283
Payen and Dumas's investigations	285
Microscopical examination of diseased roots	285
Drainage	289
Rachitis; hollowness of the beet	290

PART VI.

Feeding Qualities of the Beet.

Feeding qualities of the beet	293
Belgian manner of storing the beets when they are used for feeding purposes	296
Feeding qualities of the pulp made directly from the beet	297
Leduc's method of reducing the beet to a pulp by steam	298
The amount of fermented mass to be fed to sheep	299
The amount of fermented mass to be fed to an ox	300
Pulp from sugar factories	301
Amount of pulp to be fed to an ox	302
Pulp from distilleries; farm and distilleries of Ferme de la Briche	303
Building of Cail & Co. where cattle are fed on distillery refuse; pulp from System Leplay, System Champonnois	304
Basset's opinion of fermented pulp	305
Analysis of pulp; amount to be fed to a cow; Dr. Menrin's comparative table of nourishing qualities of beet pulps	306
Preservation of the pulp	307
Method of preservation at Ferme de la Briche	308
Leduc's improvement upon fermentation of the pulp	309
Feeding qualities of the leaves	311
Opinions of Dombasle, Boussingault, and Dumas; action upon the stomachs of animals	312
INDEX	313

INTRODUCTION.

AT the *Ecole Centrale des Arts, Agriculture, et Manufactures,* Paris, the author took special interest in chemical technology—the growth of the beet and the manufacture of sugar being one of the subdivisions of the subject—and he had the advantage of the advice of Payen, and Dumas, as well as of other eminent chemists. By these learned professors the importance of this great agricultural industry was especially impressed upon the minds of the students.

During a residence of fourteen years in France and Germany the most important beet-sugar establishments were visited, where practical and theoretical information was obtained with a view to future use; and a determination was made to plant the seed on various soils, and to ascertain the possibility of success in the United States, for if such extraordinary results were reached in Europe, why might they not be here? On returning to this country he corresponded extensively with parties—principally farmers—who were interested in the subject, and sent a printed form and circular to each, giving details of the preparation of the soil, the sowing of the seed, harvesting of the crop, etc. etc. These directions were generally followed when the cultivation was attempted; and various articles were written for the technical and daily papers either by the author himself or by others who had received information directly from him; and finally the correspondence became such that to attend to it would have consumed more time than he was able to give to it. It was then suggested that the entire subject should be written up and published in book form, where the manufacture of sugar as well as the various appliances should be given. The data which had previously been collected, with practical experience in planting and experimenting, were to be made use of. There were no authors to consult in the English language, and this fact was an additional inducement to publish such a book. It is true that Mr. E. B. Grant had written a small volume, giving a few interesting details pertaining to beet culture, in which some special lands in the Western States were recommended.

In England a book by Professor Crookes had appeared upon the Manufacture of Beet Sugar; but this was more upon the various mechanical and chemical details, with but little upon the culture of the beet itself. On the other hand, in French and German there existed a number of books pertaining to the manufacture of sugar, etc., where also some few minor agricultural principles were given. It would have been easy for the present writer to have made a translation from one of these, assuming the facts as authentic, without giving himself the trouble to test them. But these were found to be written with more or less prejudice, the one condemning the works of the other. For example, the French writers considered that the Germans paid too much attention to the sugar which the beet contained, and too little to the advantages that might be derived from the beet-pulp after a portion of the saccharine principles had been extracted; whilst the Germans argued that the French made an error quite the opposite of this.

A special visit to Europe was considered to be of the first importance, and this was undertaken. The sugar factories working only in the winter months, it became necessary to sail at that season, and the author arrived out in the midst of the sugar campaign in France, going thence to the other side of the Rhine, and visiting Belgium on his return. Provided with several letters of introduction, a most cordial reception was in all cases given him, and the new information from the manufacturer, chemist, and farmer was carefully noted. These, differing from each other in many cases, had for effect the origination of new ideas, which had not previously been published. The Paris Exhibition of 1878 being then held, the author took advantage of it to obtain further information, after which he returned to the United States.

It would have been easy, with the amount of information here given, to have written a much more extended treatise, but it has not been deemed advisable. Efforts have been made to make the book as complete as, if not more so than, any previous one—if such exists on the same subject. No mention has been made of the processes for the manufacture of sugar and alcohol, as it is proposed to follow this up with such treatises when the importance of the plant itself is fully understood, the author having for several years made a special study of plans of buildings, machines to be made use of for the manufacture of alcohol and sugar.

Evidently the matter here treated is so varied that errors have doubtless occurred, but every effort has been made to prevent them, and it is hoped that any, if such there be, will not be of such importance as to be the direct cause of misleading the reader.

The book has not been written solely for the so-called practical man, as it would then have been impossible to enter into numerous technical considerations; but, however intricate these may at first appear, they will finally be understood by all, as it is a remarkable fact that the American farmer is no longer a man who works blindly upon rules of husbandry which have been transmitted for generations from father to son, but investigates for himself. Knowing these facts, it is probable that the theoretical portions will not be out of place in his hands. There are some well known agricultural principles which the farmer is neglectful in carrying out, and the author has therefore called attention to them with a view, if possible, to produce a change for the better.

As shown, in a complete history of the numerous changes which have taken place in the beet-sugar industry, the fluctuations have been mainly due to absurd systems of internal taxation in France, which have discriminated against a great domestic industry which was of immense value to the people and the country; whilst, on the contrary, in Austria and Germany a steady increase in the number of factories has taken place,—the first named country, being unable to consume at home its entire product, has become a large exporter. In Russia the industry is in an equally flourishing condition.

The United States has made some few attempts to introduce the sugar industry, and the non-success of these efforts has been mainly due to the want of sufficient information, which the author has attempted here to supply. It is true we have done something in cane sugar in Louisiana, but, for reasons which he has given, he does not deem it possible that this country can be rendered independent of the rest of the world by these supplies, or by those from such sources as the maple tree, sorghum, glucose, etc. etc. The thorough and complete development of the sugar industry in this country would introduce immense economic changes as well here as in other countries, for when the $80,000,000 annually paid for foreign labor in the form of sugar is paid to our own people, it will become a source of wealth equal to its entire annual amount—adding to our productions this whole sum, and, at the same time, rendering the soil more productive for other crops.

The author has made a study of the many varieties of beet, all containing sugar in different proportions; those of high percentage being small in size, and most desirable when sugar is the chief object. The large will give greater satisfaction to the farmer when the sugar is not of importance. There are other types, however, which are a sort of compromise between the sugar manufacturer and the farmer. The soils on which they give the best results have also been mentioned, and an opinion has been advanced which does not entirely correspond with those given by seed growers representing interested parties, but rather from the author's experience in growing beets on various soils in this country. This latter subject has been well and carefully studied, and it is, he considers, clearly demonstrated that the physical properties of a soil are of more importance than the chemical, as these last can readily be changed by a judicious selection and use of fertilizers, while, on a soil having no subsoil, the idea of producing the beet would be irrational. A comparison of analyses of soils of France and other parts of Europe has for this country been considered of interest.

The general examination of the beet has been done with equal care; and the possibility of ascertaining the quality of the root by its exterior signs, as well as the various opinions of chemists as to the locality of the sugar in the root, and the manner in which it is formed, has been given. The tillage of the soil being effected in a manner somewhat different from what one is in the habit of seeing, care has been taken to give the details of the same, including the methods of working and types of ploughs made use of, but no particular plough has been recommended, as our agricultural implements are far superior to those used on the continent of Europe. The various mechanical devices which the American farmer has at his disposal would doubtless enable him, while paying higher for labor, to produce the roots as cheaply as is done in Europe—cheapness in the end being more certainly reached through that intellectual development which enables men to avail themselves of the forces of nature, than through that brutalization of human beings which shuts out all possibility of doing more with them than merely using them as we do beasts of burthen.

The weeding, under ordinary cultivation (drills), cannot be satisfactorily accomplished, and efforts have been made to show the advantages of the cultivation in hills, which is without doubt better for beet culture, and especially in America, where the importance of using a subsoil plough does not seem to have been as yet well understood. At the present day many of the European farmers have discovered, now that it is too late, that better results would have been obtained both to their lands and their crops if it had been adopted years ago—the only objection being that it requires a special appliance. But in a country where the root has not yet been planted, where a given type of implement is no longer an obstacle, it should be the system.

The author has made a thorough investigation of the various manures best adapted for given soils, and regards the advantage as being with a chemical fertilizer, this being indorsed by the greater number of scientists in a theoretical way, and by farmers practically.

It is true that barnyard manure is most excellent, and has held its own for years on all soils and in various portions of the globe, but in the special case of beet culture, given soluble elements are requisite, and these must be placed at the disposal of the root at given periods. This organic manure is obliged to undergo changes before any benefit can be derived from its use. Then, again, on analyzing it, it is found that a comparatively small quantity (a little over 2 per cent.) is of any use. The natural green manures and oil cake and guano have their advantages and disadvantages, which have been pointed out. As for the mineral fertilizers, they are divided into four classes, each corresponding to the element the plant requires, these being nitrogen, phosphoric acid, potassa, and lime. As shown, when used in a judicious manner, they will yield most excellent results; if in excess, they will produce the contrary effect. The nitric fertilizer, for example, in too large quantities, will ruin the soil and sugar of the beet, exhausting the former, and introducing into the latter, chemicals which have for effect the destruction of its commercial value; this type of fertilizer being the most important for the growth of the root when in certain quantities. The advantages of phosphoric acid have been pointed out, as well as the mistake in using non-soluble phosphates, as Liebig and several others have done for years.

Potassic fertilizers, however successful they have been in Germany, the author considers that their use should be to a certain extent restricted, as they do not facilitate the formation of the sugar, and few advantages can be derived from their employment. The calcareons fertilizers, as shown, are of the highest importance when the soil does not contain sufficient lime, these facilitating the action of the acids of the stratum below. To make even more evident the advantages of the chemical fertilizer over barnyard manure, comparative experiments have been given which clearly show the truth of this apparently mere hypothesis. Knowing these facts, what manures can be recommended? Evidently these vary according to the localities; and the author has endeavored to give the various methods of ascertaining the most suitable for a given soil, these being principally based upon experience. Besides these, various fertilizers are sold, and highly recommended for beet culture, the composition of which has been thought of interest.

The advantages of a small or large seed have been carefully studied, and the importance of each farmer growing his own has been pointed out. These seeds after being placed in the soil germinate under the influence of certain agents. Touching the advantages or disadvantages of activating the germinating principles with chemicals, the author has bestowed great pains, as well as to the sowing and the time, which have a considerable influence. Mechanical sowing seems of late to be much preferred, as greater regularity can be obtained. No special machine is given, for reasons mentioned above.

The importance of planting the roots in close proximity has been clearly shown, to this the author has added many other arguments, as to the advantage of the beet being grown on the angle of a rectangle or a lozenge, and finally the various operations which follow the sowing are given. For many years past it has been clearly proven that with proper selection the roots can be greatly improved, and most remarkable results have been obtained. There is no reason why similar improvements should not be made on our American soils. The possibility of growing a seed which will become acclimated, is an important consideration, and the knowledge of the manner in which the mother roots are planted in the soil, and the resulting seed harvested, renders the problem most easy. Besides these principles, the author has explained the importance of a correct rotation of crops, which is most beneficial to the growth of the plant, and renders the possibility of exhausting the soil far less probable. A rotation that gives satisfaction on one soil may not on another, the principles being the same in all cases; great advantage will be derived for the crop immediately following the beet, as the soil is in a most excellent condition for its reception. The ploughing is not in this case a necessity, and it is but just that the last planted crop should bear a portion of the expense of the cultivation of this root.

Various estimates of cultivation for Germany and France have been given, from which one can form but a slight idea of what may be done in this country; but, from the author's experience and from letters received from farmers where their opinions have been advanced, a fair surmise may be made as to the possible cost in the United States. These beets should be paid for not in accordance, as many suppose, with their weight, as the buyer would then purchase an article from which he might suffer considerably. Paying for the roots proportionately to the sugar they actually contain is far more rational, but unfortunately in Europe it is up to the present day rarely carried out. The farmer's and manufacturer's interest being so radically different, a method giving satisfaction to both is most difficult. The author advocates a new principle, by the application of which the farmer produces an excellent root, for which can be justly paid an excellent price. The beet has leaves, the functions of which are similar to those of other plants; but the possibility of ascertaining the quality of the root by the exterior signs of the leaves, makes them of immense interest in this special case. They form an enormous portion of the crop, and are good for feeding purposes, but, as here shown, should not be utilized, but permitted to fall on the ground and act as a fertilizer, as the necks of the beets would otherwise become large. As to their effects as a food, upon the animals, the author has gathered some most interesting facts.

The advantages or disadvantages of using the beet and pulp for feeding purposes, as practiced on a large scale in France and Belgium, at the farms the author had occasion to visit, and where several practical points were obtained, are here communicated to the reader. When we remember the vast amount of straw that in the Western States is burned, the knowledge of being able to utilize it for feeding purposes is considered of great interest—the fermented mass being much relished by the cattle. Slicing the root is advocated by some, but reducing the total to a pulp, with straw, is far preferable. As for the pulp refuse of the sugar factory, it contains a large amount of nitric fattening elements, which, when utilized, will, as shown, give excellent results. There still remains the pulp from the distilleries, these existing in all countries where the beet-sugar factories are established. The author visited Ferme de la Briche, owned by Cail & Co., one of the largest sugar-beet distilleries in the world, and of which a general description is given. The possibility of preserving this pulp during the entire year renders its study of great interest.

The question as to the best method of harvesting the beets is of the highest importance; if this work be not properly done, considerable loss may ensue. Harvesting with a plough often gives excellent results, especially in the case of cultivation in hills.

As soon as the roots are taken from the soil they require certain care, to which attention is called, this being previous to transportation. This latter operation has been carefully studied, and the account is far more complete than any thing of the same sort, to his knowledge, written up to the present day; he, having visited the farms and factories where these different devices were working, had the advantage of judging of the results to be expected. Each plan gives satisfaction in different ways, and for this reason they are all of interest, and every possible circumstance that can present itself is here given, which permits of the carrying of the beet from one place to another.

As to the *silos*, the author has made a considerable effort to point out their qualities and defects, as they are of great importance for Americans, as any loss of sugar produced by the excessive cold, fermentation, etc., would be a direct cause of failure in many cases, which would be attributed to poor beets, and which in reality was in consequence of neglect. The situation of these silos is also important. With this the various methods proposed and adopted for the conservation of the root, such as desiccation, or uniting the juice with lime, to render all alteration impossible, have been given.

The study of the ravages of the enemies of the beet has been done with equal care. Similar cases may have to be contended with in America. Efforts have been made to ascertain the causes of the same, and methods adopted to prevent their renewal. As for the insects, these will not in all probability be identical, but, without doubt, of the same entomological classification. The habits of those unknown will be somewhat similar to those existing in Europe. The author's idea in giving these is to show the reader how methods of destruction can be deduced from a knowledge of their manner of living, and, however numerous these insects are, it is possible to get rid of them; and, if collected in a mass, can find some direct industrial application. This chapter is very different from any thing hitherto presented to the public, and it is to be hoped for this reason, if for no other, it will not be without interest.

The whole treatise has been most elaborately and carefully illustrated by drawings made by the author himself, or procured from beet farmers, distillers, and others in France.

In conclusion, let it be remembered that this work on the sugar beet has not been, like others, written with a view to self-interest. The author has no lands to recommend, is not a manufacturer of a given fertilizer, etc., but has endeavored to ascertain the truth, and this with the sole idea of yielding information upon a subject of which but little is known in America, and to *assert* that in the Northern States there exist comparatively few lands which will not yield, if scientifically planted, beets equal if not superior to those of Europe; not in all cases with profit, for the elements the plant requires for its development might be wanting, and these must be furnished, and would render the expense far too great; but it can be justly said that the exceptions make the rule.

THE SUGAR BEET.

PART I.

CHAPTER I.

HISTORY OF THE FLUCTUATIONS IN THE BEET-SUGAR INDUSTRY IN EUROPE.

The Sugar Beet of to-day in no way resembles the so-called beet taken to Bohemia by the Barbarians after the fall of the Roman Empire, as it contained but few saccharine elements, and these were not in sufficient quantities to attract attention at that period, and it was not until 1705 that Olivier de Serres considered that alcohol might be obtained from the fermentation of the beet, as he was convinced that sugar therein existed. The first suggestions relating to the possibilities of the extraction of the same were brought to notice in 1747 by Margaff, a Prussian chemist. He, taking advantage of principles previously discovered, was able to extract 5 per cent. of sugar possessing all the saccharine properties that were known to exist in sugar from the cane. Some years now elapsed before any great attention was given to this important subject.

1786. Abbé Commerel published a book calling the farmer's attention to the advantages gained by the cultivation of the roots for feeding purposes. Long after this Archard, another chemist, born in France but residing in Prussia, republished and augmented considerably the researches of Margaff. The ideas of the latter, from having been too theoretical, had not until then found any practical application. Archard was encouraged by Frederick the Great, and was able, after many years of continued perseverance, to give a solution to this most difficult problem.[1] These experiments were brought to an end on account of the death of his great protector, who had been both a lover of science and of his country.

1796. They were again resumed, and a beet sugar factory was established near Steinau on the Oder.

In the treatise published by Archard he made known the methods adopted, and also spoke of the possibility of feeding the pulp to cattle, the advantages of the manures resulting, etc.; in other words, what has at the present day been realized. Here we must not only admire a man of science who was able to predict events years in advance, but also one of honor, as $30,000 had been offered him by a society in England[2] to make the world believe that his attempts had not been a success. This proposal was fortunately rejected, and two years later a new offer was made of $120,000,

---

[1] See reports written by Napoleon.
[2] See Annales de Chemie, 1799.

which had the same fate as the first. In Archard's report he considered that there could be no doubt that it was possible to extract the sugar from the beet at f. 0.65 ($0.13) per kilog. (2.2 lbs.), and if the existing methods were improved upon that this cost would be greatly reduced. A committee was appointed, consisting of Chaptal, Parmentier, and others, to ascertain the truth of this assertion; and unfortunately it was found to be erroneous, as but little over 1 per cent. in sugar had been extracted. Under these conditions, it would have been practically impossible either to sell or manufacture. Soon after this Napoleon endeavored to destroy the prosperity of Great Britain by excluding English sugars from the French market. Evidently under these circumstances the possibility of home manufacture became more favorable, and a second committee of chemists was formed, composed of Chaptal, Crespel, Delesse, Barruel, and Isnard. These gentlemen's ideas combined led to many improvements on the processes that had heretofore existed. During this period the English made a third attempt to destroy this future industry. Sir Humphry Davy published his work on beet sugar, in which he made most positive assertions that this sugar was far too sour for consumption. Notwithstanding this fact, every power in Europe commenced taking a most active interest in a scheme, by the application of which in the future, it would be possible to produce at home an article of daily need that formed one of the greatest yearly imports.

In 1812 Delessert, who had been studying the subject for eighteen years, announced to Chaptal that he had succeeded in obtaining sugar from the beet under favoring circumstances. This was repeated to Napoleon, who immediately visited the factory at Passy. Samples of this sugar were afterwards exhibited in the palace of the Tuilleries as being one of the greatest wonders of the day, as it was thought that there existed a possibility of France being independent of England. A decree was that very day issued in order that this industry should be made a success. The factories of Barruel and Chappelet with two others formed establishments where a special and practical education was to be given concerning the fabrication of beet sugar. The total number of students was not to exceed 200.

In 1812 and 1813 over 2,000,000 kilog. of sugar were manufactured.

In 1814 and 1815 the wars and excessive rain caused here again a most unfortunate change. The Cossacks were encamped on the very soil on which beets were grown for the supply of these years.

During the period of the Restoration the small home and colonial protection that had heretofore existed was now again at an end, and to sustain competition with foreign sugars became impossible. But one factory was able to survive. Soon after this various essays on the Sugar Beet were written wherein new processes were proposed, and by the adoption of the same 5 per cent. of sugar could be practically extracted, this being a great advance over the 2 per cent. that the factories up to this date had been able to realize.

1822 to 1825. New efforts were made, and over 100 new factories came into existence, giving a total yield of 5000 tons.

1829. The amount of sugar produced and consequently the number of acres planted in beets was satisfactory, but just at this period the first discussion arose in the Assembly concerning the importance, as they considered, of an increase in the taxation. The bill was carried, and to go into effect in the coming year.

1830. The Revolution prevented this taxation being carried out.

1831. The most interesting researches of Pelouze were brought to light, these proving that the quality of the sugar varied with the beets, and the importance of a selection of the same. This idea added greatly to the progress realized.

1836. The number of factories in existence was 436, and the colonial importers became alarmed and endeavored to influence the government to tax the home production in such a manner as not to interfere with the imported article.

1837. The number of factories was at a maximum, but the Comte d'Argout proposed the establishment of a system of taxation on home sugars, to go into effect in 1838 and to be increased in 1839, etc. The consequence of this was, that 166 factories completely disappeared.

1840. It was proposed to suppress the culture of the beet, and for this purpose the government was to purchase the existing factories; but Thiers carried the house, he having made a most eloquent speech proving the absurdity of such a scheme, but, on the contrary, showed that, if left alone, or better still, encouraged, benefits would result to the French nation.

1843. The government proposed again to purchase the existing factories after which they were to be abolished, but here again Thiers objected and carried his point.

1847. The colonial and home sugars are equally taxed. That is to say, the duty on one was equal to the tax on the fabrication of the other. The only rational law passed during this period was the prohibition of the importation of foreign refined sugars, and in this manner the French refiners were protected.

1848. The French Republic being in existence, slavery in the colonies was abolished; this was an immense advantage to home production, the tax still remaining the same.

1851. A new law unfortunately nearly brought about a panic; it consisted in obliging all Beet Sugar establishments to have each a given room where the government authorities could have the production under their direct control. This should be closed with lock and key and opened only with their permission.

1853. Alcohol was selling at a high figure, and many of the factories were transformed into distilleries.

1854. Some 80 others followed their example.

1855. The war in the Crimea, by the withdrawal of men for the army and other circumstances, caused a considerable change, which was injurious in its results.

1860. The system of taxation that existed in 1847 was again re-established, and the struggle still continued between those interested in home and colonial sugars, and it was again feared that the state would purchase the factories. Notwithstanding this fact the production had nearly doubled.

1864. The tax was again augmented, and new factories that were to have been built were abandoned. Between 1860 and 1865 international treaties were

Holland, Prussia and other nations, making special concessions to the exports of each country.

1865. The manufacturers were greatly encouraged, as the government had declared that the existing system of taxation was not correct, and promised an immediate revisal.

1871, '72, and '73, etc. Instead of a decrease, this tax has been augmented.

As shown, France has been obliged to go through many difficulties before the beet sugar industry has been established on a solid basis, and even at the present day the success would be greater than it is if many of their foolish laws were abolished.

We consider it of interest to give a complete table showing the amounts produced for given years, which will form a synopsis of all we have above said.

Production of Beet Sugar in France 1826–78.

Years.	Number of Factories.[1]	Production in Kilog.[2]
1826–27	—	2,400,000
1827–28	—	2,700,000
1828–29	—	2,896,000
1829–30	—	4,400,000
1830–31	—	7,000,000
1831–32	—	9,000,000
1832–33	—	12,000,000
1833–34	—	20,000,000
1834–35	—	30,000,000
1835–36	—	40,000,000
1836–37	436	48,968,000
1837–38	580	49,236,000
1838–39	560	39,199,000
1839–40	420	22,000,000
1840–41	385	29,939,000
1841–42	389	31,234,000
1842–43	383	29,560,000
1843–44	322	28,660,000
1844–45	290	36,457,000
1845–46	302	40,546,000
1846–47	298	53,795,000
1847–48	305	64,316,000
1848–49	280	38,639,000
1849–50	287	62,175,000
1850–51	300	76,151,000
1851–52	325	68,583,000
1852–53	335	75,275,000
1853–54	299	76,951,000
1854–55	204	44,669,000
1855–56	275	92,197,000
1856–57	281	83,126,000
1857–58	337	151,514,000

[1] The number of factories given above is in many cases only an approximation, obtained by taking an average of the various reports published, but few of which seem to agree.

[2] A kilogram = 2.2047 lbs.

Years.	Number of Factories.	Production in Kilog.
1858–59	349	132,650,000
1859–60	335	126,479,000
1860–61	334	100,876,000
1861–62	346	146,414,000
1862–63	360	173,677,000
1863–64	362	108,466,000
1864–65	398	149,014,000
1865–66	418	265,489,000
1866–67	435	204,069,000
1867–68	452	224,767,000
1868–69	456	206,885,000
1869–70	463	282,159,000
1870–71	482	282,109,000
1871–72	494	324,429,000
1872–73	320	395,255,000
1873–74	527	383,219,000
1874–75	524	437,996,000
1875–76	524	462,320,000
1876–77	530	235,000,000
1877–78	513	325,000,000

These figures are sufficient to show the rapid increase of this industry in the last 50 years. As will be noticed, the yearly production does not depend upon the number of factories in existence, as in 1837 these were 580, and the sugar manufactured was 49,236,000 kilog., whilst at the present day, with only 513, we have a yield of 325,000,000. This has been owing to the absurd system of taxation mentioned above, causing in many cases complete failures, or again, the season had been unfavorable, and the crops were not then sufficient to supply a given factory, and consequently the owner preferred and was frequently obliged to wait for the coming year.

The beet sugar establishments are mostly situated in the northern portion of France, for example, in the Department du Nord there exist 150, in the Pas de Calais and Aisne 91 in each, while in Yonne, Meuse, Nièvre, Loiret, Marne, etc., but 1 in each. The most important arrondissement in the Nord is Cambrai.

We know of no better manner of proving the evident progress realized and the general good done to the community than the recalling of a few figures.[1] From 1826 to 1835 but 9 factories existed in Cambrai, and during the last portion of 1835 the amount of sugar produced was 700,000 kilog., working 14,000,000 kilog. of beets. The pulp and resulting molasses were scarcely utilized, and produced consequently little or no alcohol or meat. The amount of land under cultivation in beets was 360 hectares,[2] and was worth but 3000 francs per hectare. The production of wheat amounted to 400,000 hectolitres,[3] and 18,000 head of cattle were raised.

In 1875, in this same arrondissement, the number of factories existing was 32; in these the motive power was 3248 H. P., using 93,900 tons of coal. As many as seven thousand workmen were employed in 1875-76; the number of kilog. of beets worked was 694,580,000, yielding 38,474,365 kilog. of sugar, 173,750,000 kilog. of pulp, sufficient to produce 1,700,000 kilog. of meat, besides which 24,525,000 kilog. of molasses, yielding 60,000 hectolitres of alco-

---

[1] See Reports of E. Macarez, "fabricants de sucre de l'arrondissement de Cambrai," Paris Exposition, 1878.

[2] Hectare = $2\frac{1}{2}$ acres. [3] Hectolitre = $26\frac{1}{2}$ gallons.

hol at 100° B.[1] The hectare of land is now worth 7000 to 8000 francs. The production of wheat is 684,416 hectolitres, and 32,500 head of cattle are yearly fattened. This industry represents a capital of twenty-five millions of francs. We have not considered in the above the numerous other factories that depend entirely upon the existence and activity of the beet sugar industry.

Germany.

From the time of Archard's failure until 1830 but little sugar was manufactured. Then some few attempts were made, but it was not until Schubarth returned from France that any great progress was realized. This gentleman, having studied the matter, became afterwards an expert, and it is principally through his influence that the present success has been achieved. During the twenty years that had elapsed the Prussians watched with every possible attention the various scientific improvements that had taken place, and had seen the struggles to overcome various difficulties, after which they did not simply content themselves by exactly imitating what had been previously done, but, on the contrary, saw the defects and prevented their renewal.

The factories that were established (the same rule holds good at the present time) had a general organization for the purchase of the beets from the surrounding farmers, who were also financially interested in the success of the enterprise. The roots were paid for in

---

[1] B. means according to Beaumé's scale.

accordance with their actual value for sugar manufacture. The consequence of this was and is that the yield per acre in roots is not as great as in other countries (Russia being excepted), as here the beets are raised for their sugar alone.

The system of taxation also is most excellent, this is on the green roots. The amount is constant, it being on a supposed yield of eight per cent. in sugar. It seems at first not just that this tax should be the same for soils where the percentage of sugar and yield is greater than on others where the circumstances are unfavorable. Evidently, on the contrary, the cousequence of this method is that the beets are of a better quality than in other countries, owing to the special attention given by the farmers to the subject, and an increase of over two per cent. in the yield of sugar is obtained.

We would call attention to the fact that in 1850 the production of sugar was 1,066,979 cwt., and in 1864 this was 3,413,214, or more than three times as much. This increase is greater for a given time than is to be found in any other country in Europe, Austria excepted; at the present day it surpasses that of France. The factories are in great numbers near Magdeburg. Of the most important in Germany may be mentioned that of Waghaeusel, near Carlsruhe, 3500 men, women, and children finding employment; also that of M. Schuetzenback, in Gallicia, where 82,000,000 lbs. of sugar are yearly manufactured. As a general thing the sugar made in the Zollverein is of a fine quality.

Production of the Beet-Sugar in Zollverein,[1] *1836-65.*

Year.	Factories working.	Roots utilized, cwt.	Production, cwt.	Consumption per head, lbs.
1836-37	122	506,923	28,162	0.11
1837-38	156	2,763,942	153,552	0.40
1838-39	159	2,904,208	163,158	0.62
1839-40	152	4,405,637	253,198	0.85
1840-41	145	4,829,734	284,102	1.03
1841-42	135	5,131,516	314,817	1.11
1842-43	98	2,475,745	154,734	0.81
1843-44	105	4,349,667	286,162	0.70
1844-45	98	3,890,404	259,360	1.04
1845-46	96	4,455,092	303,068	1.03
1846-47	107	5,633,848	402,418	1.14
1847-48	127	7,676,000	536,837	1.52
1848-49	145	9,886,000	717,154	2.25
1849-50	148	11,525,671	847,475	2.75
1850-51	184	14,724,309	1,066,979	3.13
1851-52	234	18,289,901	1,261,372	4.01
1852-53	238	21,717,096	1,696,948	5.25
1853-54	227	18,469,890	1,420,761	5.13
1854-55	222	19,188,402	1,572,820	4.61
1855-56	216	21,839,799	1,747,184	4.84
1856-57	233	27,551,208	2,071,519	5.58
1857-58	249	28,915,134	2,409,594	7.06
1858-59	257	36,668,557	2,887,288	7.76
1859-60	256	34,399,317	2,915,196	9.10
1860-61	247	29,354,032	2,530,520	8.23
1861-62	247	31,692,394	2,515,269	7.51
1862-63	247	36,719,259	2,760,847	7.37
1863-64	253	39,911,529	3,023,600	8.17
1864-65	270	41,641,204	3,413,214	9.01
1874-75	....	55,072,412	5,011,589	

Austria.

Archard, in his book,[2] mentions the existence of a factory as early as 1802. After this very little was

---

[1] Zeitschrift des Vereines für die Rutenzucker Industrie im Zollverein, 1866, 67.

[2] Fabrication de Sucre de Betterave, 1812.

done until 1831, when others were built. The general conduct of this industry is shown in the table below.

Average Annual Production, etc., of Beet-Sugar in Austria, 1834-67.

Years.	No. of Factories working.	Roots utilized, cwt.	Production	Exports.	Imports.	Consumpt. per capita, lbs.
1834-39	37	605,616	30,270	38	518,193	1.52
1839-44	42	1,577,995	78,875	89	574,470	1.42
1844-49	59	1,729,280	103,757	150	568,955	1.81
1849-54	97	5,196,896	311,814	324	787,478	3.01
1854-59	119	11,712,692	820,080	88	581,489	3.00
1859-64	135	17,798,429	1,246,090	21,058	71,125	3.51
1864-67	139	19,201,861	1,344,136	506,074	2,115	2.36

The most striking feature of these figures is the enormous increase in the exports in eight years' time.

The system of taxation is at the option of the manufacturer, this being either on the beets, as in Germany, or on the capacity of the existing machines.

Belgium.

Nothing of any special interest is to be found here, the historical events having depended entirely upon France, and the sugar manufactured is of an inferior quality. But at the same time the total production per head is greater than in any other country in Europe, this being 19 kilog. (41.8 lbs.). This figure being in excess of the consumption, the difference is exported. The system of taxation is upon the juice at the rate of

1,500 grammes[1] of sugar to the hectolitre at 15° C.[2] (59° F.[3]).

Holland.

This industry is making yearly and rapid progress, and the beets are of a most excellent quality. The number of factories in 1867 was only 10, and at the present day is over 40.

The system of taxation is at the option of the manufacturer, either from the juice,[4] as in Belgium, or on the amount of sugar actually produced.

Russia.

Here, also, within a recent period the beet sugar industry has been yearly increased. The beets are good, but their quality seems to vary according to the zone in which they are planted.

The system of taxation is based on an estimate established by experts. This consequently varies according to circumstances. If the manufacturer can produce more than indicated by the government authorities the surplus is free from tax.

The general production of beet sugar in Europe and the number of factories and consumption per head are as follows:—

---

[1] Gramme = 15.43 grs.

[2] C. means Centigrade scale of the thermometer.

[3] F. means Fahrenheit scale of the thermometer.

[4] As the beets here are much richer in sugar, the supposed basis is consequently considerably higher, it being 1,635 grammes to the hectolitre.

Countries where factories exist.	Production in 1877–78.	Approximate consumption per capita.	Factories existing.
Germany	375,000,000 kilgs.	6 kilogs.	330
France	325,000,000 "	9 "	513
Austria, Hungary	245,000,000 "	2 "	248
Russia, Poland	250,000,000 "	2 "	288
Belgium	50,000,000 "	6 "	153
Holland, Sweden, Denmark	25,000,000 "	8 "	42
	1,270,000,000 "	. . . .	1574

The above figures also show the difference in the results obtained in Germany over France, with 200 less factories.

CHAPTER II.

SYNOPSIS OF THE ATTEMPTS MADE IN THE UNITED STATES TO INTRODUCE THE BEET SUGAR INDUSTRY.

THE following has but little interest, as the success has been but negative, owing to the fact that the experiments have, as a general thing, been made by those having but little knowledge of principles which, if not observed, will in all cases result in failure. The earliest attempts were made in 1830, by a company formed in Philadelphia, having for presidents John Vaughn and James Ronaldson. But little or nothing was accomplished, as *practical information was then wanting*. In 1839, the "Northampton Beet Sugar Co." was organized by David Lee Child, and 1300 lbs. of sugar were obtained, but here for similar reasons ended.

In 1863 a small company was formed in Livingston County, Illinois, and has since been transferred to Stephenson County, in the same State.

In 1864 Gennert Brothers purchased a large farm at Chatsworth, Illinois; their beets were said to be good in quality, but their capital was too small for the enterprise. The farm was purchased by the "German Beet Sugar Co.," but the lands were badly selected, and with this poor seed, and the entire establishment was removed to Freeport, Illinois.

The next factory was established in 1866 at Fond du Lac, Wisconsin, by Bonestel & Otto. It was contended that great success was attained with a small capital, and that the soil was well suited to the enterprise. Strange to say, that in 1870 they removed to California, where the Alvarado Co. was formed. The following year, it, as well as the Sacramento Beet Sugar Co. commenced operations. The first had a capital of $75,000, and the second but $15,000 was under the direction of a French Count. The latter has not since been heard from. The Alvarado Co. achieved a fair success, but owing to the bad management of several so-called technical directors, bad machinery, and small capital had for a final result the breaking up of the works. In this same State we may mention the Soquel and Isleton factories. These have accomplished but little.

During 1870 Tyler Beach, Secretary of the Santa Clara Valley Agricultural Society, informed the State that a beet sugar company had been organized at San José; shortly after this an enterprise was started by Germans, who formed a company at Black Hawk, Wisconsin. The success was not as great as was expected, on account of the small supply of water at their disposal.

In 1877 Mr. Joseph Wharton attempted the growth of the beet near Elwood Station, N. J.; the soil being principally sand, these experiments were not a success.

It would be impossible for us even to mention the various minor attempts that have been made in nearly every State of the Union; the most absurd were those in the Southern States. The Agricultural Department of the United States has done all in its power to encourage the industry for years past, and beet sugar machinery has been allowed to enter free of duty; besides this, several States have offered special inducements. In April, 1872, the Legislature of New Jersey enacted that for a period of ten years beet sugar factories should be exempt from taxation. The most deserving of all the States is Maine, by which several thousand dollars are to be yearly given to any company that will organize a beet sugar factory, and besides this, a premium for every pound of sugar produced; in consequence of which a factory was started at Portland in 1878. During their working period they manufactured several thousand pounds of sugar. In 1879 this company contracted with the growers for large quantities of beets and will utilize these the coming season. These inducements are great, and we are convinced that ere long that State will set the true example. We are glad to add that during this season the Delaware Beet Sugar Co. will also make its first attempt.

The State Agricultural Society of California reported in 1874 that the total production of beet sugar was—

In 1870	500,000 lbs.
" 1871	800,000 "
" 1872	1,125,000 "
" 1873	1,500,000 "

Which shows an increase, but these figures are not in accordance with the addition which should be looked for from the number of new factories that have already been mentioned.

For years past many of our prominent men, among whom may be mentioned Henry Clay, have predicted great results from the introduction of this industry into the United States, and we have every reason to believe that if the ideas presented in the following pages are adhered to, success will, in the not distant future, be certain.

CHAPTER III.

THE PRESENT CONDITION OF THE SUGAR INDUSTRY IN THE UNITED STATES.

OF all the articles entering our ports from foreign countries sugar is the most important, not only in its actual value but its cubical volume; hence for this, if for no other reason, the importance of adopting some plan by means of which the millions that are sent elsewhere for the employment of foreign capital and labor shall remain at home, as a country should grow and manufacture, as far as possible, all products which it consumes. The importance of this was fully demonstrated during our late war, as well in the South as in the North.

Unlike many of our imports, sugar does not enter into immediate consumption, but passes through a refining process, which industry alone gives employment to 10,000 men, and requires an annual capital of $15,000,000. The following table shows the fluctuation in the import of this article for years past. We would call attention to the fact that the consumption varies with the times, and it may generally be considered that if in a given year the consumption *per capita* is great during that same period, the general financial condition of the country has been good. As shown, there exists a slow increase *per capita*, which has not

Consumption of Sugar in the United States.

Years.	Consumption.		Imported, in tons (2240 lbs.).	Domestic, in tons (2240 lbs.).
	Total in tons (2240 lbs.).	Per capita in lbs.		
1860	415,281	29.56	296,250	119,031
1861	363,819	26.14	241,420	122,399
1862	432,411	30.73	241,411	191,000
1863	284,308	25.00	231,398	52,910
1864	220,660	19.00	192,660	28,000
1865	350,809	24.08	345,809	5,000
1866	391,678	25.00	383,178	8,500
1867	400,568	26.13	378,068	22,500
1868	469,533	29.78	446,533	23,000
1869	492,899	30.35	447,899	45,000
1870	530,692	31.00	483,892	46,800
1871	633,314	36.80	553,714	79,600
1872	637,373	35.96	567,573	69,800
1873	652,025	35.71	592,725	59,300
1874	710,369	37.00	661,869	48,500
1875	685,352	35.39	621,852	63,500
1876	638,369	38.00	561,369	77,000

as yet in all probability attained anything like a maximum, as sugar has not the general usage in the United States that it has in England, where it is as high as 60 lbs. There also it is about one-third cheaper than here, and the consumption varies with the price. As shown, the greatest consumption was in 1874, and during that year quantities and values[1] of sugars, molasses, etc., imported into the United States were as follows:—

	Quantity.	Value.
Brown sugar	1,594,306,354 lbs.	$77,459,968
Refined "	39,259	3139
Molasses	47,189,837	10,947,824
Melada, syrups, etc.	106,952,236	4,424,356
Candy, etc.	56,443	13,916
		$92,849,203

[1] Cost per lb. 7 88 cents, this being much less than it had previously been.

These came from various countries, and were for 1877—[1]

Country of export.	Quantity in lbs.	Aggregate value	Value per lb.
Cuba	926,163,842	$52,702,160	5.70 cts.
Porto Rico	62,733,886	3,182,734	5.07 "
Other Spanish Colonies	161,089,740	5,219,809	3.28 "
China	17,842,724	623,950	3.50 "
Brazil	74,327,436	3,155,078	4.25 "
Dutch East Indies	39,676,415	1,569,029	3.95 "
Dutch West Indies	7,756,758	303,376	3.91 "
British East Indies	4,413,021	166,621	3.77 "
Danish West Indies	3,558,716	126,359	3.55 "
British West Indies } British Guiana }	127,140,363	6,426,803	5.05 "
French West Indies	48,210,896	2,274,019	4.72 "

To the above we must add a certain amount from Mexico, England, Germany, Belgium, etc., giving a total of 1,584,162,824 lbs., having a value of $81,187,-504, representing an average of 5.12 cents per pound.

Besides the above sugars we have a certain quantity of home product of various origins, such as *maple sugar*. The latter in consequence of our forests being steadily cut down has largely diminished. To give some idea as to the exactitude of this statement, in 1860 it was 40,120,000 lbs., and in 1870 only 28,000,000 lbs., and to-day is very much less. There can, therefore, be no hopes of any great increase in this special direction. We now have a sugar made from *sorghum*. It may be remembered, that some years ago it created

---

[1] Report of David A. Wells, 1878.

maintenance of the navigation of the Mississippi River, which now seems probable, a commission having been provided for by a late Act of Congress. Even then the results will not be wholly satisfactory, as it must not be forgotten that the yield of sugar per acre is 1200 lbs. to 1900 lbs. This is small when compared with the West and East Indies or Mauritius, where it has frequently been 7000 lbs. This difference is not owing to the inferiority of our soil but to the methods of working the same; with this inferior seed and poor drainage, or a too frequent crop on the same land, and not ploughing sufficiently deep. The "cane-mills" extract but 60 to 65 per cent. of the juice; the boiling in the greater number of cases takes place in open kettles, &c. A complete change is necessary before these acres will be able to yield all that is demanded by the country. And until then (if some other plant be not introduced) the sugar difficulties will continue to exist.

Without any great knowledge of this special line of business it can easily be understood that any trade where frauds exist, having for effect the deceiving of the government, should be stopped when possible. For example, for years past the so-called Dutch Standard has been the one adopted by customs authorities. Thus working on a wrong basis, that of color, which cannot be relied upon, because varying with circumstances, while a given hue pays a given price, the law supposing that the saccharine percentage in this case is constant, or nearly so. This is absurd, as a sugar made in the vacuum pan can be actually within a few points of chemically pure and at the same time enter into our ports as an inferior article; or again sugars that are of the very best may be artificially colored to suit the occasion.

If a uniform duty be established it will exclude the lower grades from our market, thus doing much harm to the refining business, and will permit the higher to compete with our home product.

The *ad valorem* principle is good, but can not be relied upon, as there is danger of undervaluation by the seller. The "polariscope"[1] is without doubt the best, but here again important errors would occur if the instrument be not used by those having sufficient scientific knowledge. Errors even then occur, frequently due to the existence of "dextro-glucose," which has been fraudulently mixed with the raw sugar.[2]

It would require much time to discuss the above in all its details, but it is sufficient to say that none of them are perfect, but it is to be hoped that the time is not far distant when the country will not be subjected to such uncertainty in the collection of the duty upon this article.

[1] This is an optical instrument based on the property that saccharine solutions possess of turning a certain angle, the plane of polarization of a cluster of ordinary light passing through; the so-called *dextro-glucose* causes this ray to turn to the right to a greater extent than would the ordinary sugar, thereby causing an error.

[2] It is admitted that the above never exists in normal sugars.

The laboring man requiring his pound of sugar as well as the rich man, the first-mentioned, forming the greater portion of our population, should be most considered. The increase *per capita*, as shown in the foregoing table, is owing to the fact that sugar now forms one of the essential elements of food for man, and has ceased to be regarded as a mere luxury.

Have we not at our disposal a root called the *sugar beet* from which is extracted the greater portion of sugar consumed in Europe? Have we not millions of acres of land willing to do all that is necessary to give satisfaction to any one who will bestow sufficient money and labor upon their cultivation? There are but few who actually appreciate the result that would be produced upon the entire country if this industry could be successfully introduced, and we are entirely satisfied that it could and finally will be.

CHAPTER IV.

PROBABLE RESULTS WHICH WOULD BE PRODUCED BY THE INTRODUCTION OF THE BEET SUGAR INDUSTRY IN THE UNITED STATES.

As shown, we send $80,000,000 yearly to foreign lands for the importation of sugars, which should and might be expended in the employment of home labor. The capital in our own country is entirely sufficient to enable us to build 900 beet sugar factories, here supplying our home market with 1,654,747,854 lbs. of sugar.[1] This would necessitate the cultivation of 800,000 acres of land in beets; and, if due allowance for the rotation of crops be made, would require 3,200,000 acres. The beets thus produced would be 27,000,000,000 lbs. The working of these would require about 4,000,000,000 lbs. (1,730,000 tons) of coal. Besides the above sugar, we would have 5,400,000,000 lbs. of pulp, representing 30,000,000 lbs. of meat, then again about 1,000,000,000 lbs. of molasses, which, when reduced to alcohol, would be 31,000,000 gallons at 96° B. The above would give employment to 270,000 men, women,

---

[1] In the above calculation we do not even consider what would be required in some twenty years from to-day, but take the consumption of 1877, and base the calculations upon the results obtained in the arrondissement of Cambrai, France.

and children. The resulting manure from the feeding of cattle would be 2,800,000,000 lbs. We would thus give a new market for coal, coke, bone-black, limestone, matches, brooms, various brushes, cords, leather, lime (hydraulic, etc.), plaster, oil of various natures (to grease the machines, etc.), potassa, sulphur, sulphate of iron, salts of ammonia and soda, bisulphide of lime, muriatic acid, etc., various wires (copper and iron), iron and copper rivets, bolts, and also lead, zinc, tin, borax, tar, flax oil, colza oil, various kinds of putty, white lead, various sizes of window panes, etc. etc. etc. Besides the above, many millions of tons of iron and copper for the building of the various machines in and out of the factory, and hundreds of millions of bricks to construct the walls of the same. We would, in this manner, give employment to engineers, chemists, agriculturists, and to every possible branch of industry. We would thus have an increase in the demand, and the number employed in manufacturing the same would thereby be augmented. Besides this, it would increase greatly the yearly traffic on railroads, canals, steamboats, etc.

We would consequently see small clusters of houses forming around the factories, these lodging the workmen, the stores supplying their domestic wants, the roads (public or private) would be transformed into streets, and the towns would become cities, and they would there have three elements required by man—meat, bread, and sugar. The first would be the consequence of the fattening principles, the second would be lessened by the extra yield of wheat, thus diminishing the average price of bread, and the sugar resulting would furnish to the laboring man an article now considered by him a necessity, and which would have been beyond his reach in a few years to come.

Any new and successful industry springing into existence in a country is likely to be overdone; as capitalists are only too glad to find, as they imagine, a good investment for their money, and, as they are numerous, they do much harm to each other, bringing about financial failure, resulting from an over-production.

This has been the case with iron, coal, oil, etc., and at the present day they do not bring the price per ton or gallon they did when the first iron was manufactured or coal mined or oil discovered.

If several large beet sugar factories be started, and these prove profitable, there will be hundreds of others built, and numerous failures resulting from the same; the sugar thus produced would be far in excess of the demand, and but two solutions would remain: a fall in the value per pound, or an export of the sugar.

On the other hand, if we consider that there are few countries where this could be shipped—Brazil largely supplies the South American market, and Continental Europe is independent, the same can be said of China, etc. Here are great points gained in favor of beet sugar, but there remain to be mentioned several others, the most important being the increase of the yield per acre when planted with wheat, corn, barley, etc. The following table shows what the American yield was in 1876:—

Seeds grown.	Aver'ge yield per acre (bushels).	Average price per bushel.	Average value per acre.	Aver'ge yield per acre for 20 years.
Indian corn . . .	26.1	$0.37	$9.69	32
Wheat	10.4	1.03	10.86	10.9
Rye	13.8	0.66	9.28	9.9
Oats	24.0	0.35	8.44	25.3
Barley	21.9	0.66	14.56	13.5
Buckwheat . . .	14.5	0.72	10.53	76.8
Potatoes	71.6	0.65	48.14	
Tobacco (lbs.) . .	70.5	0.07	52.33	
Hay	1.22	9.74	11.96	
Cotton (lbs) . .	178.6	11.00	19.64	

These figures represent a general average for the total production of the United States. As shown, the crop having the greatest value is tobacco, being $52.33 per acre. We have been informed that in Lancaster Co., Pa., the yield has amounted to $300 per acre in some special cases, but unfortunately it requires but a short time to exhaust the soil to an extent that will render it for years useless, notwithstanding the extra quantity of fertilizers placed thereon to restore the same, during which time attempts will be made to grow other crops with but negative results. Now, compare these with an average yield of beets, such as we may expect in America, which is 15 tons[1] per acre;

---

[1] In Europe it is 20 tons per acre.

if these are worth $4.00 per ton, we will then have a total of $60.00. It is true in this case the preparation of the soil would require more care, time, and money, but here exists a compensation, as the following year the ground would be in a condition to require but little or no ploughing. Then again, strange to say, it has been noticed that on all beet growing farms the crops that follow this root are most extraordinary; the wheat is heavier, the straw much stronger, etc. This may perhaps be due to the fact that subsoil ploughs have been made use of, and with this the deep penetration of the roots; having for effect the removal of the elements beneath to the surface, which would not otherwise have been able to exert their influence.

As a general thing it may be said that all the above crops exhaust the soil, as but few of the substances extracted are returned.

The sugar beets are grown for their saccharine principles, which are mostly, as is supposed, taken from the air. After they have been utilized for the extraction of these saccharine principles, there still remains a pulp containing a large amount of the original salts, etc., the rest being in the resulting molasses, which passes into the distiller's hands, and, if not utilized for the manufacture of potassa, these will still remain, and can be utilized on the soil as a useless product, the alcohol having been extracted by fermentation. The pulp, being then fed to the cattle, will yield a manure containing nearly all the remaining elements. We consequently conclude that this root will give better present and future results than any other crop; will return to the ground a greater amount of the salts, etc., extracted than will any other plant; will increase the future yield and quality of the resulting grains (wheat, barley, etc.); the cattle and general feeding stock for miles around will concentrate at that given point, thus rendering a previously non-feeding country most prosperous.

Of all the community the one deriving the greatest benefit from the introduction of the beet sugar is the farmer. In America, like all other countries, the man who tills the soil has occupation for but half the year, this ending at the very time the beet harvest commences; the consequence is, many of the inhabitants of the country, not able to find sufficient occupation during the winter months, will leave for the time being, to seek employment in the cities, where they unfortunately but too often remain. Now, compare this with what would occur with the cultivation of the beet. The weeding is done by the children during their vacation, this being a healthful exercise. The factories working during the winter give an intellectual employment to all interested, as they acquire notions of chemistry, mechanics, etc., which they would not otherwise have possessed. Under these latter circumstances the farming population will increase yearly.

In travelling through Europe one cannot but observe the amount of labor bestowed upon the soil to obtain a good crop, and which, in all probability if in the United States, would not have been considered worth the trouble, the general fertility of our lands seeming to be such that with but little labor wonderful results are obtained. The farmers do not feel it is worth their while to bestow time and money when the crops are satisfactory, but how long will this last? Will they not in time discover that the land requires more attention than has heretofore been given? Will it not then be too late? Is it possible to convince them of these facts? We doubt it much, and for that reason they will not till the soil as in older countries is done.

Here above is presented one of the greatest difficulties to be contended with in the introduction of the beet culture in America. If subsoil ploughing is neglected there is no possibility of making the manufacture of sugar from the beet a profitable enterprise. These facts being known, it might be well to have European farmers brought here.

The beet sugar enterprise has, like all other new industries, many opponents that advance various theories pertaining to the probability of its success, the most important being that it may not struggle against the cane, and, as long as there remains sufficient land for the cultivation of the latter, it will be impossible to think of sugar from any other source. In answer to these we would refer the reader to facts mentioned above,[1]

---

[1] See Sugar Industry in U. S. A., p. 45.

where it is shown that in Louisiana and elsewhere many difficulties are yet to be overcome. As to the possibility of beet sugar being able to compete with the cane sugar of Cuba there can be no doubt, as the yield to the acre in France is frequently 5000 lbs., which is greatly in excess of any results yet obtained on any *ordinary* sugar-cane plantation. It costs but little more to extract the saccharine principles in one case than in the other, and there still remains from the beet sugar manufacture a pulp having a considerable value. This diminishes the first cost in an important degree. Admitting that the expense of manufacture in both cases is the same, there would still remain the cost of transportation and the duty. Then again it has been argued that the beet could only be grown on a given soil and in a given climate, but these ideas have long since changed, and one can readily be convinced of their absurdity on considering the various soils and the number of European countries where the beet is grown. Then, again, it has been feared that even if a success, it would do much harm to the country, as the space devoted to other crops would be lessened. The same argument was advanced when the potato was first brought to the Northern States; but, on the contrary, the number of acres will be increased.

The following table[1] of agricultural products gives

---

[1] To have the exact number of hectares it will be sufficient to multiply by 1000 the figures in the above table. The approximation given is sufficient for practical purposes.

official figures for the arrondissement of Valenciennes, Department du Nord, France:—

Proportional Area Under Cultivation.

Years.	Nature of the products in hectares, 2½ acres.				
	Wheat.	Rye.	Barley.	Oats.	Beets.
1854	14.08	2.42	1.87	4.35	6.96
1855	13.42	2.41	1.69	5.10	6.82
1856	15.27	2.24	1.71	4.61	6.50
1857	15.19	2.01	1.73	4.11	8.22
1858	14.83	2.49	1.81	4.41	6.89
1859	15.70	2.64	1.85	4.74	6.13
1860	15.86	2.47	1.58	5.22	6 95
1861	15.60	2.38	1.59	4.99	7.95
1862	16.09	2.38	1.46	4.97	8.56
1863	16.18	2.38	1.44	5.28	7.64
1864	15.72	2.43	1.35	5.28	9.56
1865	16.12	2.50	1.40	5.29	8.43
1866	15.98	2.60	1.39	5.53	9.03

(Barley excepted, the number of hectares cultivated, as shown, has increased.)

We have talked with sugar men upon this subject, and they contend that the government will tax home sugar, and in this manner the possibility of competing with foreign markets can no longer be thought of. If this tax was not imposed there would be a yearly decrease of $40,000,000 in the revenue by reason of the loss of duties of foreign sugars. This taxation might be adopted, but it would not be owing to any difference in the yearly government receipts, as, on the contrary, these would be considerably augmented. If the entire molasses derived from beets be transformed into alcohol, the taxation on the same would be $44,000,000.[1] This would not be the case, but we are quite sure that the increased revenues from this source would amount to considerably more than the present duties on sugars. It is quite probable that distillers would find the beet more profitable than the utilization of grain. Up to the present day one of the great drawbacks has been that a beet sugar factory cannot be worked on a small scale, and a large one requires an enormous capital, which, as many suppose, is invested on an uncertainty, but such is not the case, unless some great blunder is committed in the start, such as selecting a bad location near the sea,[2] or where there is likely to be a scarcity of water, or where within a few years forests had been cut down, these, in many cases, having left their roots remaining in the soil; or again, at some distance from railroads, canals, rivers, etc., thus rendering the transportation difficult, which would greatly enhance the first cost of the sugar produced; or again, many other errors which cannot be pardoned.

[1] The above calculation is made with the present taxation as a basis, $0.70 for each proof gallon.

[2] Here the land would be greatly charged with chloride of sodium, this would have a most serious effect upon the quantity of sugar the manufacturer would be able to extract.

PART II.

CHAPTER I.

VARIETIES OF THE BEET.

THESE may be divided into three classes:—
1. Those used as food for man.
2. Those used as food for animals.
3. Those used for the manufacture of sugar and alcohol.

The last category is of the most interest, but we think it important to say a few words concerning the others.

As may be imagined, each of these classes has many subdivisions, and it would be impossible to give them all, so that we will content ourselves with the most important.

1 (α) *Red Beet*, or *Red Castelnaudary*.—The type growing in our gardens is the most preferred for salads, has a reddish flesh, with a root growing but little out of the ground.

(β) *Yellow Beet*, or *Yellow Castelnaudary*.—The flesh is of a darkish yellow, and skin slightly on the orange; grows almost entirely beneath the surface; is very sweet, but not as much used as the type (α) on account of its color.

2 (α) *German Red Mangel Wurzel* (Disette d'Allemagne).[1]—This grows two-thirds out of the ground, and when fully grown measures from sixteen to nineteen inches in length, and has a diameter of five to nine inches. The flesh is white, and, when cut in two and examined, zones are visible, these being slightly on the red. This variety has seldom side roots. The skin is red under ground and brownish above. The yield per hectare (two and a half acres) is supposed to be 10,000 to 40,000 kilog. (22,000 to 88,000 lbs.), and it contains, according to Vilmorin, seven per cent. of sugar.[2] The leaves are green, and stems slightly on the rose.

(β) *Long, White, Green-top Mangel Wurzel* (Disette blanche a ecollet vert).—This type also grows greatly out of ground; when fully developed has a length of thirteen to nineteen inches, and a diameter of about six inches. The portion exposed to the air is green, and beneath the surface white. The yield per hectare (two and a half acres) is supposed to be the same as (γ), and contains, according to Vilmorin, 7.4 per cent. of sugar. The leaves are green and of a good size.

---

[1] "Mangel wurzel" is derived from the German, and means scarcity-root, when, on the contrary, it is in great abundance. The French have adopted "disette," which is also irrational. These roots were known first to exist in Germany, and afterwards transported to England by Dr. Lettson.

[2] The above figures are only approximate, as the yield and per cent. of sugar vary according to the climate, soil, etc.

(γ) *Long, White, Red-top Mangel Wurzel* (Disette blanche à collet rose).—At one time was planted in large quantities, and for cattle is preferred to the green-top, but at the present day the last-mentioned has the preference. It grows well under ground, and the yield per hectare is about 40,000 to 50,000 kilog. (88,000 to 110,000 lbs.), and has about seven per cent. of sugar, according to Vilmorin.

(δ) *Yellow Globe Mangel Wurzel* (Bettrave jaune globe).—This is of spherical shape, and grows almost entirely above the surface of the ground. The skin beneath the ground is yellow and above yellowish-brown; the flesh is white, and the zones are slightly on the yellow. It has but few leaves, and each of these is small. The yield to the acre is about the same as the above. This constitutes a most excellent and economical food for cattle; has the advantage of being early harvested; grows well on a calcareous and shallow soil.

(ε) *Red Globe Mangel Wurzel* (Bettrave globe rouge).—The shape is also spherical; the color of the skin is reddish under ground and brown above. The flesh is white; the leaves are green, with a few spots of red. Yield per hectare (two and a half acres) is 70,000 kilog. (154,000 lbs.), and has a percentage of 7.95 of sugar, according to Vilmorin.

Besides the above there exist the so-called long-yellow, red-oval, yellow-oval, etc.

3. Here we have a variety of beets, which the greater

number of farmers cannot understand the importance of cultivating. The yield per acre in all cases, it is true, is much less than with those just mentioned, but the percentage of sugar is greater, hence a sort of compensation. Those that have grown beets in America frequently argue that with the ruta-baga[1] or the mangel wurzel the percentage of each in sugar is less, but the yield greater, and, all calculations made, more sugar can be obtained from a given area than with the finer quality (where the roots are small). Even if this were true for feeding purposes it is absurd when the manufacturer's interest is at stake, as it is generally forgotten that the amount of water is greater, and the foreign substance also. The first must be evaporated and the second gotten rid of, as the elements other than sugar (when in great quantities, as those that we have grown in the United States) have a chemical action, changing this into glucose or non-crystallizable sugar.

In Europe also it is frequently impossible to convince the farmer of these facts. This being the case, contracts are made where given seeds are to be planted. But even then frauds occur, and it is found that the only possible plan to obtain good results is for the manufacturer to sow the seeds after the ground has been tilled by the farmer for that purpose. As may be imagined, here a most difficult problem presents itself: this consists in giving satisfaction to both in-

---

[1] This is a Swedish turnip, and contains seldom over two per cent. of sugar.

terested in obtaining a maximum yield of roots and sugar.

We will now examine the different types of beets that have been acclimated, and to each affix either the name of the country in which it originated or the grower.[1] The most important of this class is the first mentioned, and the others are but the same type degenerated.

White Silesian (fig. 1).—This type has been known in Germany for many years, and it is supposed that Mathieu Dombasle was the first to introduce it into France. It grows mostly under ground, and gives a yield of 25,000 to 30,000 kilog. (55,000 to 66,000 lbs.) per hectare (two and a half acres), and has a percentage of about 16 in sugar. Strange to say, since it has been acclimated its volume has increased. The skin and the flesh are very white. The varieties[2] that have been derived from this by selection are numerous, and the most important is the so-called

Magdeburg.—This root is long and regular, has but few side roots, and grows well beneath the surface. The yield to the hectare (two and a half acres) is about 25,000 kilog. (55,000 lbs.), and it has a percentage of 14 of sugar.

Imperiale (fig. 2).—Has a green neck, and grows greatly beneath the surface. Was obtained for the first time by Knauer, and brought to France by Vil-

---

[1] We counted in the Paris Exhibition of 1878 twenty exhibitors pretending that they had obtained better results than had heretofore existed.

[2] See culture of the grain.

morin. This beet is very light, and contains about 13.50 per cent. of sugar. It adheres to the ground, and for that reason the harvesting of it is most difficult.

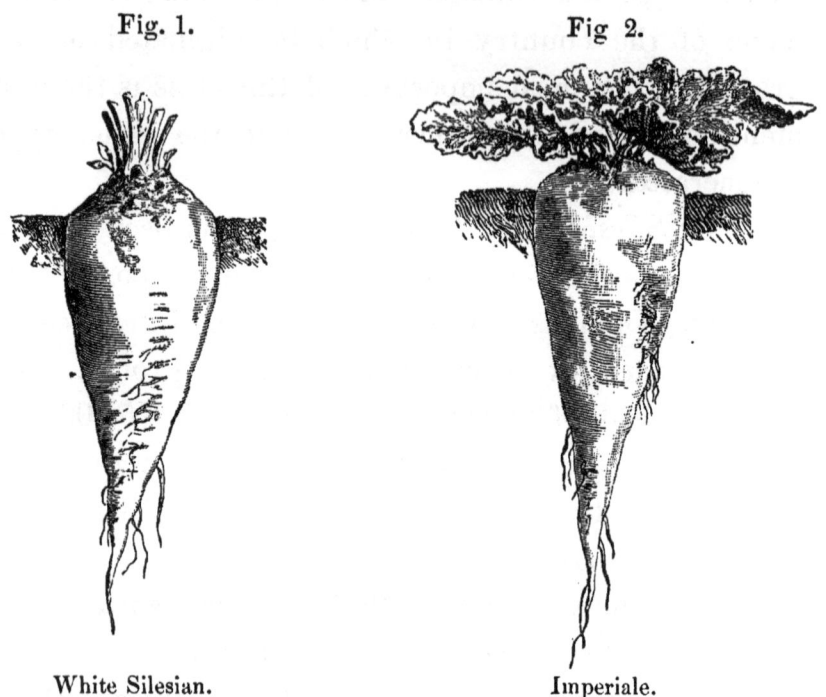

Fig. 1. White Silesian.   Fig 2. Imperiale.

We now have some few direct sub-varieties known as the *Breslau* and the so-called *Electorale*, also brought to notice by Knauer. These are rather larger than the *Imperiale*, but they do not contain the same amount of sugar; also a white variety of German beet having a green top, known as "Blanche de Pologne," and contains about 13 per cent. of sugar. Besides these there exist several varieties acclimated in France, having also the same origin, but they are much degenerated.

VARIETIES OF THE BEET.

White Silesian Green-top (fig. 3) (Bettrave race Française collet vert).—Strange to say, this variety is not as much in public favor as in years past. The portion above ground is slightly green, the root is long, and the skin white, smooth, and watery. Portions of this are slightly hairy, and without small adhesive roots, and the yield per hectare (two and a half acres) frequently attains 55,000 kilog. (121,000 lbs.).

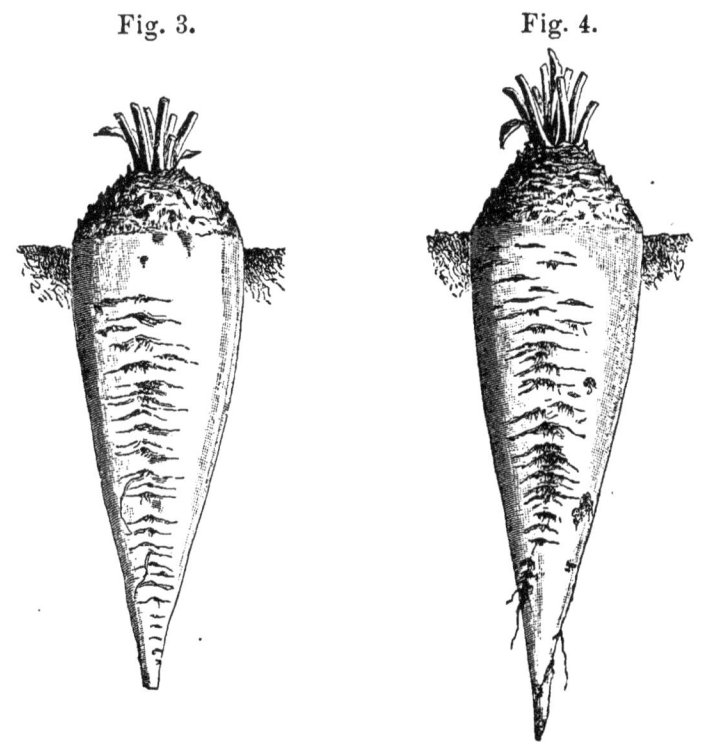

Fig. 3.   Fig. 4.

Variety so-called Green-top.   Variety so-called Rose-top.

According to Vilmorin a maximum of 8288 kilog. (18,233 lbs.) of sugar has been extracted from the yield of one hectare (two and a half acres). The leaves are numerous and green.

White Silesian Rose-top (fig. 4) (Bettrave race Française collet rose).—This type has become very popular of late. The skin is white under ground, and the neck, exposed to the air, rose; has no extra roots. The leaves are abundant, and the yield is considerable, this being to the hectare 70,000 kilog., yielding 10 to 12 per cent. of sugar. According to Vilmorin the greatest yield in sugar extracted from the same was 8881 kilog. (19,538 lbs.) to the hectare (two and a half acres).

The French were not contented with the varieties just mentioned, but have several others, "*variétés bouteuse*" and "*demi-bouteuse;*" easily extracted from the soil; grow partly out of the ground, but contain much less sugar, and give a larger yield to the acre; under these conditions but few advantages are gained over the ordinary *mangel wurzel.*

White Sugar Grayish-top (fig. 5).—This variety is but little used for beet sugar manufacture. It is very large, and grows two-thirds out of the ground. The neck is green and the skin gray; yield per hectare (two and a half acres) 110,000 kilog. (242,000 lbs.) as a maximum; contains about 6.50 per cent. of sugar. It is considered that with proper selection of seeds great improvements might be obtained.

Improved Vilmorin[1] (Bettrave blanche améliorée Vilmorin).—The first type was brought to notice in

---

[1] Mr. Vilmorin has rendered in this case and in many others an immense service to the beet sugar industry in France.

1860. Efforts had been made to obtain a large percentage of sugar without considering the resulting shape, which was irregular, and the neck large, and a

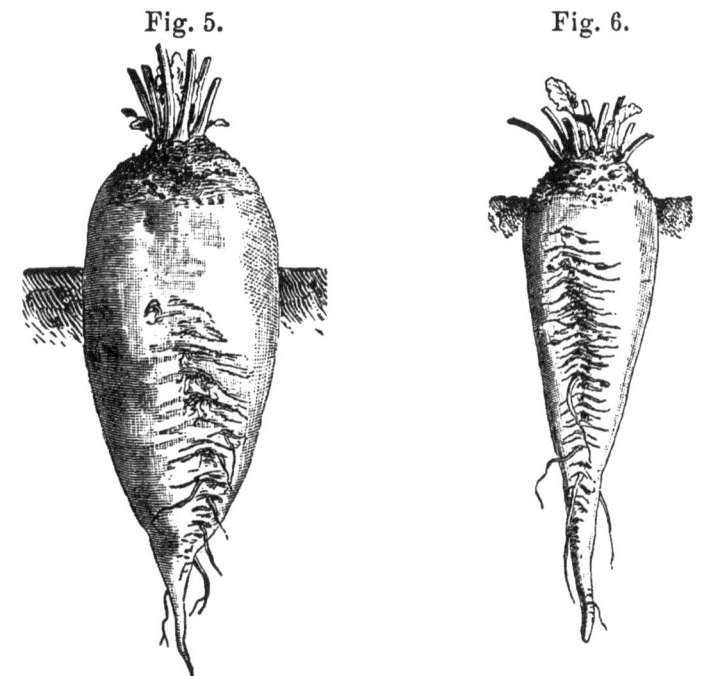

Fig. 5.   Fig. 6.

Variety so-called "Collet Gres."   Variety called Improved Vilmorin.

great number of small roots grew on its exterior surface; under these conditions the harvesting was almost impossible. It had an average of 15 per cent. of sugar, and gave a yield to the hectare (two and a half acres) of 20,000 kilog. (44,000 lbs.). In 1870 another type was brought to notice, which was the same root much improved both in shape and quality. These gave 15 to 18 per cent. of sugar, and a yield of 40,000 kilog. (88,000 lbs.) to the hectare (two and a half acres). It has been found that it is impossible to much surpass this, as the roots would not have then sufficient strength to resist the variations of the weather. But this shape was not as yet entirely satisfactory, and in 1875 another new type was brought to notice (see fig. 6), which was rather pleasing to the eye. This root grows entirely beneath the surface, and has an average weight of 0.500 kilog. (1.1 lb.) and contains about 15 per cent. of sugar. The harvesting is difficult.

Improved Deprez.[1]—Here we have three important varieties, known as types Nos. 1, 2, 3. These were created some few years ago, and much credit is due to Mr. Violette, Professor to the Faculty of Lille.

No. 1. The root is white, and frequently has a rosy tint, and contains 15 to 16 per cent. of sugar. Grows entirely beneath the surface, and the roots are very long, and give an average yield of 30,000 kilog. (66,000 lbs.) to the hectare (two and a half acres).

No. 2. White or rose; contains 12 to 14 per cent. of sugar; grows slightly out of the ground; gives a yield of 50,000 kilog. (110,000 lbs.) to the hectare (two and a half acres), and is supposed to come nearer to the solution of the problem before mentioned, which consists of satisfying both the manufacturer and farmer.

No. 3. We have here the acclimation of the various types mentioned above, such as Magdeburg, White

---

[1] Deprez et Fils have the largest agricultural laboratory in France, and have the facility of making 2000 analyses daily.

Silesian, etc., improved as the yield is supposed to be greater. The percentage of sugar remains constant. These have no small roots and grow well under ground when the soil on which they are planted is suitable and thoroughly worked. The average yield is 50,000 kilog. (110,000 lbs.) to the hectare.

We now have several types created by Simon Legrand, the most important of which is the "Franco-Allemande." This variety is white, and has a green or rose neck, and contains from 13 to 14 per cent. of sugar. It requires a deep subsoil. There are also a great number of sub-varieties not of the same interest. Of the less important types existing in France might be mentioned " Bettrave dit Dervaux" and " Bettrave dit Tollet," each of which claims from 13 to 14 per cent. of sugar, and last of all in England the Improved Carter[1] sugar beet, which is supposed to give a high percentage of sugar.

[1] Experiments which we made in Pennsylvania and New Jersey were not satisfactory with this variety.

CHAPTER II.

EXAMINATION[1] OF THE BEET.

WE have had frequent occasion to examine the structure of the beet, and are only too glad to state that the results reached by Decaisne were in nearly every case similar to our own.

If a section be made through this root several zones or concentric circles are thus made visible, but here our examination would end if we had not at our disposal the principles of botany, chemistry, and micrography, and even then the various observations do not agree with others that have previously been made. We will follow nearly the same order of examination as this learned professor mentioned above which we consider most excellent.

1. *With Microscope.*—The first period being when the two small leaves are visible above ground. Let a horizontal section be made through the young plant, and examine the same with a microscope; we will then see a row of epidermic utricles, then a layer of cortical parenchyma[2] also formed of utricles, and in the

---

[1] There are many botanical principles which have not been mentioned in the above, as we consider it would lead to arguments in which the reader would have but little interest.

[2] This has frequently various colors, which are apparent through the epidermic tissue.

EXAMINATION OF THE BEET.

centre the vascular groups which are, as a general thing, cylindrical. If we make a vertical section (see fig. 7), great regularity of the cortical utricles will be apparent.

Fig. 7.

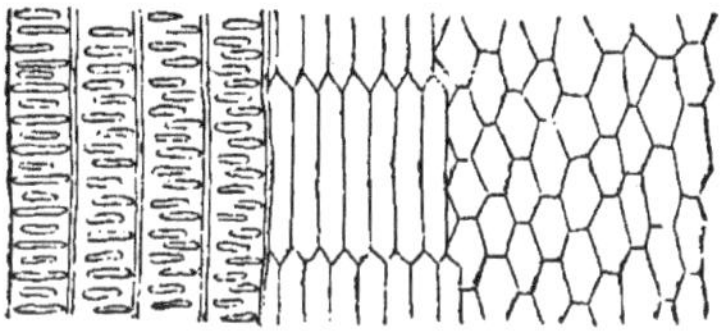

Vertical Section.

The utricles are very transparent; the vessels that occupy the centre of the root are shown in fig. 8. The

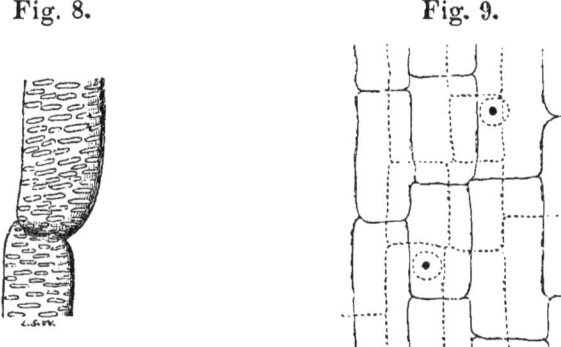

Fig. 8.   Fig. 9.

Vessels that occupy the centre.

young beet soon gives out small radicles, which generally form near the vascular tissue, become conical, and present in their centre elongated utricles. Some of these have a nucleus that possesses a luminous spot, these seem to form one over the other. (See fig. 9.) These small particles will come in communication with the vessels in the centre of the mother-root and then penetrate the cortical parenchyma.

If we now examine a plant having two leaves more than the above, in the exterior zone of the parenchyma can be seen traces of a transparent tissue. Little by little this becomes larger, and will finally form a complete circle, and the vessels will soon become apparent, the new formation is consequently composed of vascular cells, and a transparent zone situated on the other side. This is separated by a medullary zone that was before colored, and the utricles situated between each zone of the vascular groups have diluted communication, while those of the centre become isolated. The new groups that appear near the circumference are composed of elongated utricles. The root consequently increases in size when the diameter of the utricles becomes large, and others form, this occurring at the same time. Knowing the above facts, we should conclude in advance that in all probability each cycle of leaves[1] corresponds to a given zone, and, as the new formations are concentric to the first, the outer or older leaves[2] communicate with the inner zone the richest in sugar.

Several of the most prominent men have made nu-

---

[1] We have analyzed upon various occasions the various zones, and found for the outer zone 9.6 per cent. of sugar, 2d zone 10.2 per cent., 3d zone 11.3 per cent., 4th zone 12 per cent., etc. See "Leaves of the Sugar Beet."

[2] Basset contends that the above is not correct, and that if there existed any communication between the zones and the leaves it would be in a different manner; in other words, that the outer cycle of leaves corresponds to the outer zone; the former having a new development from the centre, the same phenomena should exist with the latter.

merous experiments to ascertain what this relation was; the most important of these were by Walkhoff, Scharcht, Bretschneider,[1] Champignon, and Pellet,[2] etc., and from these there can be no doubt as to the truth of the above hypothesis. If a beet be examined when it is a little larger than the above, we can see that the various new zones[3] have continued forming in exactly the same manner, and the utricles have remained perfectly transparent. (See fig. 10.) Mr. Decaisne tells us that in the greater number of roots the vascular group is central and unique, and becomes larger with age, and is surrounded by a layer of various thickness of cortical parenchyma composed of utricles.

[1] Mr. Walkhoff gives in his book experiments of Bretschneider, these being to ascertain the proportions existing between the number of zones and leaves.

	Leaves developed.	Concentric zones of the root.	
The 20th July	9 to 10	4	
9th August	15 " 18	5 to 7	
31st August	18 " 28	7 " 8	Many of these
15th September	18 " 28	7 " 8	leaves were yellow and were
30th September	18 " 28	7 " 9	partly gone.
16th October	18 " 28	8 " 9	

[2] The experiments of Champignon and Pellet are even more interesting. These gentlemen suppose that each zone is subdivided in two.

	Per cent. of sugar.	No. of leaves.	No. of zones.
Vilmorin's seed,	15.7	42	48
	14.8	39	36
	13.8	31	32
Ordinary seed,	12.2	23	28
	11.	19	20

[3] Some authors contend that the number of zones in matured beets is limited to 7; to those going to seed the following year 10; but we cannot indorse this statement, as it seems to vary greatly, and consequently no rule can be given.

In the beet these two elements are to be found, but the parenchyma is replaced by a utricular tissue of the medullary vascular zones, which, instead of being one against the other, are separated by a mass of utricles of variable thickness If a thin horizontal slice be made in a beet and examined with the microscope, it will be seen that the vascular groups are composed near the centre of a considerable number of vessels, having variable sections and a reticulated transparent tissue.

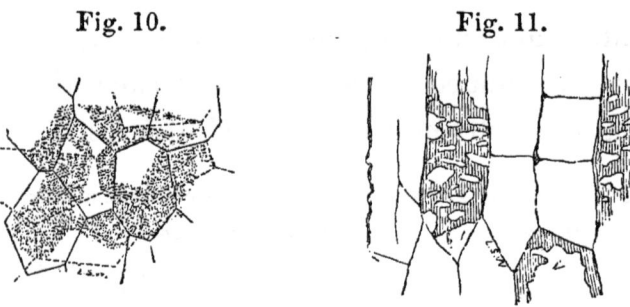

Fig. 10. Fig. 11.

Horizontal Section showing the Transparency of the Utricles.

If these be examined, commencing from the centre, they will be seen to diminish in size from zone to zone, and finally become invisible in the exterior ones. These are mainly formed by the utricular tissue that surrounds the vascular groups in the central portion of the root. (See fig. 11.)

The utricular tissue that exists between each group is extremely transparent; this greatly diminishes when the root has matured. When the beet pulp is washed in alcohol and dried, these utricles become so compressed that they cannot be separated without destruction. (See fig. 12.) Then in water they assume their primitive form. (See fig. 13.)

If the neck above ground be examined some curious facts will be made known. A considerable number of utricles here exist; these are filled with crystals (fig. 14); the latter become more and more numerous as the

Fig. 12.   Fig. 13.

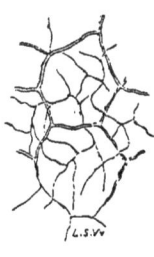

After being Washed in Alcohol.   After being Washed in Water.

length of the neck increases. Strange to say, none of these exist in the portion of the beet below the surface. As the age of the root advances the central utricular portion here disappears, and leaves a cavity which is considered to correspond to the "moelle" in vegetables.

As Mr. Decaisne justly remarks, here is a characteristic difference between the neck and the root.

We will now examine the contents and composition of the various cells mentioned above, these being very numerous, and corresponding to the size and age of the leaves. For good beets they are about 0.23 of an inch in width, and the quality of the root will decrease as these become larger.

Fig. 14.

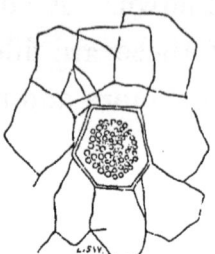

Section in the Neck.

2. *Chemical Examination.*—The composition of the tissue of which the beet is composed, as well as the contents of the cells, is most varied. If merely a sugar solution existed, the difficulty of working the root would be much reduced, as it would then be sufficient to reduce the total to a pulp, press and concentrate the same by boiling; operations that could take place in every house. The manufacture of sugar would then be within the hands of all.

The epidermic tissue is composed mainly of *cellulose*. This is with or without color or taste, and is not soluble in water, alcohol, or ether. When this coloring matter exists it is *chlorophyl*, a substance of which very little is known. According to Sacks the color does not at first exist, but forms in consequence of the action of oxygen and light. It is a compound mainly of four elements, of various colors. The portion of the root growing beneath the surface having but little color, the quantities of this chemical are small, but considerable near the neck. If the cellulose undergoes an oxydation, a substance called *suberine* will result. Frequently a certain amount of *tannin* also exists in considerable quantities, and excellent effects are the consequence, as it combines with the albuminoids and forms a non-soluble compound. We would consequently not be far from the truth in saying that the quality of a beet depends upon the percentage of this acid. If a transformation should continue *pectose* will form; this frequently changes to *pectic acid*, and, if the root be mutilated, to *pectine*. If a small slice of beet be placed in a solution of water and a few drops of hydrochloric acid, this pectine will after several months be dissolved. We now have *albumine*, the most important element contained in the beet. Its property of coagulating renders it most easily gotten rid of. Of the entire substance there still remain *betaine* and *asparagine*. The first, if in water, will crystallize in a most remarkable manner—and its taste is sweet; the second is soluble in hot and cold water, and not in ether or alcohol at 96° B. Several acids exist besides the one mentioned above; the most important, *malic acid*, was studied by Payen. This, as may be understood, forms various salts with the different bases. The beet contains, for example, malate of potassa, malate of lime, malate of soda, malate and bi-malate of ammonia, etc. A small amount of *oxalic acid*, must exist, as various salts formed by the same have been brought to notice by Payen, Dubrunfaut, and others. The most important are oxalate of potassa and soda and small quantities of oxalate of ammonia. If oxalate of lime exist or not we have not been fortunate enough to decide, but consider in all probability that it does, as all other plants of the same family as the beet (chenopodees) contain it. Decaisne asserts that it does not, while Payen and others contend that it does.

We must now say a few words regarding the mineral substances which have a most important effect upon the final results. Fortunately, the greater portion of these are to be found in the neck, which is sliced off[1] before working, and in this manner many of the difficulties of fabrication are gotten rid of. We do not think we would be far from the truth in saying that the amount of sugar in the beet varied indirectly proportional to the salts, as hundreds of experiments have proven this statement. These minerals and other salts seem also to affect the general form of the root, the beet being a plant that absorbs a portion of each of these in quantities that vary with the composition of the soil and fertilizers[2] made use of. Champignon and Pellet consider that an absorption may in certain cases take place without a combination.

Saltpetre exists in quantity sufficient to cause much harm. A series of *sulphates* also do considerable harm.

---

[1] See "Harvesting."   [2] See "Soils and Fertilizers."

These are principally to be found in the upper portion of the root near the neck, the most important being the sulphates of lime and potassa. The *phosphates* are of potassa, magnesia, and lime.

We now have the *chlorides*. For many years it was thought that the existence of these would prevent, to a certain extent, the formation of sugar, but it has been generally decided that this was an error. These are principally to be found in the upper portion of the root; the most important we may mention are chloride of potassium, chloride of sodium, and hydrochlorate of ammonia. Of late Dubrunfaut tells us that beets contain a certain amount of silica and sulphur, also copper, rubidium, and cæsium. Comparatively few of all the above can be detected by chemical analysis. We have no doubt that hundreds of other chemical compounds or elements will in time be discovered.

The total chemical composition varies with thousands of circumstances. To give any seems to a certain degree absurd, but the analysis made by Payen some years ago seems to have held its own, and is as follows:—

Water	83.5
Sugar	10.5
Cellulose, pectose, pectine	0.8
Albumine, asparagine, and other neutral nitric elements, malic acid, pectic acid, gums, fatty substances, chlorophylle, oxalate and phosphate of lime, etc.	3.7
	100.00

84   THE SUGAR BEET.

According to R. Hoffmann—

		1st type.	2d type.	3d type.
Water		89.20	83.20	75.20
Sugar		4.00	9.42	15.00
Non-nitric elements	soluble	4.13	3.34	4.23
	cellulose	1.01	1.50	2.07
	pectic, coloring sub. etc.	0.00	0.00	0.00
Nitric substance		1.00	1.64	2.20
Cinders		0.66	0.90	1.30
		100.00	100.00	100.00

3. *Sugar in the Beet.*—The formation of the sugar in the beet, as before stated, seems mainly but not entirely due to the leaves, as the root takes an active part on soils where these are small and the saccharine percentage large. Various causes, such as weather, fertilizers,[1] size, soil, etc., will greatly influence the amount of sugar contained in the beet. We know that there exist several zones, some of which are transparent and others opaque.[2] Payen admits that the latter contain the sugar, and consequently the greater their number the richer the beet. Figs. 15 and 16 give the reader a good idea of the general distribution according to Payen; whilst Charles Violette, on the other hand, clearly demonstrates by analysis that there is very

---

[1] See "Leaves of the Beet."

[2] These are, according to Violette:—

Translucid Zones.		*Opaque Zones.*	
Sugar per cent.	{ 1st 14.5 2d 13.4 3d 10.0	Sugar per cent.	{ 1st 15.7 2d 15.5 3d 11.2

little difference[1] in their saccharine composition. As for the mineral salts, etc., it is more striking. The amount of sulphuric acid is greatly in excess in the

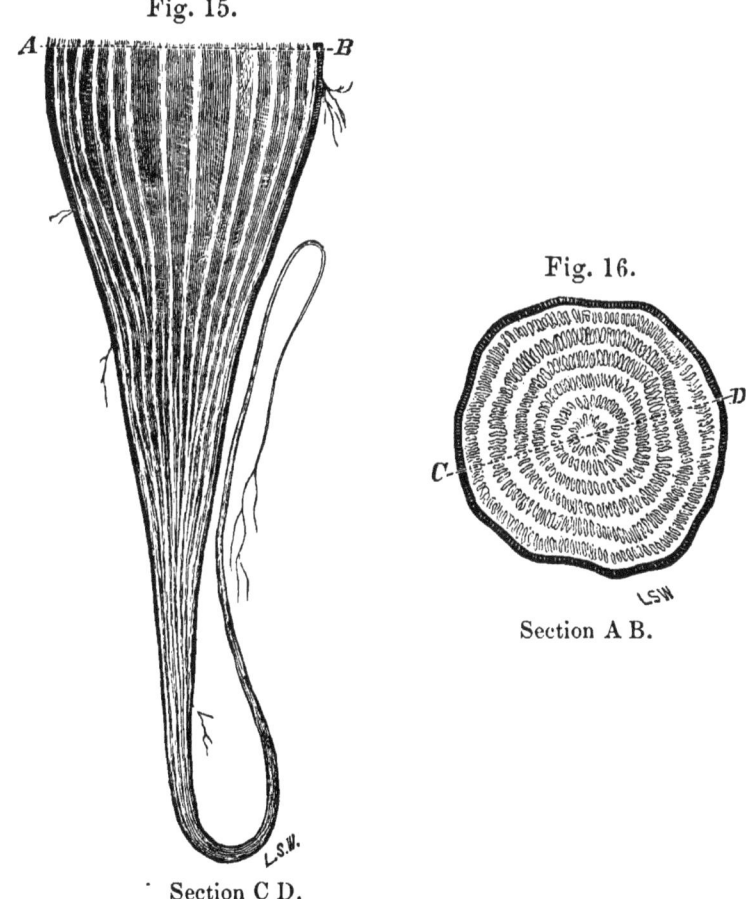

Fig. 15.

Fig. 16.

Section A B.

Section C D.

opaque zone; this is considered to be principally owing to the excess of albuminoids existing therein. The upper portion of the root contains more salts than the

---

[1] See Chapters on Fertilizers, Soils, etc., Shape of Beet, etc.

lower. The sugar increases from top to bottom.[1] In the distribution according to Payen this is also apparent, the extremity being mainly composed of cells having a large amount of saccharine elements in their interior. We have made several sections in the root, which demonstrate this:—

    1st section . . . . . . 9.35 of sugar
    2d   " . . . . . . 10.02 " "
    3d   " . . . . . . 10.05 " "
    4th " . . . . . . 10.42 " "
    5th " . . . . . . 10.97 " "
    6th " . . . . . . 11.03 " "

(On the other hand, Dubrunfaut would attribute the difference in the saccharine percentage to an osmotic effect, and thereby explain why a small root should have more sugar than a large one. The argument is that the vascular tissue is in connection with the leaves and adhesive roots, thus absorbing the saccharine and saline principles. The sugar will pass into the cellular tissue by the principle of osmose, and the proportion existing here between the chemical composition of these tissues no longer exists in large roots.)

---

[1] According to Champignon and Pellet—

	Analysis near the neck.	Analysis at the extremity of root.
Water	86.64	84.48
Sugar	7.30	9.70
Cinders . . .	1.02 ⎫ 6.06	1.26 ⎫ 5 82
Organic substance .	5 04 ⎭	4.56 ⎭
	100.00	100.00

The cellular tissue separating the opaque zones when of considerable thickness is watery, and corresponds to a root rich in sugar. In what state does this sugar exist in utricular tissue? This question we do not think decided. Decaisne tells us, that if examined with great care no foreign substance can be found to exist, it being perfectly translucid. On the other hand, several of the most prominent chemists have declared that it is impossible to make an exact observation, as the color changes so rapidly when in contact with the air. The tissue of the cells also alters from light red to black. The rapidity of this change seems to be proportional to the sugar the tissue contains. Decaisne tells us that when these changes are examined with a microscope it can be seen that the color is due to a multitude of crystals or granules, and the combination of their mass has a dark appearance.

The beet when fresh and in a good condition contains very little glucose, but, if mutilated, it will form, thus causing a proportional loss of sugar.[1]

4. *External Qualities; Shape of the Beet.*—As before stated, the method of cultivation, the fertilizers, etc., exert great influence on the size and consequently on the saccharine elements the beets contain. Evidently, the longer the root the greater the depth to which it penetrates and the greater the amount of nourishment it extracts. If the various shapes be examined[2]

---

[1] See "Conservation of the Beet." [2] See "Variety of Beets."

and their analysis made, we will discover that the short and fat ones contain far less sugar than the type mentioned above. To express this idea geometrically we will suppose an axis A B and a line cd forming an angle γ with the same (see fig. 17); evidently if this revolves it will thus engender a cone, if a curve $\alpha\beta$ (see

Fig. 17. Fig. 18.

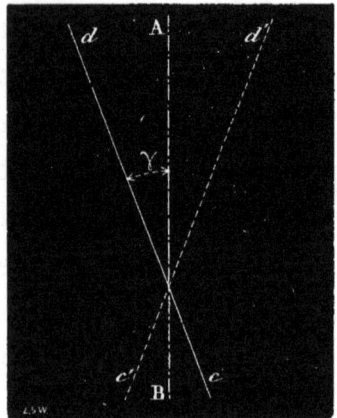
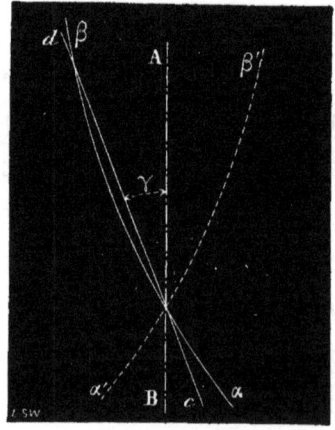

fig. 18) takes the place of this, the volume thus formed will greatly resemble the rutabaga or roots having but 3 to 4 per cent. of sugar; now, if this curve be concave (see fig. 19), the surface will then represent a type containing 15 or 16 per cent., or most favorable for beet sugar manufacture. The necks in this case are short and small, and in the other long and large. This consideration holds good for the greater number of cases, but, as Peligot first remarked, beets having many small adhering roots contain more sugar than others

that are regular.[1] If this be owing to the greater power of absorption or other cause, we are not prepared

Fig. 19.

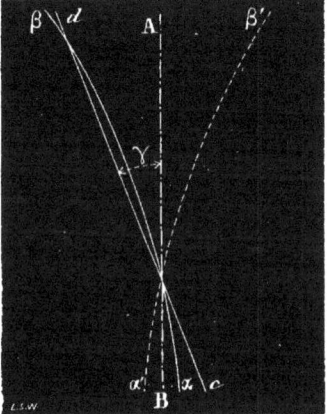

to state; but this type[2] cannot be recommended, as the washing and working would be most difficult.

For many years it was argued that the shape depended upon the variety of the seed. This evidently has much to do with it, but is not general, as a given seed planted in different soils will frequently yield beets entirely different from those expected. This is mainly due to the condition of the ground; if compact and not well worked, in all probability the resulting roots will be forked, but if, on the contrary, the soil be tilled as it should be the shape will then be, with proper seed, most satisfactory, and correspond to the

[1] See Chapter on "Leaves."
[2] See "Variety of Beets, types Vilmorin."

variety type that they represent. The importance of small necks and growing well under ground has been before explained;[1] this will also result when the above named care is given.

[1] This being the case, it would lead one to suppose that the saccharine elements were drawn principally from the soil, and not from the leaves, as before stated. See "Leaves of the Sugar Beet."

CHAPTER III.

LEAVES OF THE SUGAR BEET.

There can be no doubt as to the important role which the leaves play in the beet culture. As before stated, their exterior signs give evident proof in many cases of the qualities of the root to which they belong.

The functions which they have to fulfil are most interesting. These we consider have for an object the formation of the greater quantity of the final sugar in the root, the most important element being carbon, which is partly or entirely absorbed as carbonic acid; the latter being partly decomposed, a certain quantity of the oxygen is thrown out. The remaining carbonic acid seems to circulate for a time in the tissue. During the growth of the leaves the root increases but comparatively little in size, and, as soon as complete, the contrary action takes place. Evidently the greater their size the larger the amount of the elements which they are able to extract from the surrounding air, and their total weight is up to a certain period greater than that of the root. Each leaf has apparently communication with a given portion of the beet, and supplies it with the nourishment it requires.

The outer corresponds to the inner portion of the

root; these representing the older leaves, we may conclude that they have furnished the larger portion of the saccharine elements.[1] These facts being known, we consider that the quality of beets for sugar manufacture improves with the number and weight of its leaves. A series of experiments made by the writer and others[2] will be sufficient to demonstrate the seriousness of this hypothesis.

The roots which we analyzed gave the following results:—

Saccharine percentage in the root.	For 100 lbs. of beets weight of leaves.
15.0	55 lbs.
14.8	53 "
14.7	57 "
14.3	52 "
14.0	50 "
13.7	45 "
12.0	41 "

Such being the case, we made several new tests, and found that it not only held good for a given weight of roots, but for each one in particular.

---

[1] See "Study of the Sugar Beet."
[2] Experiments by Champignon and Pellett:—

		For 100 k. of root (224 lbs.).	Sugar per cent. in the root.
1st.	Grams vilmorin ameliorée	56^k of leaves.	14.5
	Simon Legrand	33 "	13.3
	Ordinary	20 "	11.8
2d.	Ordinary seed	52 "	13.2
	Ordinary culture	28 "	11.8

Variety of seed.	Sugar per cent. in the root.	No. of leaves on the root.	Av. weight of each leaf.
Simon Legrand	15.2	40	108 grains
	14	35	105 "
	13.8	32	104 "
	13	29	103 "
Carter seed	12	27	102 "
	11.3	27	100 "
	10	18	92 "

As a general thing it is admitted that the weight of the leaves in a given crop is about equal to one-half that of the roots, and one-fourth to one-third for beets containing 8 to 9 per cent. of sugar.

Corenwinder was the first to prove that the amount of cinders in the leaves in general augmented as they grew older, and that the nitric elements diminished. We analyzed leaves of the beet at different ages, and found in all cases this principle to hold good.

	Weight.	Cinders per cent.	Nitric element.
1st. Leaves, very young	7 grs. troy	20.6	25.2
2d. " 2 months old	165 "	28.2	18.0
3d. " fully grown	375 "	31.0	15.3

In other words, small young leaves contain more nitric elements and less cinders than the large ones.[1] This being the fact, we may conclude that beets rich in sugar will be possessed of leaves giving by analysis a

---

[1] Several experiments made by J. Isodore Pierre have proven that small leaves contain less water than large ones.

larger amount of cinders and less nitric elements than those of a low percentage.

Beets which have been grown on a calcareous soil, when of a high saccharine percentage, have small leaves. This is contrary to the principles stated above, and we are quite unable to explain its phenomena. If this had not been the case we might have suggested a new idea for the selection of the mothers[1] for seed culture, it being then sufficient to have a few leaves analyzed, and, when fulfilling the above condition, should be chosen. Too much cannot be said regarding the care that should be given in weeding, etc., as the slightest injury will influence the final results, and it requires but little to greatly retard the formation of the sugar; for example, the weather if rainy, windy, etc., might destroy all the leaves, but this would not prevent the roots from increasing in size, but the sugar contained therein would be small.

The temptation for the farmers to make a partial stripping of the leaves[2] from the root is great, and the harm thus done is very considerable, and varies with the age of these leaves. Evidently, when well advanced, they have nearly completed their duties, and, for that reason, it will not be as serious as it would otherwise have been. We cannot indorse the stripping of the leaves under any pretence, as the value of the meat resulting is not as great as the good that would have

---

[1] See "Culture of Seed."
[2] See "Feeding Qualities of the Leaves."

been derived when permitted to fall naturally on the ground, as thus a large amount of the salts, etc., that have been absorbed by the plants are returned to where they justly belong, and these are as a general thing considerable, and are, according to Vivien—[1]

Total Elements taken up by one Hectare (two and a half acres).

Nature of elements.	Elements taken up by		Total.
	Beets.	Leaves.	
Potassa	122^k.00	185^k.12	307^k.12
Phosphoric acid	24.40	48.16	72 50
Soda	34.00	48.00	82.00
Lime	19.20	56.00	75.20
Magnesium	7.20	44.80	52.00
Chlorine	33.60	59.52	93.00
Sulphuric acid	10.00	28.80	38.80
Silicates	51.20	38.40	89.60
Nitrogen	110.00	62.40	172.40
Sugars	4,400.00	428.80	4,828.80
Organic substances	1,814.00	1,206.40	3,020.40
Water	33,374.00	13,793.60	47,168.00
	40,000^k.00	16,000^k.00	56,000^k.00

The whole principle is wrong. In the first place, the leaves generally taken, as before stated, are those that have commenced to change color. These are not the most nourishing; then again they are stripped from the root at different times, each having a bad final effect. If this is made a practice of, it is well to wait until the harvesting, then they are as nourishing as they were two months previous, they then being brown,

---

[1] See A. Vivien, "Traité de la fabrication de sucre," 1878.

and the harm done is comparatively small, although it nevertheless exists.[1]

We had a most curious experience in **New Jersey**. Having planted a given area in beets, when these had four and a half months' growth, the pigs of the neighboring farm made their escape and indulged in eating the leaves of some and left those of others untouched. We analyzed the roots in both cases one and a half month afterwards, found 6 per cent. of sugar in the mutilated and 11 per cent. in those untouched. Here the difference was most striking. During the interval other small leaves had made their appearance, which they always will do. The number of the new growths will correspond to the number of leaves pulled from the beet; the consequence is, the neck becomes much longer, and the loss of sugar seems to be proportional to the length of the same. But, as before stated,[2] the neck contains a greater amount of foreign substance and less sugar than any other portion of the root; the consequence is that there is not only a loss of sugar resulting from the stripping, but the difficulty of working the beets for the extraction of the saccharine elements is greatly increased. It is apparently better to cut the neck from the beet, thus permitting this also to remain on the ground, but the operation has many

---

[1] The above is somewhat in opposition to Payen's idea, he contending that more benefit will result from feeding them to cattle than permitting them to remain on the ground.

[2] See "Study of the Beet."

disadvantages.[1] At one time it was argued[2] that this stripping of the leaves was of great advantage, as it thus permitted the root to receive an airing which it would not otherwise have had; this is absurd, for reasons before explained. The Germans were the first to

Fig. 20.

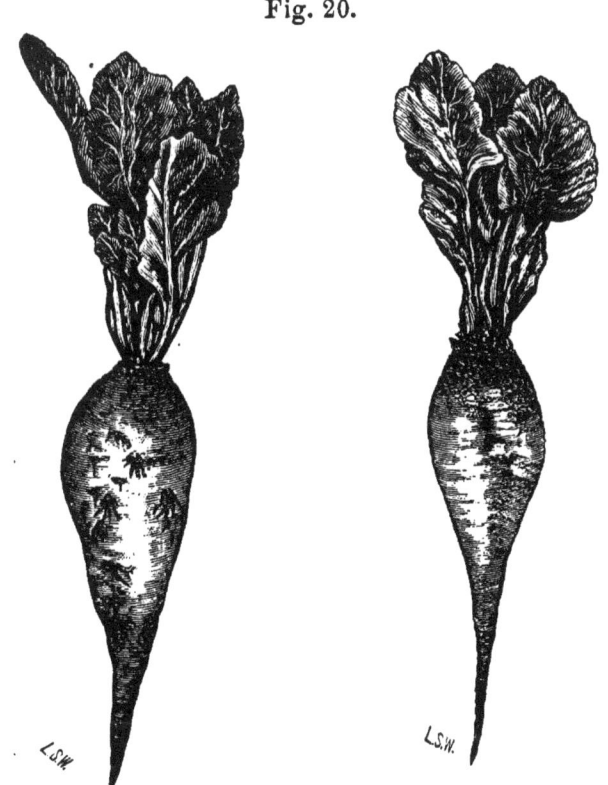

call attention to the fact that the advantages gained on one side did not compensate for the loss on the other, and

---

[1] Harvesting. See "Preservation and Conservation."

[2] J. Isodore Pierre contends that the stripping of the leaves influences but little the nitric elements contained in the roots.

98 THE SUGAR BEET.

for years past hundreds of experiments have been made to ascertain exactly the harm done. The most interesting have been those of Corenwinder, he having grown a certain area in beets, one-half of which were stripped and the remainder were untouched, and he concluded that the operation caused a decrease in the yield of roots

Fig. 21.

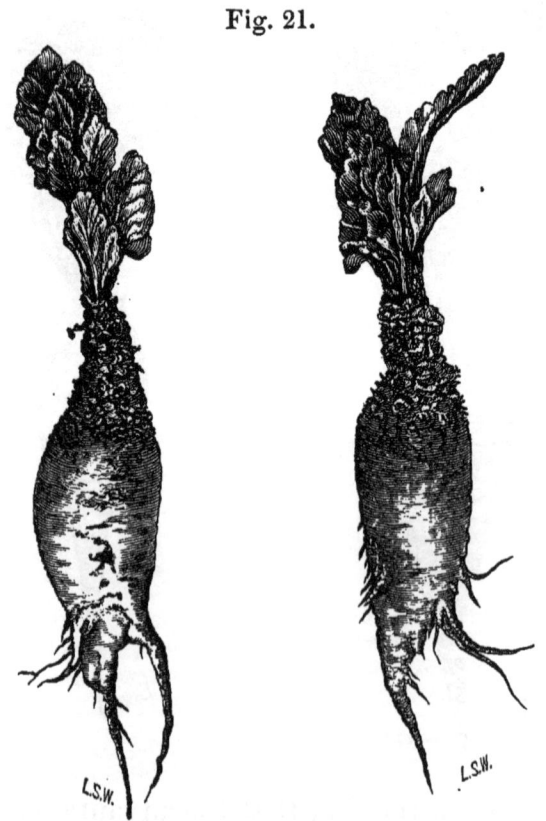

of 14,500 kilog. (31,900 lbs.) to the hectare (two and a half acres). The necks had greatly augmented in length, and with this an increase of 3.7 per cent. in the weight of the mutilated. Two of the average normal

LEAVES OF THE SUGAR BEET. 99

and two of the stripped were photographed (see figs. 20–21) as shown. Those that were untouched are long, have very short necks, whilst the others, on the contrary, are short, with long necks, with the many small roots adhering to the outer surface.[1]

The loss of sugar in the latter case was compensated by an equivalent of water,[2] and when this occurred a certain amount of non-crystallizable sugar was formed.

[1] The results obtained by analysis were:—

	Beets untouched.	Beets stripped.
Water	85.600	88.250
Sugar	9.320	6.210
Nitric elements	4.360	4.559
Mineral salts	0.719	0.981
	100.000	100.000

[2] Schwartz, a Belgium agriculturist, considers that if 100 represents roots untouched, 98 would be the yield if stripped once, and 58 twice, etc.

PART III.

CHAPTER I.

SOILS. GENERAL CONSIDERATIONS.

ONE of the principal reasons given by Americans why the beet culture has not been introduced into the United States is that our soil is not adapted to it. But never was an error greater than this, and we can justly say that with few exceptions on all land found above latitude 38° the beet will flourish, and with satisfactory results, if grown according to scientific principles. Evidently, over a space of many thousand miles the general composition of the soil both physical and chemical greatly varies. The first is by far the most important, as the latter can be brought with proper fertilizers to a given standard.

Apparently this would not be judicious, as the money thus expended would not be compensated by the resulting yield of roots, but the contrary has been the experience of farmers in Europe.

In the following pages we will pass in review the most important elements requisite for a soil on which the beet is to be grown, and it is advisable in all cases to adhere to the same; to those interested it will be a great saving of trouble and money, and will permit a given beet sugar establishment to render competition impossible. There are many examples which we could give of factories situated within ten miles of each other, where one is realizing large profits and the other only paying its expenses, owing to the bad selection either of the ground or to the want of men versed in the new scientific agricultural discoveries.

The color of the soils seems to vary from a light yellow to dark brown, and in many cases to black or nearly so. The last has been known to give excellent results in Russia. Those we have seen near Magdeburg, in Germany, have a darkish hue.

No given color can be named as being the best, for in many cases it is owing to an oxide of iron producing a bad effect upon the vegetation. In cold climates, where the warm season is of a short duration, the heat absorbed by the soil, and facilitating the various chemical actions produced upon the plant, should be in a given time a maximum, and for that reason a darkish hue is preferable.

Some years ago elaborate theories were advanced wishing to demonstrate that a soil to yield roots of a given quality must be of a given composition.

The following analysis is of nine samples of soils where the beet has been grown and where most excellent results were obtained in Prussia: (Schiepzig, Salzmunde, Quillschina, Dölitz, Besenstedt, Schnittersdorf, Friedeburgerhohe, Galgenberg, Benkendorf.)

SOILS. GENERAL CONSIDERATIONS.

Analysis of Prussian Soils.[1]

Composition.	Average.	Maximum.	Minimum.
Sand and clay	806.7	866.4	770.8
Mineral soluble substances .	132.0	195.4	99.2
Ferreaux.	39.8	48.5	34.4
The mineral substance contains:			
Potassa	5.93	11.83	2.33
Soda	3.86	10.14	0.60
Lime	14.57	31.42	4.07
Magnesia	5.47	10.16	0.69
Oxide of iron . . .	29.75	34.59	22.10
Oxide of manganese. .	0.92	1.72	0.25
Alumina	42.40	60.47	26.08
Sulphuric acid . . .	0.63	1.54	0.29
Phosphoric acid . .	0.76	1.50	0.31
Silicic " . .	43.87	68.75	17.49
Carbonic " . .	6.72	20.59	0.10
Chlorine	0.214	0.799	0.0007

Evidently, in making a choice of land for beet culture, if we take these as a basis, or a series of others having given good results, we cannot be far from the truth, but it would not necessarily follow that because the ones in question contained more of a given chemical and less of another that little or no sugar could be expected; for example, when we compare the soils of Prussia, apparently heavy, and those of France.

---

[1] See Grogven, "Journal de l'association allemande," also Walkhoff, "Industrie de sucre."

Analysis of French Soils.[1]

Number of experiments:	1.	2.	3.	4.
	Dep. Somme.	North.	Aisne.	Somme.
Organic substances	5.600	4.840	5.70	8.200
Silica	81.800	82.500	79.00	42.000
Alumina	7.240	8.620	8.50	3.91
Lime	0.510	0.420	0.25	23.220
Peroxide of iron	2.880	2.180	3.50	2.310
Phosphoric acid	0.070	0.077	trace	0.385
Potassa	0.064	0.140	"	0.044
Soda	0.085	"	2.85	0.058
Carbonic acid	0.400	0.700		19.050
Various elements	1.851	1.523		0.823
In this there existed for the total—	100.000	100.000	100.000	100.000
Nitrogen	0.088	0.120	0.154	0.270
Ammonia	0.013	0.030	0.016	0.010
Sand	72.100	80.000	62.000	35.770
Clay	22.000	9.000	30.000	10 to 12.000

The analysis of each is very different, but good results are obtained in both cases; proving that this alone cannot be relied upon, and, strange to say, even up to the present day but little is known, and for that reason it is far better to plant the roots and have them analyzed and conclude their value for manufacturing purposes than to operate in an opposite direction, as then the elements which are wanting can be furnished, whilst those in excess are diminished. In all cases it is not well to consider the apparent exterior

---

[1] The first three soils above gave beets containing 12 to 14 per cent. of sugar, whilst the fourth very secondary results.

signs alone, for the subsoil is as important as the surface above. If this be not sufficiently deep the beet cannot penetrate to the required depth, and will therefore grow partly out of ground. If we suppose a soil to be formed on a granite foundation, for example, it would in all probability be barren, or nearly so, and if on shales and sandstones indifferent or bad, whilst those on nearly pure calcareous limestone might be most productive.

Then, again, the upper surface is frequently very inferior to the lower, and combining the subsoil with this the yield of roots might be most satisfactory.

It frequently happens that the subsoil is compact, and prevents the passage of water, thus producing disease,[1] etc., but can be improved by proper drainage. On the other hand, if too dry, all vegetation becomes impossible. The beet in growing, like other plants, requires three principal elements: water, carbon, and nitrogen, each of these having a special function to fulfil. As they are not all contained in the atmosphere, we can only conclude that they partly exist in the soil. The carbon is required for the formation of the sugar and the oxygen for the development of the root, etc., but of the mineral elements that are found in analyzing the plant, what their purpose is we cannot exactly say, but evidently their presence is necessary, not in excess, as the saccharine qualities would be diminished, but in certain unknown propor-

---

[1] See Chapter "Diseases of the Beet."

tions, and each having a special effect upon the resulting root. It is generally admitted that the soils should not be new, as the excess of organic matter would produce bad effects, but in opposition to this Walkhoff tells us that those of Russia give excellent results, and far better than others having been in use for many years.

The beet in growing, from the germinating to the harvesting period, requires a soil of a texture such that but little resistance will be offered, as otherwise the root instead of being long and thin would, on the contrary, be short and stout, a shape not desirable. It must also be understood for the same reason that small stones should not exist, as the growth of the plant would take place on both sides of the same, producing a forked *root*, and containing the obstruction in its centre; this alone might be the cause of much harm in working the beet. Theoretically speaking, a pure and sandy soil would have the best physical texture, as far as the resistance went, but the silica here existing would offer but few of the nourishing elements which the plant requires, and as here the porosity would be such that but few of the nourishing constituents the beet requires, such as water (humidity), would remain at its disposal, but simply passing through, the necessary organic matter would in all probability be found many inches below and in some cases beyond the reach of the root. When these sandy soils are from alluvial deposits from a river bed, and are subject to a yearly overflow, most excellent roots will result. These roots have a strong texture, and contain a high percentage of sugar; but, as these soils are not common, the combination with some other soil becomes necessary. We have at our disposal various manures and fertilizers, but these, unless in very large quantities, will not produce the desired effect.

If we now consider various clays, having alumina in great excess, these will produce roots also very inferior, as here the powers of absorption are too great, and but little evaporation will follow, and when in wet, cold climates they will be shortly choked with aquatic cryptogamia. These varieties of soils, more especially when pure, offer great resistance to the penetration of the plant, and in many cases the cultivation of any root could not possibly take place. Here then, again, it becomes important to have combination with another soil. As a pure calcareous one will have many of the above disadvantages, it should also be combined in given proportions with an argillaceous or sandy one in order to obtain satisfactory results. The sablo-calcareous are excellent on the condition that they contain a certain amount of humus. The action of the chalky portion is not exactly known, but it is generally admitted that when this is in large proportions the quality of the root is much improved.

The researches of Leplay on this subject have been most interesting. It would be difficult to say what this action is exactly owing to, but some contend that the lime has taken an active part in decomposing, under the influence of heat, the various chemicals, for example, in neutralizing the alkaline carbonates from the acids, and thus preventing the formation of glucose in the root; or, again, a portion of the carbonic acid being set free, the plant absorbs the same, throwing out the oxygen and keeping the carbon, etc. Leplay contends that the soil in close proximity to the root will contain less lime than others that are at a distance. The *argillo-sandy* soils also give good results. They contain about 30 per cent. of clay, 70 per cent. of sand, and 5 per cent. of carbonate of lime, and have not the inconvenience of many soils of an argillaceous nature, as the air and water penetrate with ease.

We now have the argillo-calcareous, containing about 33 per cent. of clay, about 45 per cent. of sand, and the remainder of carbonate of lime. It is much liked for beet culture, but we do not recommend this as a type.

We must, as a general thing, admit that soils that are composed largely of argil will give a satisfactory yield, but the roots will be watery, containing but little sugar and a large amount of foreign matter. The calcareous ones, on the contrary, give small crops, but desirable roots.

There are various chemicals[1] that are said to produce or to be most favorable to the formation of the sugar.

---

[1] See Chapter "Fertilizers."

What these exactly are has been questioned for years past. Whatever the physical or chemical properties of the soils may be, if not ploughed in the proper manner to permit the air, etc., to penetrate, they will in all cases give bad results, and even then the variation of the weather and temperature will have the same effect, but these are beyond the control of man, for which he cannot be blamed.

CHAPTER II.

PREPARATION OF THE SOIL, OR TILLAGE.

The importance of bringing the elements of which the subsoil is composed to the surface has been before explained. This might, as many suppose, be done in one operation with a good subsoil plough, but bad crops would then follow, for the reason that the air could not penetrate into every portion of it, this being requisite for the healthful growth of the root. The preparation of the soil is more complicated than may at first be supposed, and evidently varies not only with each country but also with each variety, as the absorption or reduction of the various gases would not be the same in a sandy as in an argillaceous texture, and the needs in each case greatly differ. We cannot enter into the practical details of the numerous cases that might present themselves, but will consider the various operations in one of an average composition.

In Europe the tillage of the soil for beet culture is effected according to two methods, neither of which is perfect. These are:—

1. *Drills*, or on nearly horizontal levels.
2. *Hills*.

The first is now the general practice, and we can

with difficulty understand why it should be, as the second has many advantages which do not exist in the cultivation in drills.

1. *Cultivation in Drills.*

The first operation is with a small light plough shortly after the crop, wheat or rye, which precedes the beet, has been harvested. This should be done as soon as possible, as the soil is then comparatively damp. If several weeks have elapsed, evaporation would have taken place, and it would not be so easily worked. The roots of the small weeds are thus exposed to the sun, they then dry, and are no longer to be dreaded. Shortly after this a harrow is passed over the land thus worked, and destroys the remaining parasitic plants, and is in most cases very effectual. An ordinary plough is now made use of, penetrating the soil as deeply as possible, then this is again harrowed. The land is now in a condition to be exposed to the variations of the weather, snow, ice, and rain. The effect produced is the pulverization of the entire mass, which is at the same time left in a state of humidity most satisfactory. The airing is complete, this being partly aided by the decomposition of the organic vegetable matter, the resulting gases which make their escape into the atmosphere leaving behind openings through which the air can freely pass, and which are in the spring at the disposal of the beets, that penetrate to a very great depth on the condition that the soil is again turned over with the assistance of *spring ploughing*.

This is done in various directions, the object being to unite well the different soils brought to the surface. The ploughs used are of numerous types, a description of which would have but little interest for the American public. The double ones are much preferred, as they have the advantage of throwing the ground to the left or the right, as the case may be. Their weight varies from 300 lbs. and upward, and they are drawn by horses or oxen, the number of which varies with the physical texture of the soil. Steam ploughing has many advocates in Europe, and we are convinced it is the only system for culture on a large scale, as the work done is far superior and at the same time cheaper than with animal traction. When this is complete a harrow is passed over the field. At Magdeburg we have seen them repeat this with the harrow inverted, thus breaking up masses that had not been sufficiently pulverized. The rolling of the field before the sowing is strongly advocated by some, but we do not consider it advisable.

Hoeing is the next operation, and is frequently done before the plant has shown itself above the surface, and in many cases will have a most extraordinary effect, as it loosens the outer crust, thus facilitating the entrance of the air and lessening the resistance the young root has to overcome. The young weeds that are becoming visible between the lines are then gotten rid of.

Various mechanical devices have been brought to notice, and in many cases adopted, these working principally when the young root is about two inches in height. They are generally assisted by hand labor, as it would be dangerous to the final crop to approach within several inches. In Germany they prefer hand labor, and we can only indorse their ideas, as the results of the use of machinery brought to our notice were far from being satisfactory. It is advisable to rid the soil of the weeds by hand rather than with a hoe for the first ten days, as the slightest vibration produced upon the ground in proximity to the final desired root might result in considerable injury, whilst, on the contrary, when the plant has attained the size shown in fig. 22, the danger is over.

The thinning out is the next operation. The methods vary with the practice in sowing. When this is broadcast the labor is greater than when in lines, as in the first case the roots must be destroyed in such a manner that a given distance will be left between the various remaining plants, whilst in lines, the space between each is only to be considered. If the thinning out be not done with care, the crop will be ruined. Some reject the use of the hoe and advocate the knife, only penetrating the ground to a sufficient depth to destroy all roots between the desired ones; this is most wise when the sowing has taken place in clusters or even when but one seed has been planted in a given spot, from which have resulted three or more roots. If these had been pulled they would in all probability have loosened the ground and caused the remaining ones

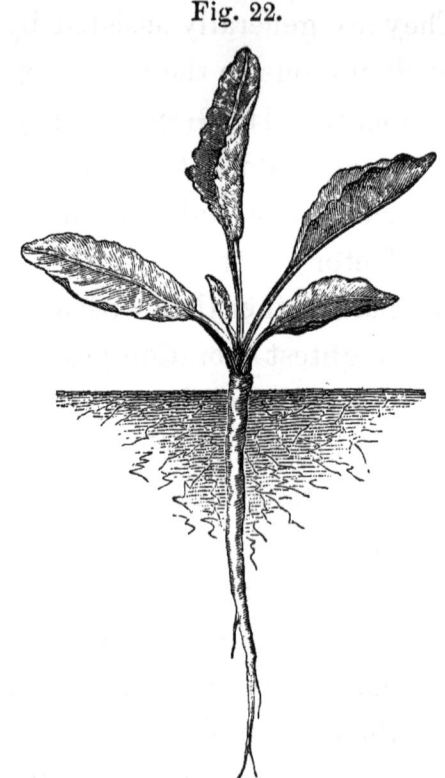

Fig. 22.

Showing the general appearance of the plant when thinning out can commence.

to perish. When the seeds are planted in lines we consider that a hoe could here be utilized within a few inches of a cluster, and finishing these as before stated. In this way there would be two operations, the first being completed by the second, and shortly afterwards

PREPARATION OF THE SOIL, OR TILLAGE.

a second hoeing is desirable. From this time forward the last operation should be repeated over and over again. As a general thing it must be admitted that no economy will result from this neglect. In France it is considered that, when the land has been hoed three times after the thinning out, this is all that is required, whilst in Germany (where far less weeds exist, the ground being there more thoroughly worked), this is repeated five and even more times. It is well to choose dry weather for the hoeing, and, when sandy soils are cultivated, it is desirable not to penetrate too deeply with the hoe, as the evaporation would become excessive. The hoeing has for a general effect the development of the leaves, which results in a greater formation of sugar, but should be continued only until the root has attained its full growth, and would then have the general appearance shown in fig. 23. If we should continue, the leaves would become still larger, at the very period that the saccharine elements are increasing, and the latter would be diminished if the general foliage became too excessive. The weeds then are no longer to be dreaded, as they are not exposed to the light, and receive but little air, and are consequently smothered by the leaves of the beet.

In conclusion, we would mention that in France they frequently pass a roller over the field before the thinning out; this loosens the ground, and is supposed to facilitate the coming operation, after which the entire

116 THE SUGAR BEET.

crop has the aspect of being ruined, but the next day the young plants grow with renewed vigor. This we

Fig. 23.

Showing the general appearance of the root in the soil when the leaves have attained their full growth.

do not advise, as it can be done only by experienced hands.

At the Paris Exhibition a device for thining out was exhibited. It consisted of a cylinder formed of slats, the distance between each represented the space to be left between the remaining roots.

The plants on which this passes are crushed, while those passing through between the slats are left untouched. This is more theoretical than practical, and its use is not desirable.

2. *Cultivation in Hills.*

The idea of cultivation in hills dates back to the middle of the last century, and is at present adopted for various house-crops, corn, etc. Our American farmers understand the good here realized, and we are convinced it is the only method of cultivation to be adopted for this special case in the United States. The cost per acre is less than in drills for beet culture, and many difficulties of cultivating the soil are gotten rid of. Of late years Mr. Champonnois[1] has made much effort in this direction, and through his influence numerous experiments have been made. These are most satisfactory, and many farmers consider that, if this system of beet culture had been adopted ere this, the general condition of the ground would have been far better than it now is, and it is considered that it comes near to the solution of the problem, a large yield and a high percentage of sugar.

---

[1] We have exchanged letters with Mr. Champonnois upon this subject.

The soil when heavy is prepared just before the winter, the frost, etc., having the same effect as mentioned above. Subsoil ridge ploughs are here made use of, these penetrating the ground some twelve inches; the earth is thrown to the right and left, each forming a portion of the coming hill, which is completed on the return trip.

These hills are about thirty-one inches apart from summit to summit (see fig. 24) which distance varies with the height of the same. Their inclination is 45°, this being considered the best for facilitating the flow of water resulting from the rains, while at the same time their general shape remains the same. On light soils it is not advisable to form these before the winter, but only some weeks before sowing.[1] In the first case the manure is added, and, after the ploughing is complete, a heavy roller is passed over the entire mass. This renders it more compact, and it is then better able to resist the variations of the weather, and when the spring arrives another ploughing takes place, and, to complete the hill, a roller is made use of having the final desired shape. It now becomes important to compress the hill with a heavy roller in order to have this adhere to the surface below. The special roller is again made use of (see fig. 24), and the soil is now ready for the sowing. If we have a light sandy soil to contend with, all these operations should take place within ten days of the time of sowing. The thinning out is effected

---

[1] See "Sowing of the Seed."

by hand entirely, and immediately afterwards the hoeing commences. This hoeing is done with a mechanical device approaching within a short distance of the plant, and is repeated as often as possible, until the weeds are no longer to be dreaded. When the roots are matured the harvesting can be done with a plough, leaving just sufficient earth to keep the root in a vertical position. They can then be extracted by hand with the greatest ease, in soils of the closest texture.

To make more apparent the advantages here gained, we will suppose two beds (see fig. 24), *A B* and *C D*

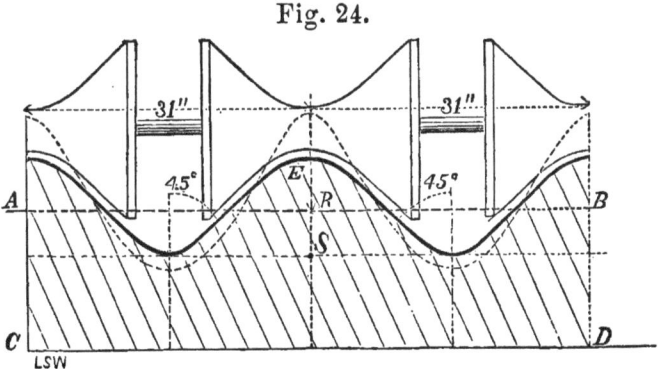

Showing the shape of the hill before and after the roller has passed upon the same.

the distance between each representing the stratum in which the root will grow to advantage; below *C D* it cannot for various reasons penetrate. The dotted line represents the hill produced after one ploughing, and the other, or the black undulated, the final one, *E R*, represents the portion above the first level, and *E S* the height of soil that has become loosened by this system. Here the first apparent advantage is that, the beet having sufficient soil to penetrate, the neck will not grow above the ground, and, having but little resistance to overcome, the root will become long and thin, which shape is desirable.

There no longer exists the danger of the ordinary method of planting, which is a dread of crowding when nearer than seven inches, but, on the contrary, they can be planted as close as six inches. This alone greatly augments the yield per acre. This distance of thirty-one inches between lines permits a cart to enter to collect the roots after harvesting, or to bring the required manure.

If we consider the manner in which the root here grows, great advantages will become apparent. (See

Fig. 25.

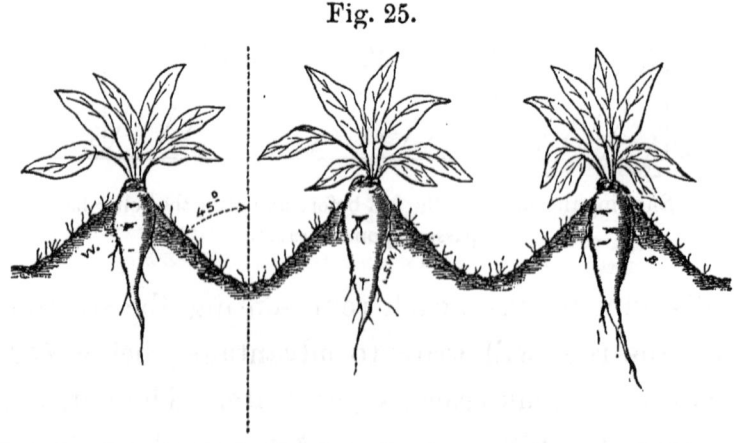

Showing the roots in their places during the last period of their growth.

fig. 25.) In the ordinary system of cultivation the leaves soon cover the ground and prevent the soil from

PREPARATION OF THE SOIL, OR TILLAGE.

receiving the light, heat, and air which are requisite for the growth of the root. But here, on the contrary, they are elevated, the air can penetrate freely, the light also, as the distance between the lines is such that even an excessive growth of the leaves will not obstruct the same, and if it does, nothing prevents augmenting the distance between the hills from summit to summit.

If heavy rains occur they find an easy passage, and the subsoil filtration producing disease, etc., is but little to be dreaded. The air circulates most freely between these hills, and keeps the soil in a perfect state of moisture, and the formation of hard crusts on the surface is not to be dreaded.

The leaves, which long before harvesting commence to wither in the ordinary system of cultivation, in consequence of the radiated heat from the soil, will remain in a perfect state until the full growth of the root. There remains to consider the hoeing. In cultivating in drills we would not recommend any mechanical device for this operation, as there exists a continual danger of harming the young root, and it has to be accomplished by hand labor, and even then there is continual danger of cutting the small roots adhering to the exterior portion of the beet, which, as some admit, greatly help the formation of the sugar. This is but little to be dreaded when the beet grows in hills, as these are out of reach. The mechanical hoe drawn by one horse can enter between the hills with perfect ease, and produce little if any harm. This being the case, it will be understood that great economy of labor will result. We would at the same time advise that some personal attention be given to that portion of the hill in proximity to the root, this to be attended to by hand, as it frequently occurs that the beet has a portion of its neck above surface and wants hilling up.

Some farmers with whom we have talked advise the placing of the manure between the hills during the growth of the root, this having for advantage the keeping of the soil damp, but the infiltration of various elements preventing the formation of the sugar is not desirable, and, contrary to the opinion of some, we cannot believe that an exposure of this sort would be advantageous to the quality of a fertilizer to be used several months subsequently.

In addition to the above, we can only say that many difficulties of the ordinary cultivation are here gotten rid of, and it is to be hoped that the cultivation of beets in hills will be the system of the future. We have consequently many agricultural implements to make use of for the tilling of the soil, and these should be of the best and in sufficient number not to necessitate any loss of time. Practically speaking, ploughs, etc., of any description can be utilized in the cultivation in drills. The hills require a special appliance, and for that reason the system has not been put into practice in many cases, but in a new country like our own this cannot be an objection.

CHAPTER III.

VARIOUS MANURES.

How unfortunate it is that a country like our own, most productive in every way, yielding crops on soils and in a manner far excelling those of other nations, should not have at the same time a greater number of men sufficiently versed in scientific agricultural principles, or even its elementary rules, to fully appreciate the probability of exhausting the soil, and the certainty of rendering it sterile, if a change for the better does not take place ere long. There might be some excuse if we had not before our eyes examples such as Sicily, which furnished the grain for the Roman Empire, and where the soil was quite equal in fertility to our own, and which, from neglect and exhaustion, is now worthless or nearly so. This exhaustion takes place with every plant, and in a manner that varies with the soil, etc., and, in order that things should remain normal, it becomes necessary to restore what has been taken away. As far as the direct chemicals are concerned it is not difficult, as science will exactly tell what these are, but when we are obliged to consider organic compounds, the problem is changed, and becomes most complicated. But, as a general thing, a perfect manure, so-called, is one that contains all the elements a plant requires for its development. What these exactly are we do not know, but are obliged from that fact to admit theories advanced by the agronomists of the period. In analyzing the crops harvested we know exactly what has been absorbed, and what consequently must be returned. Apparently the use of the barnyard manure resulting from the cattle that have been fed upon the crops would come nearer to a solution of the problem than any other, but unfortunately these cattle are not in sufficient number (in a majority of cases) to entirely consume the same, and, admitting that this system of fertilization were perfect, this manure is seldom, if ever, in sufficient quantities to supply the demand. On the other hand, if we remember that in the manufacture of sugar from the beet, or growth of the grain (wheat, rye, etc.), or the fattening of live stock, etc., we produce elements that are sold, and we therefore take from the land principles that should remain. If these had again been returned nothing would have been lost to the soil, but it would have necessitated the killing and utilization of every portion of these products, which would have been practicably impossible. In the case of beet culture, as already stated, the necks and the leaves return a large portion of what has been extracted, but there still remain elements requisite for a perfect fertility. On the other hand, we may consider that soils may have a too high or too low percentage of a given chemical, and to render beet culture possible these must be increased or diminished in given quantities. With the barnyard manure it is not possible to produce these changes, and it is most natural to direct our attention to some other system of manuring, where we can have the growth of the plant more under our control; and for this reason we cannot endorse the opinion advanced by some, that organic manures are the only ones that yield satisfactory results. The plant should find at its disposal during each period of its existence all the principles it requires, and for that reason the various elements should be soluble at given times. Here we have an argument in favor of the mineral fertilizers over the barnyard manure. These facts for a long time were not fully understood or appreciated, and even men like Liebig committed errors, as he manufactured a fertilizer that contained non-soluble elements, contending that if they possessed the contrary qualities they would be soon carried off by the rain, etc. In the case of barnyard manure it is obliged to undergo various changes, produced by fermentation, before any portion can be absorbed by the root, and these, as a general thing, are in excess, which is most disastrous when beet culture be considered, as these organic nitric elements, as well as the chlorides, etc., prevent the formation of the sugar. The absorption of these seems to vary with the humidity of the soil.

Chemistry has been able, through the exertions of George Ville, as well as of other men of scientific fame, to produce a fertilizer taking the place of barnyard manure, not only giving equal results as to the yield, but at far less cost. If these mineral manures had been advocated only by given manufacturers of fertilizers, they would have had but little interest, but such is not the case, as the farmers have given them their endorsement, not without considerable discussion. It was argued that the organic fertilizer contained elements (humus, etc.) that did not or could not exist in any chemical compound, and that the results obtained with the latter, however surprising at first, would have for a final ending the exhaustion of the ground; but, as we shall presently see, this is not the case. Evidently these, like all others, have at times been utilized in a most irrational manner, producing a bad effect both on the soil and the crops, but these are circumstances we have not here to consider.

Whatever be the plant, it is composed of fourteen elements:—

1. Carbon,
2. Hydrogen,
3. Oxygen,
4. Nitrogen,
5. Phosphorus,
6. Potassium,
7. Calcium,
8. Sodium,
9. Magnesium,
10. Chlorine,
11. Iron,
12. Silicum,
13. Sulphur,
14. Manganese.

The first four, with the exception of a portion of the nitrogen, come from the air, rain, etc. These evidently have nothing to do with the exhausting principle. If we consider the last seven they are contained in all soils in abundance, and even in those nearly sterile they exist in sufficient quantities. There remain, 1st nitro-

VARIOUS MANURES.

gen, 2d phosphorus, 3d potassium, 4th calcium, that are taken away, and must be returned, and any fertilizer to be *complete* must contain all of them in quantities that vary with the soil and plant, and one that does not contain them is imperfect, unless the wanting chemical is in excess in the soil under consideration. We have for this purpose various manures, which may be divided in two classes, 1st organic, 2d mineral, these are used singly or combined.

1st. *Organic.*—The most important is the barnyard[1]

---

[1] Mr. George Ville gives the following composition for barnyard manure, it being considered an average:—

Water	80.00	Without value for plants as it is found in great abundance in the soil, being the result of rains, etc.
Carbon	6.80	13.29. Without value for plants; arise in sufficient abundance in the air and rain.
Hydrogen	0.82	
Oxygen	5.67	
Silica	4.42	5.23. In sufficient quantities in all soils, and thereby form elements of but little value, and the returning of them is no longer necessary.
Chloride	0.04	
Sulphuric acid	0.13	
Oxide of iron	0.40	
Soda		
Magnesia	0.24	
Nitrogen	0.41	1.48. The soil contains these in very limited quantities, and the return of them becomes necessary.
Phosphoric acid	0.18	
Potassa	0.49	
Lime	0.56	
Total	100.00	

This learned professor tells us that the 13.29 of carbon, oxygen, and hydrogen mentioned above represent undecomposed fibres that have become black on account of the alteration that has taken place. Consequently the only active principles form but 1.48 per cent. of the total, which can only produce its effect after a given time.

manure, giving large crops of beets when used in excess, and when in the soil undergoes great changes; if the weather is too rainy the nitric elements making their escape either in a free state, as ammonia or organic complex alkalies. Here, in all probability, is a great loss, or perhaps a gain, resulting from the transformation of the nitrogen into nitric acid in combining with the oxygen of the carbon elements in the plant. If this organic substance is in a damp oxygenated soil the amount of nitrogen if it remains will, as a general thing, be in excess of what is actually required, and for that reason increase the size of the root, but diminish at the same time its saccharine qualities. If, on the contrary, the weather is dry, the decomposition will not entirely take place, and the beet will not derive the expected advantage from the same. The composition of this varies with the animal and straw from which it was produced. The amount of phosphoric acid[1] it contains is extremely small; this being advantageous to the formation of the sugar, it is advisable to add the same in the shape of a phosphate; evidently on calcareous soils the general decomposition is greatly facilitated.

These manures are generally from cows, horses, sheep, and pigs. The combination of the first two yields the best results. If we consider other excrements of similar sorts it is advisable to mix the same

---

[1] In beets we have analyzed the quantity of sugar is directly proportional to the above, and this varies with the amount at its disposal in the soil or manure.

with a certain amount of coal dust; in this manner the odor is greatly diminished, and in small quantities will give tolerable results as a fertilizer. For beet culture this last we do not recommend, unless in urgent cases. The same can be said of blood, waste meat, etc. We now have the most natural of all, which are called—

Green Manures.—These represent the fertilizers evidently known during all periods of civilization. The principle consists in sowing a given crop with the idea of utilizing it as a manure, harvesting the same before the blossoms show themselves. If the seed had appeared they might give considerable trouble. The whole is buried with a plough several inches beneath the surface, gives life to various elements, which render soluble many portions entering into the composition of the soil. The great disadvantage here existing is that it does not return any of the mineral substances the previous crops had taken away, and for that reason to make it perfect it is necessary to add the same. The crops generally used for green manures are clover, mustard, flax, etc., and in all cases should be buried before the winter sets in, as their action upon the coming root might be the direct cause of considerable harm. This system of fertilizing is good for poor soils, and we are convinced that it would render most satisfactory results in the Western States, where transportation is difficult.

Oil Cake.—Of various origins this has a most active

influence upon the vegetation, as it decomposes with great rapidity, and more especially after a heavy rain. It is generally desirable, when used, to mix this with pulverized bones or any other phosphate; for beets going to seed its use should be rejected.

We now have various waste products from the sugar factories, such as strings, woollen bags, etc., but the service rendered by them is comparatively small.

Guano.—This contains a large amount of organic nitric elements but few alkalies, and its use is not desirable on soils that are heavily charged with the former. At one period this fertilizer was used in large quantities in France for beet culture, and brought about the so-called "maladie du guano," the cause of which could only with difficulty be explained.[1] But at that time the importance of other elements besides the nitric was not understood. When utilized at the present day it is generally combined with another manure acting as a complement to the same. Some contend that its action ceases before the root has entirely matured; this being owing to the solubility of the ammoniacal elements. Such being the case the beets would be easily worked. Mr. Walkhoff and others advise the mixture of the guano, with pulverized bones.

We cannot exactly decide as to the comparative practical advantages or disadvantages of this fertilizer,

---

[1] Some contend that a sort of microscopic vegetable parasite forms on the root, and comes from an exhaustion of the soil.

as in conversing with farmers we find their ideas so greatly to differ.

But it is generally admitted that guano stimulates the growth of the leaves, and at the period when the sugar is forming; this being the case, the latter is, as before stated, greatly diminished. As a general thing we cannot recommend any organic manure for beet culture, but, on the contrary, chemical compounds are superior, and from them much is to be expected.

Mineral Fertilizers.—As before stated plants require for their development four elements. To supply these we have at our disposal various chemicals that form within themselves four distinct groups:—

α. Nitric fertilizer,
β. Phosphoric fertilizer,
γ. Calcareous fertilizer,
δ. Potassic fertilizer.

α. *Nitric Fertilizer.*—There can be no doubt as to the influence of nitric elements upon the growth of the beet as well as other plants, but there is uncertainty as to the advantage attributed in the formation of sugar. A vast number of experiments have been made to ascertain what relation if any existed between the nitrogen contained in the root to that of the soil or the fertilizer made use of, but none of these agree in a manner that would convince those interested that they had been executed in good faith. There is one fact that cannot be doubted, and that is that any soil highly manured either with organic or chemical—corresponding to a nitric—fertilizer, will yield beets poor in sugar.

THE SUGAR BEET.

The albuminoids will form in its place. On the other hand, there can be no doubt, if used in rational quantities, the roots will be satisfactory. Pagnoul, Geo. Ville, and others conclude positively that the sugar augments in the beet when the nitric elements diminish; whilst others have made experiments proving the opposite.[1] We are convinced that this nitrogen has a bad effect, as beets growing on soils very rich in it are of a bad quality for manufacturing purposes. This has not been sufficiently understood, and the farmers generally add a new supply; this produces worse results than if it had been left alone, but fortunately, for the manufacturer's good, they are now restricted as to the quan-

---

[1] Champignon and Pellet made the following:—

Culture of Vilmorin and Andrews.	Varieties of roots.	Sugar per cent.	Nitrogen in 100 gr. of normal substance.
1st. { 42^k of nitrogen / 96^k of phosphoric acid	{ Vilmorin improved / Rose neck / Yellow neck	12.6 / 8.4 / 6.2	0.185 / 0.160 / 0.120
2d. { Heavy soil growth on second year's manure	{ Vilmorin improved / Rose neck / Yellow neck	12.3 / 8.9 / 5.4	0.168 / 0.170 / 0.113

Second series by the same, as above—

Saccharine per cent.	Nitrogen per cent.
14.4	3.1
14.0	3.2
13.6	3.8
12.4	2.4
11.0	2.7
10.4	1.8
9.1	1.7
9 2	2.1

tities. The nitrogen is absorbed by the root in the state of ammonia or combined with an acid, and forms soluble salts; which do not all come from the soil, but about one-half from the air. Of chemicals to form a nitric fertilizer, we have at our disposal nitrate of soda and potassa and sulphate of ammonia. The advantage of the latter is that it can be taken up immediately by the plant, whilst the nitrate has to undergo certain changes, the alkali acting a very secondary part when compared with the nitrogen.

Mr. Vivien contends that the variation of the action of the nitrates is mainly due to the amount of nitrogen which the air happens to contain, and varies from year to year; for example, in 1870, with the same amount of fertilizer, the sugar contained in the beet was far less than in years previous. If a large yield of beets is desired it is indifferent in what shape this element is furnished, but when this is of secondary importance, as compared to quality, it is well not to surpass 100 lbs. of nitrogen to the acre. If a certain amount of phosphate of lime is properly united with the same the bad effects of an excess will be much diminished. From what has been said it is easy to understand what an important element the nitrogen is.

Nitrate of Soda.—For years in France this fertilizer created a great furor, and the importation from foreign countries for a given period, which was very large, all of a sudden fell to a small figure. This was caused by the final exhausting influence which experience upon the soil and sugar in the root seemed to prove, and also by reason of a most extraordinary accident which occurred at Blandain (Belgium). A sort of spontaneous combustion was the cause. This had taken place in a centrifugal of the sugar factory, the cause being attributed to a certain quantity of sulphate or nitrate of potassa the juice contained; this had been the result of a chemical change in the soil. The nitric acid had combined with the potassa contained therein, and formed a nitrate with this variation taking place under the influence of the sugar and the high temperature caused by the rapid velocity of the apparatus. Mr. Corenwinder remarked that the crystals of it were apparent, and these united with the sugar. This was owing to the fact that the crystallization of the two had taken place simultaneously. This would lead to many errors and much deception, augmenting the apparent density of the juice and yielding a sugar having but little if any commercial value. This chemical contains about 16 per cent. of nitrogen, and its use even with a superphosphate of lime to form a complete fertilizer is not desirable, and we can positively assert that any factory permitting its use alone will, within a few years, come to a bad end.

It is of interest to state that on calcareous soils it would bring about many reactions; carbonic acid making its escape, carbonate of lime and potassa would soon form, and the mineral substance the beet then contained would be greatly increased. The proportion of these nitrates in the beet is extremely variable, depending upon the variety of the root and the nature of the fertilizer made use of. If the nitrates are used it is advisable, in order to derive a benefit from them, to place them on the soil during the early part of the vegetation, as they have a tendency to descend to the lower stratum.

Sulphate of Ammonia.—This is taken up, as before stated, by the plant with great facility, and we must not forget that we have here a fertilizer that is by no means complete, and, if the lime and phosphate (small amounts) are in the soil, these will become less and less until finally the land becomes sterile. The sulphate of ammonia is more desirable on calcareous soils than are the nitrates. Many do not consider this sulphate as economical as might be desired, as large quantities are lost by evaporation. These salts exist only in small quantities in beets, and but little harm can result from their use. We have no doubt but that the combination with the nitrates is desirable, their physical properties being opposite—one rising to the surface and the other sinking to the stratum beneath. If combined with a phosphate even better results may be expected. This chemical contains about 20 per cent. of nitrogen.

Phosphoric Fertilizer.—It is now generally admitted that phosphoric acid is one of the desired elements for the formation of sugar, and its percentage in the beet varies with the amount in the fertilizer.[1] This chemical has but little influence upon the growth of the root. In opposition to this Pagnoul advances the hypothesis that its functions are as important as those of nitrogen, and, instead of preventing or diminishing the absorption of the nitrates by the beet, it facilitates it. The basic phosphate of lime which is insoluble changes and becomes soluble by combination with acids, and consequently it is desirable to use the latter on soils possessing these qualities, otherwise they will be without effect. We now have the superphosphate rendered soluble with sulphuric acid, it being thus prepared in a commercial way before it is sold as a fertilizer; thus producing a double effect, furnishing the phosphoric acid and also the lime. These penetrate the subsoil and are then at the disposal of the roots. They should not be used on acidulous soils which contain about 11 per cent. of soluble acid. We now have the precipitated phosphate, the use of which is not desirable, as it is practically impossible to detect the frauds that occur in selling it. If pure it contains as much as 40 per cent. of phosphoric acid. Here also they penetrate the subsoil. In consequence of the damp condition in which these phosphates frequently

---

[1] Experiments of Joulie:—

	Per cent. phosphoric acid in the root.
Without phosphoric acid in the fertilizer	0.45
.65^k " " " "	0.55
1.30^k " " " "	0.69
1.92^k " " " "	1.11

are, it is desirable in using them to unite a certain amount of earth, and spread the same as if one compact mass. On soils that are poor many advantages may be derived from their use, whilst, on the contrary, those of ordinary composition will be but little benefited, and for that reason it is desirable to ascertain in advance approximately what one has to contend with. The soluble phosphate of lime cannot easily be brought in direct contact with a carbonate of lime or with an alkaline carbonate without a loss of phosphoric acid, and it would then change to insoluble phosphate.

Some advocate the uniting of the phosphate with manure. The phosphate of mineral origin is indorsed by some, as its dissolution is slow, but we consider that on non-acidulous soils the phosphate of animal origin is far preferable.

Potassic Fertilizers.—Potassa is more easily absorbed by the beet than by any other plant, and, as its presence prevents the formation of sugar, its use to any extent is not desirable. The Germans for the past few years have contended that great results may be expected from it.[1] The fertilizer from the mines of Strassfurth (Germany) is composed principally of chloride of potassium, but if utilized bad results will follow, and the same may be said of the sulphate. Every equivalent of these will prevent the same amount of sugar crystallizing. The disadvantage of the nitrate of potassa has been before

---

[1] Mr. Corenwinder planted beets of various varieties on various soils both
10

explained, but as it contains 13 per cent. of nitrogen and 45 per cent. of potassa, on soils where both of these are wanting advantage may be derived; but, as a general thing, most of those of ordinary fertility are sufficiently rich, and they should consequently seldom be used. Of late years experiments have been made to ascertain the possibility of substituting soda for potassa, and it is now admitted that the plan is feasible, and that good results may be expected if chloride of sodium is added. This will, however, yield poor roots for manufacturing purpose.

Calcareous Fertilizers.—We have before had occasion to explain the various chemical changes that take place on calcareous soils which are, as a general thing, advantageous to the growth and quality of the root. When calcium is wanting it becomes evident that

of France and Italy, to ascertain if there existed any relation between the amount of potassa and the sugar the beet contained.

Origin of the beets.	Sugar in 1 litre of juice.	Potassa in 1 litre of juice.	Observations.
Modena,	59.50	3.440	These beets grew on a soil very rich in humus.
Milan,	85.00	4.613	
Bologna,	55.60	6.866	
Vicenza,	52.50	4.180	
Vicenza,	63.00	4.620	
Havrincourt,	132.40	2.166	With chemical fertilizer and ordinary manure.
Haubourdin,	99.70	2.308	Without manure.
"	96.40	2.327	With chemical fertilizer.
"	90.70	2.315	With oil cake.

From these experiments it becomes doubtful if potassa is possessed of any of the attributed qualities.

good results may be expected from its use. The waste products (defecation, animal black, etc.) contain large quantities of the same, their use as a fertilizer is most desirable, for we also then have besides a certain amount of lime, the foreign mineral elements that had been previously absorbed by the root and partly eliminated from the juice by defecation and filtration. As a general thing we must admit that certain precautions are necessary before using the calcareous fertilizers. If, at the same time, with ammoniacal salts a decomposition will take place, and thus cause a loss of nitrogen in the soil, a carbonate forming this to become soluble would require a large new supply of carbonic acid. When used as sulphate of lime it soon dissolves, and does but little harm to the other elements the soil contains; but the general advantage derived from the use of calcareous fertilizers is that it forces the non-combined acid of the soil and helps to decompose the organic. How many examples we could give in chemistry where given substances are not acted upon by acids, and when lime is added the desired effect is immediately produced. Many recommend the use of these fertilizers combined with barnyard manure, but, strange to say, the very beets that have at their disposal the largest amount of plaster are those that contain the least in their composition.

We still have a fertilizer upon which nothing has been said: this is the final molasses containing all the mineral substances that have not been returned by the waste products mentioned above, which can be united with water and readily spread over the ground.

Comparative Results Obtained with Chemical Fertilizers and ordinary Barnyard Manure.

It is now admitted that the beet will give satisfaction on soils without humus, and that the results are greatly in favor of the chemical compounds. Mr. G. Ville gives the following comparative figures:—

Expenses for 1 hectare (2½ acres).	{ Chemical fertilizer,	350^f	($70.00)
	{ Barnyard manure,	600^f	($120 00)
Yield	{ Chemical fertilizer,.	52,700^k	(115.940 lbs.)
	{ Barnyard manure,	34,800^k	(76.560 lbs.)
Value of crop . . .	{ Chemical fertilizer,	1,054^f	($210.8)
	{ Barnyard manure,	696^f	($139 2)

The fig. 26 represents the beet with a complete fertilizer used beneath and on the surface; fig. 27 represents the results obtained when on the surface only, and fig. 28 with ordinary barnyard manure. Evidently, if the size alone had been considered it would have misled the observer. Mr. Pagnoul has illustrated several of his experiments by diagrams, by which the various changes are made more apparent. (See figs. 29, 30, and 31.) The dotted line represents beets growing on chemical fertilizers and the full line with ordinary manure. One of the most striking features here shown is the rapidity with which the chemical compounds act upon the root during the time the organic manures are obliged to undergo changes. In fig. 29 we have the

VARIOUS MANURES. 141

Fig. 26. Fig. 27.

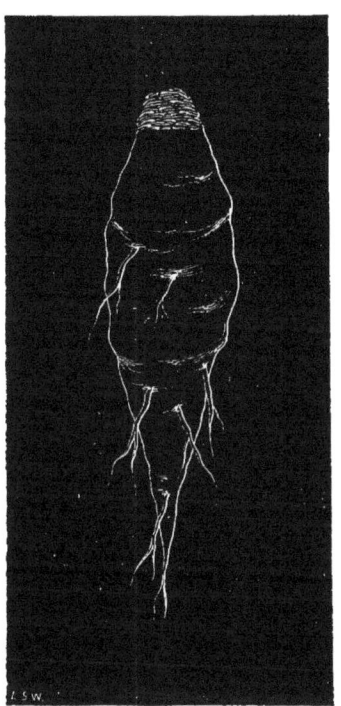 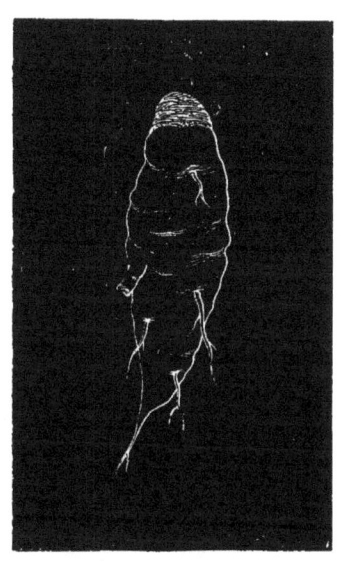

Showing the size of beet with a complete fertilizer used beneath and upon the surface.

Size of beet when complete fertilizer has been used upon the surface only.

Fig. 28.

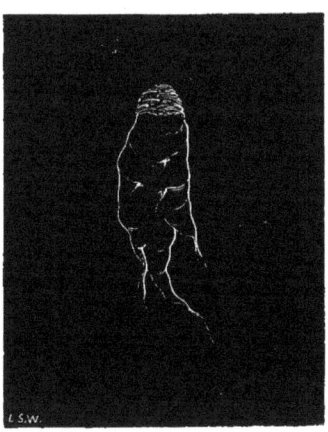

Size of beet with barnyard manure

comparative weights of the roots at different periods of their growth. From July until 5th of August, those

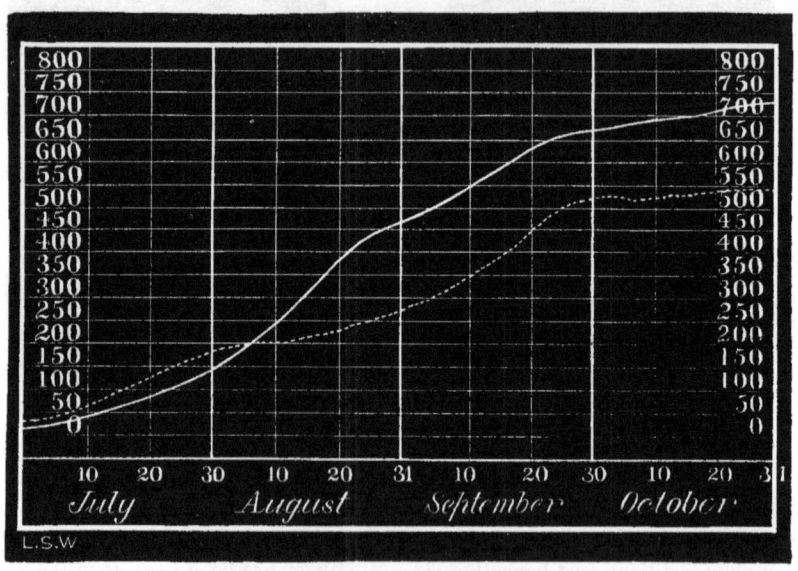

Fig. 29.
Variation in weight of roots during the growth.

- - - - - line chemical fertilizers;
———— line barnyard manure.

with the chemicals are the largest, but from this time until the harvesting period those with the ordinary manure take the lead, during which time, as shown in fig. 30, the saccharine qualities of the former are constantly superior; as for the proportion of alkaline cinders they are inferior. (See fig. 31.) We have here every advantage in favor of the chemical compounds.

Cinders of the Beet.—As a general thing lightness in weight of the cinders derived from the beet is desirable; these being composed mainly of the carbonates

VARIOUS MANURES. 143

Fig. 30.
Variation in composition of the roots.

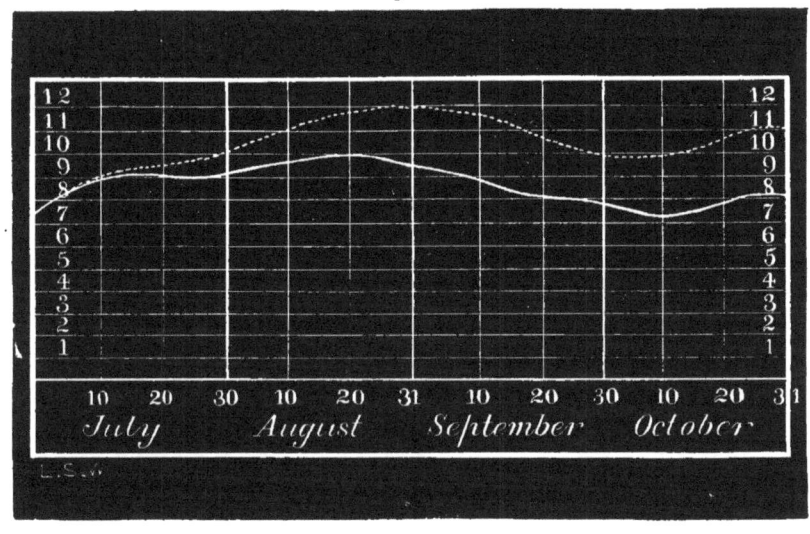

Fig. 31.

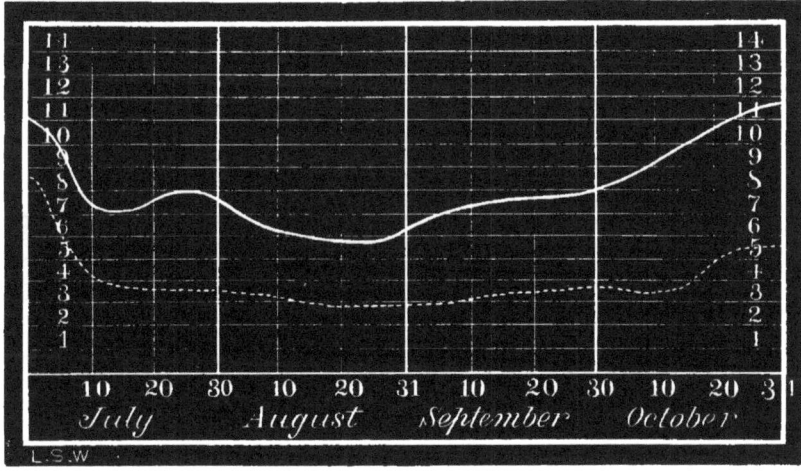

and chlorides have, as before stated, great influence on the quality of the beet. From our experiments:—

Roots containing 0.349 cinders, correspond to 12 p. ct of sugar.
"   "   0.402   "   "   11.3   "   "
"   "   0.455   "   "   11.32   "   "
"   "   0.553   "   "   10.7   "   "
"   "   0.679   "   9 2

Showing that an augmentation of the same corresponds to a decrease in the saccharine qualities, whilst, on the other hand, experiments have proven that the amount of cinders is about the same for all roots containing from 10 to 14 per cent. of sugar.[1] The various manures produce given effects upon the same.[2]

[1] Champignon and Pellet—

Saccharine percentage.	Cinders in 100 g. of beets.	Weight of cinders 100 g. of sugar.
14.4	1.05	7.2
13.6	1.13	8.2
13.3	0.95	7.1
13.1	0.93	7.2
12.7	1.06	8.2
12.0	0.94	7.8
11.8	0.90	7.6
11.2	0.93	8.2
11.0	0.77	7.0

[2] Experiments of Corenwinder.

No.	Variety of fertilizer.	Cinders for 1 litre of juice.			Soluble salts per cent. in cinders.	Composition of the soluble portion.			
						Carbonate.		Chloride of potassium.	Sulphate of potassa.
		Total.	Soluble.	Insoluble.		Potassa.	Soda.		
1	Without manure..............	7.18	4.42	2.76	61.6	65.8	15.8	11.8	5.7
2	600 k. of nitrate of soda........	8.67	6.86	1.81	79.2	57.8	26.5	10.4	5.4
3	500 k. sulphate of ammonia....	7.68	5.58	2.10	72.6	63.2	15.5	11.3	9.9
4	600 k. nitrate of soda...........	8.50	6.36	2.14	74.8	56.0	21.7	14.2	7.7
5	600 k. sulphate of ammonia....	7.30	5.29	2.01	71.1	62.1	16.9	10.7	10.1
6	600 k. nitrate of soda.......... 150 k. phosphate of lime...... 60 k. sulphate of potassa....	8.26	6.51	1.75	78.8	56.3	6.6	9.9	7.3
7	500 k. sulphate of ammonia.. 150 k. phosphate of lime..... 60 k. sulphate of potassa....	7.49	4.70	2.79	62.8	66.5	13.3	11.4	8.8
8	500 k. sulphate of ammonia.. 150 k. phosphate............. 140 k. chloride of potassium..	7.54	5.21	2.33	69.1	64.3	6.4	19.6	8.9

From Corenwinder's experiments we may conclude that when nitrate of soda is used in large quantities, the cinders from the beets having grown with the same, will contain less carbonate of potassa and more carbonate of soda than when sulphate of ammonia is used as a fertilizer. The increase of the chloride of potassium in the cinders corresponds with an increase of the same chemical in the fertilizer.

Choice of a Manure.[1]—As we have seen, the number of manures of organic and mineral origin at our disposal

---

[1] The following table shows the systems adopted by Deherain and is also most excellent; permits a comparison between the yield and cost, etc.

Nature of the manure.	Price for 100k incld'g transportation.	Manure used.		Beets harvested.		Value of crop, manure deducted
		Weight in kilog	Value. in kilog	Weight	Value 18 f. 100 k.	
	f.	k.	f.	k.	f.	f.
1. Potassic fertilizer,	13.50	1000	135	29.625	533.25	398.25
2. " "		2000	270	43.000	774.00	504
3. " "	23.50	750	176.25	49.625	893.25	717
4. " "		1500	352.50	54.750	974.25	621
5. Nothing,				56.125	1021.50	1021.50
6. { Potassic fertilizer, Phospho-guano,	13.50 35.00	1000 200 }	205	59.625	1073.25	868.25
7. { Potassa { KO fertilizer { SO_3AzH_3	13.50 40.00	1000 200 }	215	58.500	1053	838
8. { Sulphate of ammonia, Phospho-guano, Potassic fertilizer,	40.00 35.00 13.50	200 208 1000 }	285	60.225	1084.05	709.05
9. Sulphate of ammonia,	40.00	200	80	57.500	1035	955
10. Phospho-guano,	35.00	200	70	57.50	1035	965

From the above we might conclude that nothing is gained by the addition of a fertilizer. But even in a case similar to this we would be misled if the saccharine percentage had not been ascertained.

is very numerous, and a selection is most difficult; even a combination of two or three having given good results in some cases would not necessarily in others. For that reason, having a given soil, it is a question of years' experience to ascertain actually what fertilizer would be most suitable for that particular locality, for even on soils having the same chemical composition, the results would not be the same, unless their physical texture be also alike, and for that reason better apparent results have been obtained on some soils without manure than on others on which have been applied large quantities of organic or chemical fertilizers. But a question arises as to whether the quality of these roots is equal to others when the yield has not been as great, and could it not happen that a given chemical, potassa, for example, or organic nitric elements in excess, was the cause of the same yielding roots in large quantities but having no saccharine qualities, giving perfect satisfaction to the farmer while being ruinous to the manufacturer? And for this reason we consider it advisable before coming to any definite conclusion to make a comparative calculation between the yield and the quality of the roots produced. To ascertain actually what fertilizer is best calculated for a given soil many experiments are necessary, and from the results thus obtained we may conclude almost to a certainty what would be the best composition for our *complete* manure to have. These should be effected with great system, and divided into several groups:—

The 1st without any fertilizer; 2d with barnyard manure; 3d chemical compound, the latter to be composed of several sub-divisions: (α) with a complete fertilizer containing the four elements before mentioned (lime, potassa, nitrogen, and phosphoric acid); (β) without nitrogen; (γ) without potassa; (δ) without phosphate; (ε) without lime.

Each of these should again be subdivided, combining the three remaining elements in different proportions. For example, supposing that in the experiment δ (without phosphoric acid) the results had been the same as with this element, this would evidently prove that the soil contained this chemical in sufficient quantities, and the addition of the same would represent a financial loss, and for this reason, if added to the fertilizer, it should be at a minimum or in quantities requisite only for the fixation of the alkaline salts. The same argument could be applied to the nitrogen, and, however important it may be for the growth of the root, if in excess, which is generally the case, as there are comparatively few soils which do not possess a large amount in store, would do considerable harm. Evidently, after these experiments had been made it would be desirable to ascertain the rapidity with which a given soil is likely to absorb the same, but even this would vary and could not be depended upon. Many farmers with whom we have talked argue that when the waste products of the sugar factory (molasses, defecation, animal black, etc.) are returned to the soil, the possibility of exhaustion is no longer to be dreaded, but here evidently exists an error, as during the manufacture ammoniacal gases are easily detected. These represent a certain amount of nitrogen that makes its escape, and cousequently cannot be returned. For that reason it is desirable to have the roots and leaves analyzed, and the waste products as well; substract the one from the other, and whatever the difference is add as an additional fertilizer to the above, and we will then return all that has been taken away. This would necessitate the manufacturer to be a farmer, otherwise he would not consider the result compensating for the loss of time.

Then, again, it has been proposed to take the cinders as a basis, but here again errors would occur, as during the reduction of these many changes have taken place, any one of which would lead to an error.

Some soils have a most remarkable fertility, and even after several years the results will be excellent without manure,[1] but then again there is a certainty

---

[1] Mr. Pagnoul made some experiments of this sort, and the results he obtained were the following:—

	With manure.	Without manure.
Yield to the hectare (2½ acres)	51.200 k.	26.000 k.
Sugar, per cent.	14.93	16.67
Carbonates (alkaline)	0.393	0.283
Chlorides	0.045	0.007

VARIOUS MANURES.

of exhausting them if continued, and even then with proper fertilizers they can be renewed.

Mr. Vivien contends that the most rational calculation for a fertilizer is to ascertain what the soil contains, and combine this with a manure in such a manner that the total would have for composition:—

Potassa	40 per cent.
Nitrogen	23 "
Lime	17 "
Phosphoric acid	10 "
Organic substance	10 "

The above will, without doubt, give excellent results. Mr. George Ville considers that a complete fertilizer, composed as follows, is most desirable for beet culture:—

Superphosphate of lime	400 kilog.	(880 lbs.)	
Chloride of potassium	200 "	(440 ")	
Sulphate of ammonium	200 "	(440 ")	2½ acres.
Nitrate of soda	300 "	(660 ")	
Sulphate of lime	200 "	(440 ")	

On these soils the roots had been planted for eight successive years. As shown with the fertilizer it has continued to give good results, whilst on the ordinary soil left to itself having an extra fertility, the yield has decreased, but the saccharine quality of the root is augmented. In this experiment Mr. Pagnoul made use of a chemical fertilizer composed as follows:—

Superphosphates	700 k.
Nitrate of soda	400
Nitrate of potassa	300
Sulphate of ammonia	100
Chloride of potassa	100
	1600

These figures have been obtained after a long series of years; beside them we may mention those recommended by Corenwinder.[1]

Nitrate of soda . . . . 400 kilog. (880 lbs.) ⎫
Nitrate of potassa . . . 200 " (440 ") ⎬ 2½ acres.
Superphosphate . . . . 400 " (880 ") ⎭

On the other hand, Coignet advocates a fertilizer in

---

[1] Mr. Corenwinder obtained these figures by forming a table as follows :—

No.	Comparison of fertilizer, and quantity to hectare.		Yield to hectare.	Sugar in one decilitre of juice.	Cinders, sulphates in one decilitre of juice.
1		Without manure,	37.950	12.77	0.900
2	500 k. 200 240	Sulphate of ammonia, Chloride of potassa, Phosphate,	53.437	11.46	0.936
3	500 240 240	Sulphate of ammonia. Sulphate of potassa, Phosphate,	52.800	11.06	0.873
4	600	Nitrate of soda,	53.587	9.89	0.873
5	600 200 240	Nitrate of soda, Chloride of potassa, Phosphate,	52.790	9.35	1.008
6	600 200 400	Nitrate of soda, Chloride of potassa, Superphosphate,	56.210	11.69	0.873
7	400 200 400	Nitrate of soda, Nitrate of potassa, Superphosphate,	56.462	12.23	0.900
8	400 400	Nitrate of soda, Superphosphate,	54.915	12.59	0.810

As shown in these experiments nitrate of soda, when alone, will yield slightly superior results to those it did when combined with chloride of potassium and phosphate, hence the addition of the latter is of no use. With a given quantity of superphosphate the yield is much increased and the quality of the root also, and this will increase in a poor soil.

In experiment (8) 200 kilog. of nitrate of potassa have been left out, and with the same amount of superphosphate the better results were obtained.

which no soluble salts enter, and but little harm can be done to the saccharine qualities of the beet.

Assimilated nitrogen	7 per cent.
Phosphate from bones	30 "
Torrefied animal substance	50 "
Humidity	13 "
	100

Mr. Joulie considers that his so-called *engrais* is the best known on the market:—

Nitric acid	6.500 per cent.
Phosphoric acid	6.500 "
Potassa	8.00 "
Soda	9.00 "
Lime	14.00
Water, sulphuric acid, etc.	56.00
	100.00

CHAPTER IV.

SEEDS AND SOWING.

Generalities.—The grain is divided into several chambers, two, three, or even four, in each of which an oval embryo is to be found which has a white appearance; we consequently have two parts to consider, the interior and exterior, each having different functions to fulfil. Their composition greatly varies, not only with the variety of the roots to which they belong, but with each other.[1] This, with the size of the seed, seems to have an actual influence on the resulting root; and for years past there has been considerable discussion as to whether a large seed yielded roots possessing the same qualities as a small one, or, again, has the composition of the seed an important influence on the crops? Evidently, if this could be decided, when seeds are bought, to ascertain their quality it

[1] Champignon and Pellet give the following analysis:—

Composition.	Water.	Cinders per cent. of the normal seed.	Nitrogen per cent. of the normal seed.
Exterior surface	14.2	12.7	3.4
Interior "	14.0	5.5	2.2

SEEDS AND SOWING. 153

would be sufficient to have them analyzed.[1] As shown by experiments, there can be no doubt the larger the seed the larger the root, the smaller the seed the greater the amount of sugar found in the beet.[2] From

[1] ANALYSES OF CHAMPIGNON AND PELLET.

	Composition of the ashes of seeds without CO_2.		
	Ordinary seed.	Vilmorin's améliorée.	Battrave, blanche or collet rose.
Potassa	21.1	24.2	16.4
Soda	8.9	12.8	10.4
Lime	25.4	17.2	20.2
	13.5	10.1	11.5
Sulphuric acid	4.	4.3	2.8
Chlorine	4.7	4.1	4.1
Phosphoric acid	8.4	17.4	9.3
Silica	13.4		
Oxide of iron	1.2	11.0	26.4
Traces of iron	0.7		
	101.3	101.1	101.1

[2] ANALYSES BY CHAMPIGNON AND PELLET.

	Water per 100.	Nitrogen per cent., no normal substance.	Ashes per cent. in normal substance.	Sugar per cent. in the root.
Vilmorin's seed—				
Large size	10.9	2.66	5.4 }	15
Small size	11.0	3.07	5.3 }	
Modern variety of beet sugar seed—				
Beets with gray necks (large seed)	12.2	2.46	6.5	10
" " green "				
German silesian (small seed)	11.2	2.80	8.2	
" rose neck				

these experiments we conclude that in many cases having a given variety a subdivision can be made by classifying them according to size; or by having them analyzed, and those containing a large quantity of nitrogen and but few ashes should be chosen, as these will yield beets richest in sugar.

Some contend that the size of the seed has nothing to do either with the resulting crops or the general saccharine average. This is contrary to the results of all experiments that have been made. In talking with farmers in Germany they led us to understand that a judicious selection could be made according to the density, and it consequently would be sufficient to place them in water, and those sinking to the bottom would yield roots richest in sugar; but we are unable to say if the direct application of this principle would be exact, as the porosity of the seed greatly varies, and the water thus absorbed might mislead the observer. But this idea within itself gives a test. If the water has greatly changed its color we may conclude that the seeds are old or have attained an age that becomes doubtful; but these dangers are only to be dreaded in some cases, and, as before stated, it is rational for each manufacturer to grow his own seed, and he is not then in danger of being subjected to fraud. In the first place it is most difficult to make a distinction between the seeds of the sugar beet and the mangel-wurzel, as their external appearances are greatly similar. Then again when it be considered that seeds over five years old[1] will no longer germinate, how easy it is for seed dealers to mislead their customers.

Evidently, seeds other than the sugar beet are seldom sold for sugar beet, as the resulting roots would give evidence against the seller, but in the case of age it is extremely difficult, unless some previous tests have been made, as seed may be warranted of a certain quality, and all appearing above the ground will fulfil these conditions. The fact that some remain beneath the surface may be attributed to bad ploughing or sowing, or, again, to a poor soil in that given spot or to an excess of fertilizers, etc. The importance of some test now becomes evident; several devices have been adopted and suggested; the general idea of these is based on the germinating principle, that is to say, if the grain be placed in a damp atmosphere for several days and signs of life become visible, the evidence of the same is a small white spot. Whatever be the care in raising the seed, one can calculate as a sure thing that about five per cent. will be worth nothing, these representing seed that have not ripened.

Germination.—From the time the seeds are gathered[2] until they are placed in the soil they remain in a

---

[1] By many it is believed that seeds should not be planted before they are two years old, but we have obtained excellent results when of the previous year, and it is certain the younger the seed the greater the germinating principle.

[2] See "Growth of the Seed."

sort of dormant state, and will not even then show signs of a great amount of vitality unless certain conditions are fulfilled, evidently the most important is humidity, then air and heat.

Humidity.—This facilitates the rupture of the exterior and hard portion called *spermoderme* and *nucleus*. In this manner the germination may continue. Evidently the amount of humidity required varies with the thickness of the nucleus; if in excess will do more harm than good, as there will be danger of absorbing the elements that are required to feed the embryo before it is able to extract what nourishment it requires from the soil.

The quantity of water which the seed is capable of absorbing varies with the temperature. The first experiments made in this direction took place in Germany, and were repeated in several of the beet-growing countries. We made several tests in New Jersey soil, and obtained the following results:—

40.1° Fahr. . . . 71 per cent. of the weight of the seed.
53.6°   "   . . . 93   "   "   "   "   "   "
57.2°   "   . . . 96   "   "   "   "   "   "
62.6°   "   . . . 98   "   "   "   "   "   "
68°   "   . . . 110   "   "   "   "   "   "

There seems to exist no exact law governing the above. We have had seeds in hot water and the absorption has been one to one and half of their own volume. We consider that it is partly on this account that it is impossible to grow the beet with satisfactory results in a warm climate. It might be well to state that the nature of the soil has also great influence on the quantity of humidity at the disposal of the seed; for example, when of a calcareous nature it will absorb more than when sandy, and retain the same in greater quantities when submitted to a higher temperature.

Heat.— Evidently there exist certain limits which in either case should not be surpassed; for example, if the seed be placed in water at a temperature of 122° F. they will no longer germinate, as all the principles of life will be destroyed. This temperature is never attained after planting, and is consequently not to be dreaded. The limits giving the best results are supposed to be between 50° and 68° F. If the seeds are in a good condition they will resist a very intense cold, remaining apparently without life, and will make their appearance above the surface soon after this cold has ceased. If their germination has not commenced the danger of destruction is not great, but, in the contrary case, considerable losses are to be dreaded.

Air.—It is impossible for seed to germinate without this element, absorbing as they do large quantities of oxygen, throwing off an equivalent of carbonic acid, thus causing many internal changes, such as the transformation of the albumen to gums, etc. There can be no doubt as to the importance of a sufficient amount of air, as experiments have been made to ascertain the possibility of germination in presence of other given gases, but were all without success, hence the importance of working the soil in the proper manner; the oxygen imprisoned will greatly help the growth of the plant; but must not be in excess, as much harm would then result.[1]

Light.—Evidently, as soon as the leaves are apparent above the surface light becomes of great importance. What chemical or physical action, if any, takes place during the germination we are unable to explain.[2] Seeds in their normal state that have been raised on a given soil forming a given variety fall to the ground as soon as matured. They here remain until the coming year, having outlived the variations of the weather, and are in a condition to give signs of life as soon as the favorable season arrives for the same. Now, if we compare these with those gathered and dried, etc., before spoken of, evidently the time required for germination of the same will be longer in the latter case than the former. The consequence of this is the weeds and other wild growth will spring up and monopolize in advance the entire soil; hence the importance of some artificial means which should not only stimulate the growth, but keep at a distance insects, which are much to be dreaded.

The exterior coating of seed being frequently extremely hard, many advocate the rolling of them be-

---

[1] See "Various Methods of Working the Soil."

[2] Besides the above, Mr. Basset wishes to attribute certain effects to an electric action. We cannot see on what ground he advances this idea.

tween boards. This also has for advantage the separating of the same, as already stated; several adhere to each other, the inconvenience of which in sowing by machinery[1] is great. A certain amount of humidity being necessary before germination commences, if we can give this before placing the seed in the soil it will evidently represent so much time gained, and for that reason the placing of the seeds a certain number of hours in water has been suggested. If for too long a period much harm will be done, as the seed will be greatly weakened[2] if too much water has been absorbed. There is then great danger of a rapid evaporation, which will thus leave the seed dryer than before, and for that reason it has been proposed to add to the water an equal volume of urine, and to place the seed in the same for about forty-eight hours, then put them in piles a few inches in height. An elevation of temperature will follow, which will consequently represent a gain in heat, as there can be no doubt a given number of degrees are necessary, this is supposed to be 248° to 266° F.[3]

---

[1] See "Sowing."

[2] The importance of these elements has already been explained. By boiling the resulting liquid we have a test; if ammoniacal gases are detected in considerable quantities it gives an almost positive proof that the maceration has lasted too long, and that the discoloration is not due to an old seed.

[3] If we suppose that the temperature for several days had been constant, 50° F., for example, it would require $\frac{266° - 32°}{50° - 32°} = 13$ days before the germi-

160 THE SUGAR BEET.

The farmers near Lille (France) make piles of their seed before sowing, and sprinkle the same with water; shortly after this they are planted. Care in all cases should be taken to prevent a fermentation, as the germinating principles would then be destroyed. Sometimes the urine contains parasites which attack the seed and do much harm. To get rid of the excess of liquid the seeds are frequently rolled in plaster or cinders, and are used only after a lapse of several days; evidently the amount permitted to adhere must be very slight, as the germination of the seed would otherwise be impossible. Some contend that there are many advantages thus gained. Evidently from this idea it was suggested to make use of a solution of lime and water, and place the seed in the same for some twenty-five hours. Good results were thus obtained, but the question now arises whether the sulphuric acid that has combined with the lime to form plaster had not also in the first case a better effect than when the lime was alone. We are convinced that a slight addition of an acid is most beneficial. Chloride and superphosphate of lime have also been adopted, but here again we consider that the chlorine took an active part, as

nation commences. If a portion of this had been gained in advance the number of days is diminished.

For example, supposing this gain $66°$, the number yet to attain would be $266°$ F. $— 66° = 200°$, and the days required $\dfrac{200° - 32°}{50° - 32°} = 9.3$ days, or a gain of 3.7 days.

Humboldt and others have proven, that the latter greatly accelerates the germination of the seed that has been macerated in water for several hours. Even with old seed the principle holds good. Frequently 5 to 10 per cent. of nitrate of potassa is added to the water. Mr. Walkhoff says that with phosphate of ammonia 71 per cent. of the seed come above ground in seven days. Then, again, saltpetre has given more striking results than any of the above. Besides oxalic acid, phenic acid, arsenate of potassa, sulphate of zinc, nitrate of soda, etc. etc., have been experimented with. We can only say to this that even if any of the above had given extraordinary results, the practical application of the same would have been impossible, as farmers as a general thing do not care to be troubled with chemicals of any description, and we consider without doubt that the solutions of equal volumes of water and urine, and the maceration with the same should last for a period of 24 to 48 hours, as mentioned above, the seeds then rolled in a small quantity of plaster, to which are added a few drops of mineral oil, which keep the insects at a distance. It is not desirable to have a too rapid growth, as much harm is liable to be done by a sudden change in the weather, and for that reason the farmers with whom we have talked in Belgium are not willing to adopt any artificial means, but content themselves by sowing some days previous to what they would have otherwise done.

The next difficulty is to know when is the best time

for sowing in order to fulfil the conditions before spoken of, that is to say, air, heat, and humidity. As a general thing this takes place either in March or April, and varies with the climate and soils, in cold ones later than when milder. It is generally admitted that the duration of the growth should be as long as possible, and for that reason the farmer has every advantage in planting as early as he can. A period should be chosen when the frosts, etc., are no longer to be dreaded. Some farmers are willing to run great risks, and argue even if the young plant is destroyed by the frost there will still remain sufficient time to recommence the sowing, but we cannot indorse this idea, as the amount of grain thus lost would in some cases be considerable. Judgment is the best guide for the practical man to follow. As for asserting that the moment has arrived when for several days there exists an equality of temperature in the ground, or when the total sum of the daily averages, morning, afternoon, and evening, be equal to a determined figure, we consider a mistake. The latter, Mr. Walkhoff tells us, is in Russia 80° R. (212° F.). The observations should commence as soon as the thermometer marks 1° R. (34.25° F.). The thermometer is placed in the ground at a depth of 4 verschocks (7.08 inches), and the observation is made at 6 o'clock in the morning. Evidently the roots rarely during their early growth (germinating period) attain a depth as great as this, and the hour chosen would lead to many errors.

In France the average mean[1] of 6° C. (42.8° F.), made at a depth of 6 to 8 cm. (2.3 to 3.1 inches) is considered to be an excellent guide, when this for several days in succession is constant.

When the seed is placed in the soil under favoring circumstances the germination commences, the outer surface swells, and, during this period, has a most extraordinary force. The embryo feeding itself on the albumen for a certain time, the radicle then shows itself by a small white point; this penetrates the soil more and more. The other extremity is where the future cotyledons appear after several days. These still have their ends in the interior of the embryo. This doubled portion then gains the upper surface of the soil, where in contact with the light and exterior heat it soon expands, and the two small green leaves become visible; radicles seem to adhere to the outer surface of the root, these greatly facilitating the extraction of the nourishment from the surrounding soil, and are assisted by the above. The portion situated between the leaves and the extremity of the plant below the surface actually represents the final root. It can now

---

[1] What we wish to convey by "average mean" is that observations are taken morning, afternoon, and evening. For example:—

Supposing 6 o'clock in the morning the temperature 36° Fahr.
" 12 " " afternoon " 48° "
" 6 " " evening " 42° "
———
126°

The average mean for the day would be $\frac{126}{3} = 42°$ F.

be understood that if we place the seed at too great a depth, we thus oblige the doubled portion to penetrate the same, which difficulty in most cases it could not overcome, or the final growth would be greatly retarded, even if it could, while if, on the other hand, the seeds be too near the surface, they will be exposed to the variations of the weather. Hence the importance of knowing as nearly as possible what this should be. No definite rule can be given, as it varies with the climate and soil, and is determined by practical experiments.[1]

Groven made the following experiments, which give a good idea of the variations in the number of plants coming to the surface, according to the time and depth :—

Seeds placed at a depth of	First roots made their appearance after	Number of roots after	
		8 days.	16 days.
0.3937 inch.	5 days.	19	24
0.7874 "	5⅓ "	14	21
1.1811 "	5½ "	15	23
1.5748 "	6½ "	15	17
1.9685 "	6¾ "	8	18
2.7559 "	8¾ "	4	14
3.5433 "	10 "	1	17

He therefore concludes that the most suitable depth is between 0.99 and 0.47 inch.

[1] We made some experiments in Lancaster County, Pa., to ascertain what this would be for that given soil, but from the farmer's neglect could not decide.

SEEDS AND SOWING.

According to Walkhoff, at a temperature of 15° C. (59° F.), the number of days required is—

13 days for seeds at a depth of 6 mm. (0.24 inch)
9   "   "   "   "   "   13 " (0.51 inch.)
9   "   "   "   "   "   19 " (0.74 inch.)
9   "   "   "   "   "   26 " (1.02 inch.)

The next important question is to know the distance most favorable to place the roots advantageously to the farmer and sugar manufacturer. This again varies with the soil, as the richer and deeper it is, evidently the nearer the roots can be placed, as a poor soil, for example, would require a greater number of square inches in surface to furnish the necessary nourishment than a rich one. No definite rule can here again be given, as this does not vary proportionately either to the size of the root or to the space; but it is certain that the greater the space the larger the root, and consequently the smaller the quantity of sugar. We might conclude from this the importance of placing them as near as possible—evidently within certain limits, as otherwise the growth of the beet would be greatly retarded.

In the beet-growing farms the most suitable distance has been sought for, and the solution varies with circumstances. The seeds can be planted in three positions: 1, squares; 2, lozenges (or oblique lines); 3, rectangles (straight lines). A glance at figs. 32, 33 will be sufficient to prove that the amount of space (*a*) lost, whatever be the distance between roots, will be greater in the squares than in the lozenges (the small circles representing the maximum limits of ex-

Fig. 32.   Fig. 33.

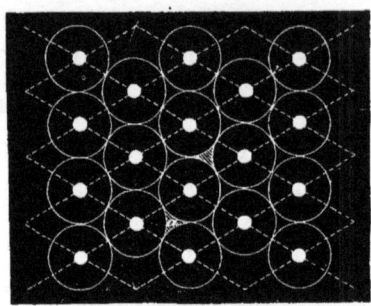
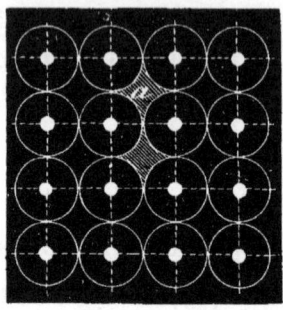

Seeds placed in lozenges. Circles represent the portion of the soil from which the root draws its nourishment; *a* is the soil not utilized, and consequently lost.

Seeds placed in squares. Circles and *a* represent the same as in fig. 32.

tracting). The latter is most excellent where weeding can be done by hand (labor being cheap), but for America space is less important than the cost of working the ground. The rectangle (figs. 34 and 35) is preferable, as horses can enter between the rows, facilitating the working of an instrument for weeding. Dr. Petermann, of Belgium, has studied this question of distance for years, and we consider him an authority. We are in hopes it may be of interest to the reader, and for this reason we give the results of several series of his experiments:—

	1st Series.		2d Series.		3d Series.	
Variety cultivated.	0.45×0.30 (17″.7×11″.8) yield to hectare (2.47 acres)	Sugar in 100 gr. of juice (0.220lbs)	0.40×0.25 (15″.7×9″.8) yield to hectare (2.47 acres)	Sugar in 100 gr. of juice (0.220lbs)	0 35×0.18 (13″.7×7″.0) yield to hectare (2.47 acres)	Sugar in 100 gr. of juice (0 220lbs)
Breslau,	37.179	10.96	47 649	11.28	46.154	11.35
Collet rose,	40.812	10.04	47.006	11.01	45.714	10.83
Flour seed,	39.742	9.76	46.153	11.07	43.077	10.92
Vilmorin's,	30.128	13.64	32 286	13.88	32.528	14.93

We conclude that in this special case the most favorable distance is 0.40 × 0.25 (17.7 × 11.8 inch) not only in reference to the yield to the hectare (2½ acres), but in the quantity of sugar. Some practical men contend that the percentage of salts contained in the roots when at short distance is greater than it would have been under ordinary circumstances. This we doubt much, as it is contrary to the results obtained all over Europe. As a general rule we may say that the distance a (see fig. 34) should never be over 16 inches, and the distance b never less than 7 inches.

Knowing the importance of growing the roots as closely as possible, the manufacturer frequently offers prizes,[1] the value of which varies with the number of plants obtained to the acre. Once the distance between the lines and the roots is determined, it becomes easy to calculate the theoretical amount a given soil will yield, hence the weight of seed that will be required; re-

[1] For example, $0 25 per ton for 30,000 roots to the acre.
     0.40 " " 40,000 " " "
     0.60 " " 50,000 " " "

membering that four or more are sown for each root, and 1 kilog. (2.2 lbs.) contains about 36,000 seed.

Fig. 34.

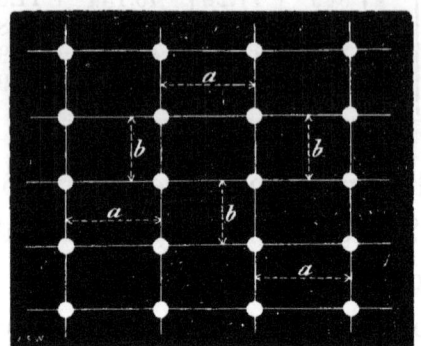

Planted in rectangles. The distance between the roots is represented by (b) and between lines by (a); this should be sufficiently wide to permit the entrance of a cultivator, horse, etc.

Fig. 35.

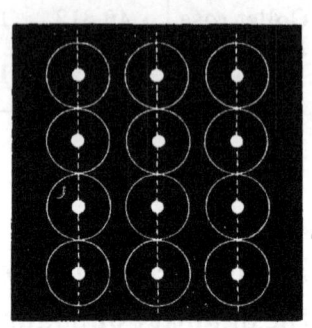

Beets placed in lines, the distance between the same not specified, at will of the planter.

The practical figure is about 7 to 10 lbs. to the acre, this representing 12, 15, and even 25 times more than would have been indicated in the above.

The sowing of the seed can be done in various ways, the most important being: 1st, broadcast, with thinning out or combined with transplanting; 2d, ordinary flat rows; 3d, rows and hills combined.

Each of these, if properly effected, will give good results. The placing of the seed in the ground can be accomplished by either hand or machine, the latter having the advantage of working with great regularity, and is generally adopted in all beet-growing countries.

In many parts of Germany, and principally near

Magdeburg, hand labor is preferred, as the fields are divided, and the average pay of a workman is less than in France.

Sowing *broadcast* has now been generally abandoned in consideration of the seed required, the impossibility of accomplishing it with regularity, and the difficulty and expense of thinning out, which in all cases must be done—the remaining roots requiring to be at equal distances or in rows. There is one case where this system cannot be abandoned, and that is when future transplanting is to be considered. Years ago Mathieu, Dombasle, Gasparin, and others advocated the latter method of growing the beet, thus giving a longer period in the soil than by any other. We are convinced that the idea is a good one. Generally the first sowing takes place on a spot well protected from the cold. When the young roots have attained a size about equal to one's finger, this operation commences. It is advisable to choose a cloudy and damp day. If, on the contrary, it is dry, it is well to water the soil with a weak solution of urine. Several days may elapse between the two periods: extracting from the ground and transplanting, providing the young roots be placed in a vertical position, ends upwards, in vats filled with earth. If the seeds have been sown in lines the middle line of roots is pulled up and the remaining thinned out, leaving between each beet the required distance. When the soil is ready to receive these a hole is dug with a stick, and in this the root is placed and the sides are closely pressed with the foot; for this purpose it has been suggested to use a transplanter. In both cases they should be placed in a given direction. The most simple is to make a cut with a spade and place the young root in the same, after which the earth is pressed as before, or, again, ploughs can be made use of, two being necessary, each forming one-half of a hill, the plant being placed in the centre.

Some twenty years ago Kœchlin called attention to the advantages gained by this method, he having been able to obtain 150,000 kilog. (330,000 lbs.) to the hectare (two and a half acres). Here the seed were planted in January broadcast, and transplanted in April. If done in the proper manner they will resist a temperature of 30° F.

The principal objection to transplanting is that it is impossible to extract the young root with its extreme end, with the loss of which the resulting beet in all probability will be forked.

Of all the varieties of sugar beet, we are informed that the *globe jaune* gives the best results when utilized for this special purpose. Whatever be the advantages of transplanting, it would be impossible to practise it on a large scale, as the expense would be great and the time wanting. It is well to have a certain number of extra beets in one corner of the field, which can be utilized for filling up the open spaces which from unknown causes exist. Some consider this is of no great importance, as when the thinning out commences there remain over a sufficient number of extra ones to answer the same purpose; but in answer to this we would state that this operation is done rapidly, and it would be impossible to bestow sufficient care in extracting the young roots. In sowing by hand the farmer can make use of a small hoe, with which holes are dug in a given direction and spot, indicated by strings having knots on them, which are placed the entire width of the field. A woman now comes and places about five seeds in each hole, and covers them with earth, after which she slightly compresses it. As for the various mechanical devices for sowing, we will not attempt to describe them, as they have but little interest when compared with our American machines, which surpass in most cases anything of the same kind existing in Europe.

The general principles of these machines are alike, and differ but little from Garrett's first idea, the problem being to open the soil to a certain depth and place the seed in this at given distances, then to cover them, after which the ground is slightly compressed by a roller. Of the most important we may mention those of Delahaye, Leferre, Fossier, Pellot-Schunz, etc. We do not consider that in climates where the weather is wet and changeable it is advisable to use rollers, as these having too great a weight will compress the soil, if damp, to such an extent that the young plant will fail to appear above the surface; if, on the contrary, some days are allowed to elapse, before passing the roller, it will pulverize the surface above, thus having a most excellent effect. The movable axis of the roller is also an important item, as the roller can then readily pass over an undulated surface.

In some portions of France we have seen them make use of a machine by means of which a fertilizer is placed in the soil at the same time as the seed. The objection to this is the evil effect caused by insects when barnyard manure or any other organic substance is made use of, or, again, if a chemical, it will frequently burn the young plant.

Of late years an invention has been brought to notice which has not these inconveniences, as the fertilizers do not come in immediate contact until the root is to a certain extent able to resist their effects. The principle is to permit the fertilizer to be the first to leave the machine, then a small device covers this with earth, then the seed falls and is covered in the same manner. We strongly advocate this for poor soils, but do not think it important otherwise.

The sowing in hills (the advantage of which has been before mentioned) is effected by various means, the most important being where the roller having the exact shape of the desired hill is passed over it. After the earth is thus pressed, lines in given directions are traced; during this operation the seeds are sown, by hand or machine, rather closer than in any of the methods mentioned above.

Changes During Vegetation.

Having at our disposal an excellent seed, planted in a good soil and in the best manner, various adverse circumstances may yet arise—over which the farmer has no control. As before stated, during the germinating period a certain amount of humidity is necessary for the development of the young plant, and, if this does not exist, but negative results can be expected. During the entire growth of the root, the same principles exist, but then the causes, and results produced are very different from what they were during the first stage. In using the manures it becomes evident that some physical force must carry to the subsoil the chemical or organic substance, and in this manner permit the root to have at every period of its growth what it requires. After the rain the air can enter more freely, etc., but as much good as can be expected from a moderate amount of rain, a corresponding harm will result when in excess, as the soluble portion of the fertilizer is likely to be carried to a depth beyond the reach of the root, and the latter would derive but little if any benefit from the same. The argument also applies to the temperature: a certain number of degrees are requisite for the germination of the seed, and for the same reason a certain number are necessary for the full growth of the root. If this is in excess, secondary results will be obtained. We consequently have two principles to consider—the effects produced by the rain and the heat.

Rain.—The sugar in the root increases during the various stages of vegetation, and this corresponds to the quality of the seed; that is to say, if a given seed will yield a root having a high percentage, this quality will be observed as existing during each period of its growth. In beets we analyzed in July this phenomenon became apparent. Mr. Walkhoff's experiments[1] to ascertain the influence of the rain are most interesting. These agree with others of a similar nature, and it is now generally admitted that if these rains come during the last months a second growth of leaves will follow, this producing a loss in sugar and frequently an augmentation in the weight of the root.

[1] Experiments of Walkhoff:—

Months.	Number of beets.	Weight.		Juice		Number of days of vegetation.	Rain-fall, weight in centimetres.	Number of days of rain.
		Leaves, total.	Each root, grammes.	Sugar per cent.	Inches of purity.			
22d June,	20	3700	50	3.7	55.2	60	11.7	25
24th "	13	3800	77	4.2	58.8	62	11.7	25
2d July,	8	1960	174	9.7	73 3	70	13.3	28
18th August,	12	852	140	10.6	70.	104	15 4	31
4th September,	8	276	127	13.4	72.4	120	16.1	32
15th "	10	450	86	7.	60.	130	32.0	36
24th "	5	900	292	6.5	63.7	139	32.4	37
6th October,	5	980	226	7.8	68.	155	32.4	37

These evidently show that from the commencement until the end of the vegetation the amount of sugar has been on the increase, until the rain made its appearance, this having for effect an immediate change; this commences about the 18th of August. Up to that time the water had been about the amount the young plant required.

SEEDS AND SOWING. 175

The absorption of the soluble salts by the roots seems also to increase during a rainy spell.[1]

The rains having a most active influence, it is well to analyze the roots during this last period, and when a rapid decrease in sugar is noticed, harvesting should commence.

Heat.—According to observations made in Europe, the total heat required is 5430° F.; this is obtained by multiplying the average temperature by the number of days. The total can be and is frequently far in excess of the above, and yet satisfactory results are obtained—probably a small loss in sugar will result, but this is of little importance. The consequence is that, as before stated, much reliance cannot be placed upon these ideal figures. On the other hand, many contend that if the total temperature has not attained within 100° of the above, poor roots will result, as they cannot possibly mature.

---

[1] Experiments of Champignon and Pellet:—

Beets growing,		The same beets taken from the ground after rain.	
Per cent. of sugar.	Saline quotient.	Per cent. of sugar.	Saline quotient.
16.8	3.8 ⎫	14.4	4.7 ⎫
16.2	4.0 ⎬ average 4.8	13.1	5.3 ⎬ average 5.2
14.7	6.1 ⎪	12.7	5.4 ⎪
14.7	5.3 ⎭	12.0	5.3 ⎭

Mr. Pagnoul experimented on two varieties:—

	Weight.	Per cent. of sugar.	
No. 1.	37 grammes.	8.8 ⎫	July.
No. 2.	13 "	5.3 ⎭	
No. 1.	568 grammes.	12.0 ⎫	September
No. 2.	556 "	10.2 ⎭	

CHAPTER V.

PRODUCTION AND IMPROVEMENT OF THE SEED OF THE SUGAR BEET.

In countries where the beet sugar industry has never as yet existed, it is of the highest importance to know without a doubt if the culture of this root would be a profitable enterprise, as it is not desirable to make these discoveries after the factory has been located and an enormous capital been invested.

The scientific knowledge that has been acquired within the last few years gives a solution to this problem, and it is important for all interested to become acquainted with the same in detail.

The hereditary principles that have long since been known to exist with the lower animals and mankind, and indorsed by Darwin, also apply to plants; hence the rational selection of the parents in order to obtain satisfactory results, in other words, beets rich in sugar-yielding seeds, these, if planted, will again bring to life a plant having the same properties. This selection will not only have for effect the production of a good seed, but will also prevent the degeneration of the beet, the laws here existing being identical with those of mixed races.[1]

The Germans were the first to call attention to the above, and their methods put into practice many years ago, and continued down to the present day, with but little change, are based on exterior signs[2] whilst the roots are still growing in the field.

Evidently, the characteristic points of beets rich in sugar vary according to the type, methods of planting, soils, and geographical location, and, for that reason, have not the same interest as they would otherwise have had; consequently, it is important for each farmer to ascertain for himself what these are.

Those growing near Magdeburg, and chosen for mothers to be planted the following year, are well beneath the surface; their tops are rather small and not conical, but few outer leaves, and these are flat and grow near the ground; at their centre, they are in a cluster, the general tint of these is bright green, and not spotted nor fringed with red. They should have been grown on a soil and in a manner best calculated to yield roots rich in sugar.[3] We are informed that if beets

---

[1] For example, if white and black races be mixed there will exist a continual tendency to return to their normal inferior state, which is black.

[2] Leplay and other French scientists have contended that there exist no outer signs. The best proof of their error is to consider the superiority of the German beet over their own, and to consider that Knauer started from a root that contained but 11 per cent., and had for final result 16 per cent. (*Imperiale*) by the adoption of these principles.

[3] See Chapters "Fertilizers," and "Sowing of the Seed."

growing and not having these signs be compared with the above, a difference of nearly 2 per cent. in the saccharine elements will, as a general thing, exist.

Some years later came into existence methods based on the density of the root. These roots were placed in a solution of salt and water, which might vary from 1° to 6° or 8° B.; those remaining on the surface at 6.5° B. would be sent to the factory, whilst others sinking and having a close texture were kept for seed purposes.

But the inconvenience of this method was the cleaning of the roots, ridding them of dirt. This would have a serious influence on the final results. Mr. Knauer brought to notice a machine which would mechanically subdivide the roots into piles according to their weight. It was then supposed that the amount of sugar was proportional to the density of the entire root,[1] but since it has been proven that many errors were thus committed, and, even if this were not the case, it would have been impossible to make the above test in a short time on millions of roots before sending the same to the factory. If several days elapse before this takes place evaporation will follow, and the roots be consequently lighter, and the density thus obtained be necessarily false. Another cause of error might be attributed to the want of care in removing the leaves, which in all cases should be done by hand, and not by slicing off with a knife.[2]

[1] We have tested beets that would have been considered worthless for seed purposes, but they contained 13 per cent. of sugar by the saccharometer.

[2] See "Harvesting."

Mr. Vilmorin, in 1851, brought to notice his method, he taking advantage of the above as a starting point; but he observed that a cylindrical piece could be taken from the root with an instrument similar to an apple corer, and that the normal condition of the root would not be altered, precaution having been taken to fill the hole thus made with sand, as soon as possible, to prevent any fermentation in its interior.

The cylinders thus obtained were placed in a series of vases filled with a solution of sugar and water, careful attention being paid to the moment when these ceased to float. Several errors here existed, the most important being the effect of endosmose, fermentation in the solution, atmospheric effect produced upon the small cylinder passing from one vase to another, etc., and the idea was abandoned for another, in which the extracted portion was reduced to a pulp with a rasp, then pressed and filtered, the exact density being had with an areometer. This varies from 1.060 to 1.075 (8° to 10° B.) for good beets. Here again we have additional errors, the most important having been noticed for the first time by Champonnois, and these were due to a certain volume of gas contained in the tissue of the root. On this account the density of the beet is not proportional to its juice. The volume of this for an ordinary root has frequently attained 45 c. c.,[1] composed principally of nitrogen and carbonic acid.

[1] Cubic centimeters.

The following will show that the volume of these gases varies considerably:—

Density of the Beet in Salt Water.	Density of Juice.	Volume of Gases per kilog.
1016	1045	26 c. c.
1012	1048	36 "
1005	1040	35 "
1012	1050	32 "

Mchay has also made many interesting experiments with a view to ascertain if there exists any proportion between the density of the juice and the entire root. He found none, but concluded that a beet having a high density and but little ash would yield a variety superior to what had heretofore existed. Of late years Dervaux has adopted, on his farm in France, a method also based on the density, but not having the disadvantage of the above, he having proven some years previous that a cylindrical piece taken from the root in a direction perpendicular to its axis has a density proportional to the entire root, at an approximation sufficient to render errors committed of secondary importance.

This being the case, the roots are chosen in the field by exterior signs alone. These are sorted by the application of Dervaux's idea. As may be imagined, here we can operate in small vases containing from 200 to 300 grammes of salt and water, with as many hands as vases, and consequently as rapidly as desired.

The advantages of this over the ordinary methods previously mentioned, are that the roots need not be cleaned nor the leaves removed, nor is it necessary to

IMPROVEMENT OF THE SEED.

have large tanks containing an enormous volume of salt water, demanding consequently a great loss of time and a considerable expense. Mr. Walkhoff considers that if we ascertain a proportion between the quantity of sugar and the saline elements, we can then make a most excellent selection; this should never be lower than 75 per cent., in other words, in 100 of solid substance indicated with the Baumé's areometer, there should exist at least 75 of sugar. Beets might indicate much sugar and saline matter at the same time, and would then have no practical value, as the proportion between the two would indicate.

The largest seed growers in France are Deprez & Co., where the roots are selected according to the sugar they actually contain. The tests are made under the direction of Chas. Viollette[1] of the *Faculté des Sciences*

---

[1] Mr. Viollette supposes the beet an exact surface of revolution, engendered by the triangle $A B C$, and that the sugar contained increases in an arithmetical progression from D to C. If $L M$ be an infinitesimal cylinder parallel to the axis $C D$, according to the above hypothesis the point S, middle of the same,

Fig. 36.

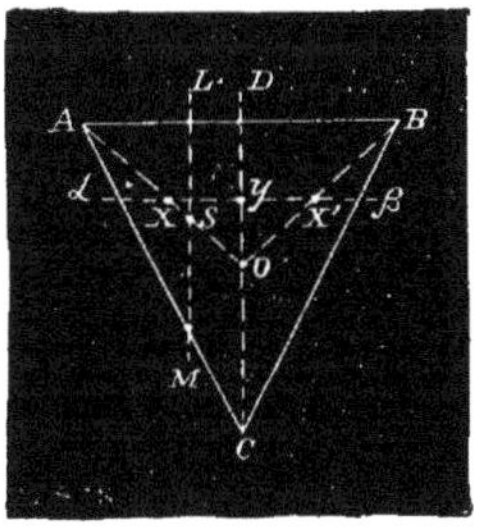

will have an average amount of sugar for this small element. The same argument will apply to O, when the cylinder having the axis $D C$ is considered.

de Lille, he having proved that the portion of the root containing the average amount of sugar is situated one-fourth the distance from the neck, and it is in this direction that the so-called apple-corer is directed.[1]

The disadvantage of the chemical test is that it requires much skill to obtain accurate results. The methods of selection that we have thus far mentioned have supposed beets rich in sugar at our disposal. This is frequently not the case, as seeds that have been bought and planted as being of the best, are of a poor quality, or sufficient experience has been wanting in

If O be joined to A and B, evidently the lines OA and OB will represent the line of all the averages corresponding to the small cylinders that it is possible to imagine as existing in the interior of the beet, and the centres of OA and OB, or X and X' will represent the exact portion of the average of all the averages, and, if each horizontal slice contains the same amount of sugar, we could then write $\dfrac{OY}{YD} = \dfrac{OX}{XA} = 1$, then $OY = YD = \dfrac{CD}{4}$.

[1] The cylindrical portion obtained is divided into small slices; five gr. of which are placed in a receiver having a capacity of 100 c. c.; to this is added 50 c. c. of water and 10 c. c. of sulphuric acid, the total is boiled, after which 10 c. c. of a caustic liquor is added; this is permitted to cool, and the remaining filled with water and filtered. One of Dr. Ures's burettes can be made use of, and is filled with the above, then 10 c. c. of Barreswill's "cupro-potassic" liquor is boiled in a testing-tube; in this the sugar solution is allowed to drop as rapidly as possible until the blue color is nearly gone; after some few minutes several more drops are added, and a brown precipitate will form, which afterwards turns red. If the liquor has still a bluish tint, it will be important to add a few more drops, and the test is at an end, when these will no longer give a brownish tint. The number of centimetre cubes of the sugar solution utilized being known, the calculation of the exact amount of sugar that could be extracted from similar beets is a simple rule of three.

planting them. Mr. Simon Legrand's idea is to have seed, for example, of French origin sent to Germany to be planted, and then the selected mothers to return to their native soil for their second year's growth. As shown, the problem is not an easy one, and opinions greatly differ as to the results obtained and the manner of producing them. There is one method which we propose for America; it is totally different from anything yet in practical use, and, from our own experience, has in every case been a success. The first thing is to obtain a location, the soil having the qualities before mentioned, and then not to import seed, which never has given satisfactory results, but to bring the roots direct from Germany; these having been previously chosen, if they are planted in any of the Northern States, will yield a seed that becomes accustomed to the American climate at the start. (We can in no way understand how Mr. Walkhoff's experience in planting seeds of one climate in a colder one has given a variety of beet superior to what had previously existed, our own experience having been the opposite—yielding roots much degenerated.) Again, if these be selected in a proper manner we will have an improved beet, possessed of all the qualities of those existing in Europe. Whatever be the method of selection or production adopted, the roots are stored in silos,[1] care having been taken to place them in layers,

---

[1] See "Preservation and Conservation of the Beet."

between each several inches of earth; the whole well protected from the cold. The preparation of the soil is in every respect similar to the first year. Some authors contend that beets should not attain to their full development the first year. But we have made several experiments to ascertain if there existed any actual advantage in the adoption of this idea, and are forced to say we found none; notwithstanding the fact that the beet is a bi-annual plant, many go to seed the first year. The exact cause of this is not known, but the fact is that the roots having small and conical necks are generally those that are possessed of this peculiarity. Some contend that this may be attributed to the age of the seed; we consider that this has nothing to do with it, for, if the resulting seed be taken and planted, it will yield roots having the same defect; therefore it is advisable to gather these, and not permit them to remain, as they will contain but little sugar and a large amount of phosphoric acid. The beets that are planted for seed are the second year placed at a much greater distance from each other than during the first. The ground to receive these is divided off in squares of three to two and a half feet; at each angle a mother is placed. A hole is dug with a spade in a slanting direction. The beets that are placed in these have their ends broken off, as they would in all probability double under and prevent, to a certain extent, the growth of the root. The earth is then filled in and pressed with the foot.

The saccharine changes that take place during the second year are most strange. The sugar seems to diminish as soon as the root gives signs of life, and shortly after this remains approximately the same until the seed commence to show themselves, and then almost entirely disappears. One might conclude from this fact that the seed had absorbed the sugar, but this is not the case, as it has been proved that a large amount of the latter passes into the small side roots,[1] which in all cases show themselves adhering to the outer surface of the mother beet. Evidently, the functions these have to fulfil are to exhaust the maximum elements from the surrounding soil.

The Chinese have for years past understood the importance of this, and for that reason, when biannual plants are grown, small slices are made in the same, these facilitating the growth of the small adhesive roots.

The mother having been planted some inches beneath the surface, the neck in growing will pass through the earth, and in this manner it will be sufficiently supported to resist the general variations of the weather.

During the first few days of August the flowers commence to appear, and should be pinched off, as they will yield a seed of a poor quality, as a general thing. By this means those to come will be somewhat strengthened. We give a drawing of the flower (see

---

[1] The opinions of scientists greatly differ as to these. Peligot concludes that they exhaust the mother root.

fig. 37) and a section of the same (see fig. 38); the pistil[1] and five stamens[2] are visible.

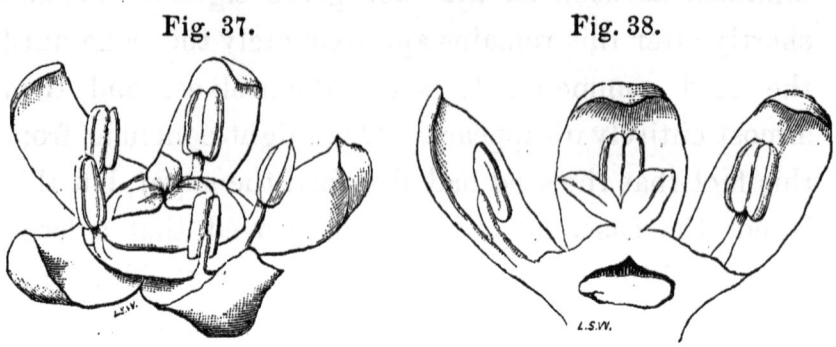

Fig. 37. Fig. 38.

View of flower showing the pistil and stamens.   Sectional view of flower.

In fig. 39 we give the fruit; there are frequently three adhering to the same portion of the stem; in fig. 40 a general idea of the stem, so-called, and the position of the fruit thereon. The fruit, for a certain period, like the leaves, decomposes the carbonic acid by day,[3] etc.

This principle of reproduction was first brought to notice by Sebastian Villiant in 1716, and can in no way be doubted.[4] The above facts being known, the

[1] The *pistil* is the central portion of the flower; the principal parts of these *pistils* are the *ovaries* inclosing the *ovules*, which become fertilized. The *stigma* is an organ placed at the top of the *style*, the latter being the prolongation upwards of the *ovary*.

[2] The *stamen* is the male organ of the flower; the fertilizing part or *anther* is composed of a series of cells, which are originally soft and pulpy; when matured, they become dry and powdery, the valves separate, and the parenchyma cells called *pollen* are now ready to be conveyed to the stigma.

[3] The *fruit* is the fertilized and ripe pistil inclosing seeds capable of producing plants, each of which has been an ovule fertilized by the pollen.

[4] Some botanists go as far as to state that it never takes place.

importance of keeping at a distance roots of another variety can be understood. If this principle be not observed the pollen of the inferior plant will fertilize the superior, and it will consequently yield a root of an inferior quality. If, on the contrary, a superior variety be placed in the neighborhood, the effect will be most advantageous, and it may be concluded from these and various other similar experiments, which we can indorse, that the resulting race will for the time being be richer in seed, and that the roots grown therefrom will contain a sugar more regular, etc., than had ex-

Fig. 39.   Fig. 40.

Fruit in clusters.   Fruit growing upon the stem.

isted in either. The roots should be placed sufficiently near each other to facilitate their fertilization. The first sign of maturity is when the fruit commences to become brown; harvesting should then take place without loss of time. The ripening will continue if the fruit is exposed to the sun. If one waits until the complete maturity, large quantities will be lost, as these adhere but slightly to the stem. The stalks of the various roots will run into these; this fact alone greatly diminishes the yield. Some authors advocate the cutting of the stems or stalks from the roots and leaving the latter to remain on the ground as a manure for the coming year. This makes a poor fertilizer, as the roots contain large amounts of mineral salts, etc., besides which insects are attracted by these, depositing their eggs in the interior; the resulting larvæ are likely to do much harm to the general crops the coming season. Whatever be the principle adhered to, the stalks are tied in bundles and placed in vertical position in the sun to complete the drying. Now comes an operation which requires some skill, and has for effect the ridding the seed of the small stems.[1] The stalks are beaten and dried on the floor; or can be separated by hand with a sort of comb having teeth of steel or wood; in this manner they can be classified according to their size.[2] It is estimated that each beet furnishes about 100 to 250 grammes of seed, and the yield per hectare (two and a half acres) varies from 900 kilog. (1980 lbs.) to 2000 kilog. (4400 lbs.), according to the variety and method of planting. It has been proved that 100 kilog. (220 lbs.) of roots will yield about 25 kilog. (55 lbs.) of seed.

[1] See "Sowing the Seed," for the advantage of the above.
[2] See "Seed Variation according to Size."

CHAPTER VI.

HARVESTING.

Some few years past the men of science asserted that beets at all periods contained the same percentage of sugar. If this hypothesis had been true there would have been no necessity for a special time for harvesting. During our travels in the northern part of France we met several manufacturers who so argued, and considered that in order that a beet sugar factory should realize large profits, it was necessary to commence operations as early as possible, and not wait for the so-called maturity; but we consider this plan a bad one, as the beets at that period have not attained their development either in size or in sugar, and the quantity of each that would have been lost in the "silos"[1] would not have been greater during the same period after maturity.

From experiments that we have made during the last three years, we conclude that the best plan for ascertaining when the harvesting should take place is to make daily analyses during the last months, and when no increase of sugar can be noticed with the saccharo-

---

[1] See "Preservation of the Beet."

meter, we may consider that they have arrived at a nearly complete state of maturity, and for that reason the desired moment is near at hand. If this is passed, a decrease of the saccharine and an increase of the saline elements will be noticed. Gasparin and several others made a series of experiments wishing to prove that before beets could ripen a certain number of degrees of heat were required, but in consequence of similar trials we made in Pennsylvania, we have reasons for doubting the truth of this theory. The numbers we obtained in multiplying the days of each month by the corresponding mean temperatures were so different for the American soil that a comparison between the two would have but little interest. Another method for ascertaining when the roots are ripe is to cut one in two. If the color changes at once they should be left for a certain number of days in the ground; if, on the contrary, the change is not rapid, turning first to red then to brown, the moment for *harvesting* is near at hand. A rule given by many, which would be absurd in America, is to watch the leaves,[1] when these turn from green to brown the moment approaches; but, when the heat of our summers be considered, above all during the early part of August, this change would have no signification whatever, and at which time a beet sugar factory could not commence operations even if the roots had attained to the requisite state. The extraction of the beets from the ground can

---

[1] See "Leaves."

be accomplished either by hand or machinery; the latter being done by ploughs of various descriptions. The machine frequently adopted in Germany consists of several coupled curved prongs penetrating the soil much beneath the maximum depth attained by the roots; the whole is drawn by horses or cattle. The objection to this or any other similar method is the traction made use of, the feet of the animals greatly bruising the roots. The pulling by hand is much the best where labor is cheap. But some device different from anything up to the present time adopted, such as steam ploughing, etc., could alone be utilized in the United States. We have noticed that if it rains several days in succession during the harvesting period, a decrease of sugar may be expected. If a sudden change in the temperature takes place, falling below freezing point, it is advisable to leave the roots for several days still in the ground. If this precaution is not taken there is danger of losing the entire crop after the thaw. If the weather[1] be dry and hot when the harvesting takes place, the beets exposed to the outer atmosphere will lose the greater portion of their water, and consequently their weight, and are thus rendered in a condition more difficult to keep in a perfect state of preservation. If, on the contrary, the weather be rainy, the soil becomes wet and a great quantity of earth ad-

---

[1] Mr. Grant in his book says: "It is advisable to select dry weather and a dry state of the soil."

heres to the roots, and all ploughing, etc., is impossible—a certain amount of water being absorbed, which has the same effect as too little. From all that we have said in the above, we conclude that the best method is the German, and that is, when possible, to do the harvesting when the day is cloudy, taking every precaution to prevent too long a contact with the air. If the leaves are pulled immediately it is advisable to cover the roots with them, if not, several inches of earth will answer the same purpose.

When the beets are taken from the ground they should be shaken in order to get rid of the earth still adhering—the fig. 41 gives the reader an idea of the roots when the harvesting takes place—if this earth were allowed to remain it would, when in large quantities, induce a second growth; if in small it would be an advantage whilst in the silos. The roots are placed in rows after having been extracted from the ground, from which plan economy of time for the cutting and the placing on carts will be realized.

The leaves are separated from the roots either with a knife or a spade. We do not advise[1] even in a case of bad cultivation (that is to say, when a portion has grown out of the ground) to chop any off but what is absolutely necessary, as the preservation would be rendered more difficult, and it is impossible not to have an

---

[1] Mr. Grant says: "A portion of the green neck should be sliced off." For the above reasons we beg to differ.

HARVESTING. 193

immense loss, as this operation takes place in a very rapid manner. Time, for the above reasons, is an item

Fig. 41.

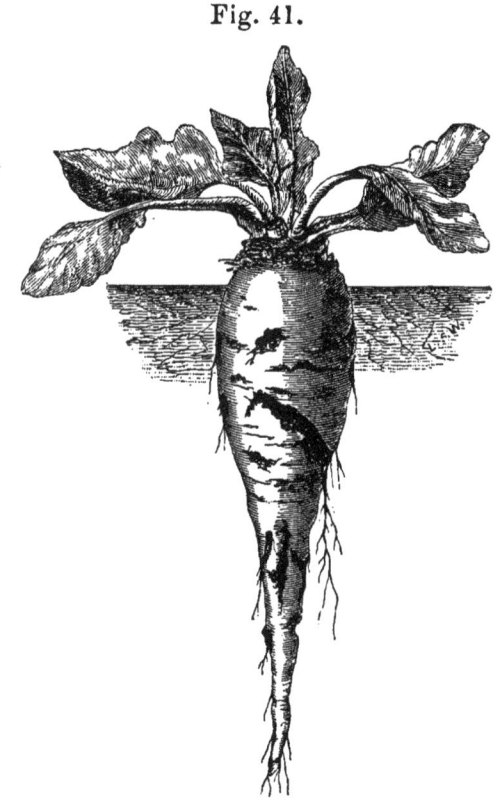

Gives an idea of a beet that has matured.

of the first importance; several inches below the neck would be accidentally extracted, this containing in all probability a large percentage of the sugar.

A question that has also been discussed is to know if the pulling of the leaves is an operation necessary before placing the beets in the silos.[1] For our

---

[1] See Chapter on the "Preservation of the Sugar Beet."

part we do not think it is, for we have seen beets kept many months with all their leaves.[1]

Too much care cannot be taken to prevent *all* bruises, each of which causes a loss of sugar and renders the preservation more difficult; when these bruises result from the careless manner in which they are thrown into the carts to be hauled to the factory they have but little importance, as fermentation has not then had time to set in. Care should be taken that the least ripe should be sent first, as these are more likely to undergo changes than when in a perfectly matured state.

In America it will be necessary not only to carry the roots required for that day's work, but also the entire crop, as the construction of silos on the ground where the cultivation has taken place, and where during the winter months in the Northern States the snow attains a height of several feet, would not be wise. A plan, if financially practical, which we consider would be the best, consists in having a number of baskets of a given capacity; these should be bought by the farmers and manufacturers, and in this way more care would be taken of them. The beets should be carefully placed in these baskets, after which on carts to be drawn in a direction not far distant from the factory.[2]

Now compare the injury done by this and the old method: 1st, bruising when the beets are thrown on

---

[1] See Chapter "Leaves of the Sugar Beet."
[2] See Chapter "Preservation of the Beet."

the carts; 2d, bruising when thrown into the house for preservation; 3d, when taken out of the same to be hauled for the second time to the door of the factory, where they frequently remain for several days, in which case fermentation is to be dreaded.

In the case we propose the only real bruise is that caused by emptying the baskets, which is the least important, as the roots are immediately utilized.

CHAPTER VII.

YIELD AND COST OF CULTIVATION.

It is impossible to give any exact figures to be expected as a yield from a given acre of land. As before shown, with certain fertilizers the crops can be made several times as great as they would have otherwise been. Then, again, the distance between the lines and each particular plant also varies, the seeds having many varieties corresponding to great fluctuations in the final yield. The variations of the weather also produce the same effect. In examples we give below the cost of working supposes that the land has been previously cultivated, as otherwise very secondary crops could alone be expected. As a principle, the growing of the beet requires more care than the cultivation of corn or wheat, etc., and the farmer can make no calculation of an exact nature, when these alone are taken as a basis. For years past we have seen many estimates made by those having never grown the beet, being otherwise interested, wishing to convey to the public mind that these roots could be cultivated with but little more care than is given to the crops just mentioned and yet have most excellent results. It is true they can be, but the sugar they contain would not pay for the cost

YIELD AND COST OF CULTIVATION. 197

of working; besides these, several other hypotheses are most erroneous.

When the roots are paid for in accordance with their saccharine value the farmer bestows more care upon their cultivation,[1] not after his own idea, but according to principles and facts long since proved in Europe to be exact. We know perfectly well the arguments brought to bear, that if large crops containing less sugar per beet should be cultivated the final amount to the acre would be more than with rich beets and a small yield. This is true, but the salts increase in the same proportion, and the only possible way of utilizing these with advantage is to discover some method not as yet known to neutralize the same; but, as this has yet to be done, we had better adhere to old principles.

To a certain extent any results obtained from experience in Germany or France will have no possible connection with those to be expected in America; hand labor being the method of cultivation on all the foreign beet-growing farms, the cost of which is, without doubt, less than here, but, on the other hand, our agricultural mechanical appliances are far superior to theirs, thus producing a sort of compensation.

The probable cost for the preparation of the soil, etc., for beet culture varies with circumstances; for example, a flat surface would be less than an undulated one; on rich soils the manure or fertilizers made use of

---

[1] See "Value of Beets."

would be less than when the root is grown on poor land, etc. The methods of sowing, as before stated,[1] greatly influence the final yield, which in itself augments or diminishes the cost of the beets per ton. As authority we may mention the estimates given by Payen for one hectare (two and a half acres).

Rent, taxes, interest of money	f115 =	$23 00
Manures	130 =	26 00
Two ploughings, two harrowings	86 =	17 20
Sowing	18 =	3 60
Weeding and hoeing	35 =	7 00
Gathering and transportation	36 =	7 20
	f420 =	$84 00

In supposing 35000 to 45000 kilog. as an average yield, we would then have for 1000 kilog. (2240 lbs.) $\frac{420}{35} = 12$ francs or $2.40, and if the 45000 kilog. be admitted, it would represent 9.33 francs per 1000 kilog., or $1.80 per ton. But in the case where the manufacturer grows his own seed, and feeds the resulting pulp to the animals, this is again greatly reduced.

If wheat or any other crop is planted the following year, this, as before stated, grows most luxuriously, and, as under ordinary circumstances the land would have received a ploughing and fertilizers, etc., it is but just to admit that the cost of these should be partly supported by that crop. If this is the case the cost per ton would be much diminished.

[1] See "Sowing the Seed."

We visited several farms in the northern portion of France, the most important in the arrondissement of Cambrai, where several figures were given us; we took an average of the same.

		Average.
Rent of one hectare of land } Taxes " " " }	f40 to f42 =	$8 20
Ploughing and harrowing	52 to 64 =	11 60
Manures	100 to 130 =	23 00
Seed	6 to 8 =	1 40
Weeding and hoeing	76 to 82 =	15 80
Harvesting, transportation, etc.	40 to 50 =	9 00
	f314 to f376 =	$69 00

If we suppose a yield of 30,000 kilog. to the hectare, we would then have roots at $2.30; but we were told that 60,000 kilog. is most common; this would then greatly diminish the same, as the cost per ton would then be $1.15. No more care or material is required for a high than a low yield. The seed represented in the above has been grown by the farmers, otherwise the cost of the same would be somewhat augmented. In France the average value of beets in 1876 was $3.00 per ton. This is not far from the general price or average for the last thirty years, including fluctuations, where in one special case $8.00 was paid, and yet the roots were worked with profit.

Several items we have not as yet taken into consideration are, that, if the leaves, necks, ends, etc., of the roots are permitted to remain on the ground, they will represent about 20,000 kilog., and be worth $14.00 as fertilizer for the following year.

The gathering of the roots and cleaning, etc., is frequently done by contract at a given sum per hectare. This in many cases gives most excellent results, as the importance of gathering rapidly has been before explained. The estimates, as we have remarked, are by no means general, and the cost of cultivation amounts in France[1] to considerably more than might as a general thing be conveyed to the reader's mind. On the other hand, in Germany, it is somewhat less. More time and attention are given to the weeding, etc., and this has proved to be to them most profitable, and they have understood the great problem that too much time cannot be bestowed upon the land. Some few figures we obtained at Magdeburg and on some of the neighboring farms we consider of interest. The most important were from Gross Wenzleben, Klein Wenzleben, Ottersleben, etc. These estimates were according to German measurements and money, but, when reduced to dollars and cents, we will have:—

The first ploughing of one acre	$4 00
Sowing	1 00
First weeding	1 20
Second weeding and thinning out	0 80
First hoeing and weeding	0 95
Second " " "	0 75
Third " " "	0 70
Harvesting the roots	3 50
Loading in carts	1 00
Placing in silos	0 90
	$14 80

[1] This is owing to the excessive amount of chemical fertilizers that have been brought to notice.

Corresponding to an average yield of 10 to 13 tons per acre, representing the remarkably low figure of $1.05 to $1.48 per ton. This is greatly reduced owing to the fact that the manures and seeds, etc., have not been considered; these are products on hand, which have cost but little, one from the cattle, and the other grown some years previously on the same soil. According to Walkhoff the cost of working a hectare of land in Russia will amount to 240 francs ($48), or considerably more than any of the above estimates; but even this, under ordinary circumstances, will leave a large margin of profit.

As for our own experience, we have planted the roots on farms in New Jersey and Pennsylvania,[1] have attained average yields of fifteen tons to the acre, and requested the farmers in each case to make a general estimate as to the probable cost of the same. These we hope to publish under a separate head later. In all cases they informed us that they were convinced with the necessary appliances they could be obtained at $2.50 per ton, and in extraordinary cases $5.00; these average 12 per cent. of sugar, or 6 per cent. of practical sugar. To this we must add the lower grades of sugar, molasses, pulp, etc. Farmers are all only too willing to introduce the beet culture on their farms when there is a possibility of selling the resulting roots,

---

[1] See "Probable Effect Produced in America by the Introduction of the Beet Culture."

which, as shown, would be more profitable and advantageous than any of the crops thus far produced.[1]

Value of Beets.

The only profitable way for a manufacturer to have beets worth using for their saccharine qualities is to pay for them not a given sum per ton (as efforts will then be made by the farmers to have large crops,[2] without paying sufficient attention to their culture with a view to sugar manufacture); but, on the contrary, according to their actual value. What basis then can be determined upon has been the topic of considerable discussion. The Germans[3] have understood this principle for years, and the results there obtained are sufficient to demonstrate the importance of this question. The French and Belgians, on the contrary, are only now commencing to appreciate it.

On nearly every farm we have visited the manufacturers specify that a given seed shall be made use of and the beet cultivated in a given manner; but even then the manufacturer is not protected, as here many complications arise, for every farm theoretically and

[1] From experiments made in Maine they came to the same conclusion; to this might be added various attempts in other Northern States, which, when on suitable soils, etc., convinced those interested that the growth of the beet on American soil would be advantageous and profitable.

[2] Then, again, fertilizers will be made use of to increase to a great extent the total yield per acre, and thereby annually the sugar in the same proportion.

[3] See "German System of Taxation."

practically requires a new regulation, the fulfilment of the same therefore becoming most difficult.

What farmer desires a manufacturer to impose upon him agricultural principles of which apparently he knows but little? Evidently, whatever these rules are they cause dissatisfaction, often resulting in strikes, frequently producing most disastrous results upon the manufacturing establishment, and for this reason we consider that, when possible, it is better for the company to own and cultivate its land.

The principle of paying for an article proportionally to its value is a just one, and we are convinced will be well understood by all interested. This plan is adopted for nearly all other merchandise, and why should it not be for beets? The farmer would then be interested, and it would no longer be necessary for the manufacturer to furnish given instructions. Then, again, let it be remembered that the quantity of salts absorbed is inversely proportional to the percentage of sugar; this being the case, the harm done to the soil is much greater with poor beets than with rich ones, in those cases where the elements taken away are not returned to it.

Among the principles which have been proposed and adopted, we may mention that in Belgium, it was thought proper that if the beets were 20 francs (\$4.00) for 1000 kilog. (2240 lbs.) for a density of 1.050 B., to augment or diminish this 0.40 franc (\$0.08) for every $\frac{1}{10}$ of a degree. Then, again, it was proposed to pay for each saccharine degree 4.50 francs ($0.90) in September, and for this to fluctuate according to the season.

This principle is wrong, as the density is no criterion; beets having a great density frequently do not contain as much actual sugar as others having a small specific gravity, these variations being due to foreign elements contained in the juice. In some cases the farmer has one chemist and the manufacturer another. The average result is considered the exact basis, and for 10 per cent. of sugar is then paid a given price, and all above or below is increased or reduced proportionally.

As before stated,[1] the proportion between the exact amount of sugar indicated with the polariscope[2] and the total substance indicated with an areometer should never be under 0.75. In other words, this would represent, when expressed in humidity, 75 per cent. of sugar to 100 of juice, and the value of the beet increase as this becomes larger. A few words pertaining to the Ventzke method, which is most simple, will be of interest. The juice is brought to a uniform density of 1.0488, corresponding to 6.6° Beaumé, and

---

[1] Several beets should be selected and a given portion of each extracted, this to be reduced to a pulp, the total heated to 59° F. and Beaumé's areometer placed in the same, this instrument gives the total of the solid substance T. To 110 c. c. of this juice is added 10 c. c. of subacetate of lead and the total filtered, and this liquid is tested in the polariscope; whatever be the indication, this should be augmented 10 per cent., representing the lead in the solution. If we have t. per cent. of sugar. T — t will be the foreign elements.

[2] See "Selection and Growing of the Seed."

YIELD AND COST OF CULTIVATION. 205

the exact percentage or degrees is doubled. This will give the so-called "quotient de pureté."[1] As a general thing it may be said that the amount of solids indicated by the areometer is greater than the reality, on account of various decompositions that have taken place in the juice, and for that reason it has been argued that a given amount of juice should be evaporated and the remaining deposits weighed. But even then small errors will exist. Too much reliance cannot be placed upon the percentage of these, as the manufacturer will greatly suffer from it. For example, the greater the mineral salts the greater the amount of bone black required in the manufacture; this increasing the expense, which would be a small item if the foreign elements could all be gotten rid of, but unfortunately these seem still to remain in the juice, and, in a remarkable degree, prevent the crystallization. Bad results may also be expected from the nitric albuminous substances, and it is important to know what these are and to what extent they exist. The effect produced by tannin has been before mentioned, and a most ingenious method has been proposed by Mr. Walkhoff[2] for its detection.

---

[1] Mr. Walkhoff indorses this principle emphatically on account of its simplicity and calls attention to the fact that a solution of pure sugar at a density of 1.0488 will indicate 50° with the polariscope, which, when doubled, will represent 100 per cent. of pure.

[2] A solution of 100 grammes of water and 1 gramme of pure tannin, or, again, 10 grammes of tannin to 1000 grammes of water, 10 c. c. of juice are united with 100 c. c. of water and 10 of a solution of alum, the total is heated

To give a long series of tables (where various calculations have been made, these having the object of ascertaining the exact price to be paid for beets) would, we think, be a mistake, as they have been based on given climates and soils, etc., and it is advisable for each manufacturer to make his own.

Close cultivation will come nearer to a solution of the problem than any other plan. To encourage this by prizes[1] will have the desired effect, and this saves considerable trouble. If a given price per ton be paid for beets, that have been grown at given distances and in given numbers per acre, we are convinced that the farmers would then produce a root containing much sugar and having every advantage that could be desired.

---

on a lamp. The tannin solution is added little by little, keeping the whole in continual agitation; a white precipitate will soon form, and this will continue as long as the nitric elements exist in the juice. The difficult part of the test is to ascertain exactly when the above has become complete. But with the assistance of chloride of iron this can be accomplished. A few drops of this will be sufficient; if a blue tint becomes visible this proves that the tannin has been added in excess; if, on the contrary, nothing is apparent, the addition of the tannin solution can be continued, etc.; knowing the amount of this made use of, the calculation as to the amount of elements existing becomes most simple.

[1] See "Sowing of the Seed."

CHAPTER VIII.

ROTATION OF CROPS.

THE importance of a rational rotation of crops has never been sufficiently understood in the United States, as our farmers are unable to appreciate the fact that there is a possibility of exhausting their soil. How many thousands of examples we could give where the same crops are grown year after year on the same land, and apparently giving excellent results; but how long will this last? Is it not possible that in many cases inferior crops have been obtained and the cause attributed to bad weather, etc., when in reality it was owing to this great agricultural principle being overlooked?[1] Evidently this is the case, as no plant exists which, if planted years in succession on the same soil, will not finally have an exhausting effect. When the demand for a given grain, etc., is great, or when the land in a given country is limited, there may be, to a certain extent, some excuse for this bad practice. For example, in France in certain cases, it has been a necessity for them to grow beets for several years on the same spot, owing to the bad location of the factory,

---

[1] See what was said on the culture of sugar-cane in Louisiana.

demanding for its supply the yearly growth of the same crop. But, in a country like our own, there can be no possible excuse, and it is to be hoped that the introduction of the beet culture will be an additional inducement for trying a rotation of crops according to scientific principles; not, however, by means of fallow lands, an idea most erroneous, and fortunately long since in most cases abandoned. It was only after a series of years that it became understood that the farmer and the general community were by this practice both the losers. In France the beet was one of the great causes that brought about this change, as this root formed or rather filled a vacant space in the rotation. In other countries the introduction of new crops answered the same purpose, but gave nothing like the same results. Great changes then took place, the rents increased, the land yielded more, and gave, from this fact, employment to a larger number of hands.

If all plants, or all of the same family, exhausted the soil in an equal manner, there would be no object in adopting a rotation, as the harm done would be exactly the same as if but one plant had existed; but when we remember that plants differ not only in the number of weeds they directly cause to grow, but also in other respects, some returning to the soil portions of what was taken or absorbed, they may consequently be classified as exhausting and ameliorating. From this we conclude that each plant leaves a certain organic product behind which forms a sort of manure, but this is not the total of the elements exhausted, and hence the importance of arranging the crops in such a manner that in a minimum time the maximum will be returned. In years gone by, on the greater number of old estates, the rotation yielding the best results was a study for centuries, and, when discovered, it was handed down from father to son as one of the great agricultural secrets. But even then time proved that this must vary, as the soil would even under these conditions become exhausted. A farmer discovers that a given plant will yield better results than another; but this is not sufficient, he must also know what would be the best rotation for him to adopt; and even then it would not be wise for him to follow the same strictly, as demand must also be considered. For example, if flour mills are in the neighborhood then wheat should present itself in the rotation more frequently than any other; if, on the contrary, dyeing or oil mills, then the corresponding plants should have the preference, and if beet sugar establishments exist, then this root should be selected. Everything consequently varies with each soil and location.

If it were possible to calculate the amount of each element which a given plant extracted or returned to the soil, a solution of this problem would be most easy; but of this but little is known. The amount of such elements remaining on the land is greater when the crops have been gathered green, and for that reason, in cases where a given grain requires more manure than another, it is advisable to adopt the principle of early reaping. Then, again, in cases like the beet culture, it is important to act in an opposite manner, for if the salts remaining were in excess the resulting roots would be worthless for beet sugar manufacture. From this we arrive at a realization of the importance of planting in such a manner as will give the best results in each case. Beets, unlike many other plants, can, with few exceptions, be planted before or after any given crops, and those, as before stated, that follow will average a greater yield than had hitherto existed, and the introduction of them in the rotation becomes most easy. Evidently, there are some few plants that are not desirable to precede this root, as bad effects might and in the great number of cases will result; for example, *clover* that has a large amount of wild seeds mixed with it (which is generally the case) would be most disastrous, and too much care cannot be taken to place this plant as far from the beet as possible, or, better still, leave it out in the rotation.

If it were exactly known to what extent the sugar existing in the root were assisted in its formation by the elements of the soil, we could then advise that plants that have a large percentage of saccharine principles should not directly follow in the rotation, as these very substances would be wanting. The introduction of chemical fertilizers has been a great help to the farmer, as with the assistance of these it becomes possible to return to the soil what has been taken away, the latter being determined by experience, or, better still, analysis;[1] and we have not the slightest doubt but that in a few years there will be a possibility of planting a given crop many years in succession with but little harm. It is well to remember, as a principle, that this should not be done when beets are grown, and, better still, these roots will never give satisfactory results when manured the year the seeds are sown. Before any plant is permitted to enter the rotation its classification, its manner of growing, and methods of culture should all be known and considered.

Lime[2] plants should not follow the same class, but potash[3] plants may come immediately in the rotation; then, again, those that draw their nourishing elements from the air, and consequently penetrate the soil but little, should be followed by those that penetrate deeply and plants that absorb large amount of sulphates and phosphates should not be followed by roots that are planted for their seed, as these chemicals are important for the formation of the latter.

The great guide to the rotation of crops is experience, and no definite rule can be laid down for beets. The bi-annual rotation of wheat and beets has been adopted in many portions of France. The ground under this system does not receive sufficient rest, and is producing bad results. The first year the wheat is grown on a manured soil, then the third on chemical fertilizers.

---

[1] See "Fertilizers."

[2] Lime plants are those wherein this chemical predominates.

[3] Potash plants are those wherein the plants contain one-half their weight of soluble alkaline salts.

The reasons for this have been before explained. The tri-annual system existed when fallow land was advocated, but has now been abandoned, and the most popular is the quadr-annual, which has many advantages. The land receives a sufficient variety of plants to produce a most excellent effect. The number of acres of land under cultivation varies with the system of rotation, and the complications resulting increase in the same proportion. It would be of little interest to give all the combinations that have been adopted in Europe, but a few we consider important. The following is adopted in the northern part of France:—

    1st year . . . . . Wheat
    2d year . . . . . Beets
    3d year . . . . . Oats
    4th year . . . . . Clover

Or, again:—

    1st year . . . . . Wheat
    2d year . . . . . Grass
    3d year . . . . . Flax, colza
    4th year . . . . . Beets

Or, when large quantities of land are at one's disposal, a five-year system can be and is adopted:—

    1st year . . . . . Wheat or rye
    2d year . . . . . Beets
    3d year . . . . . Barley
    4th year . . . . . Clover
    5th year . . . . . Wheat

The wheat in this case being the object of rotation.

Then again on some farms we have visited tobacco

has been grown as well as beets. This forms a most excellent crop to precede the root on rich soils:—

1st year	Tobacco
2d year	Beets
3d year	Wheat
4th year	Clover
5th year	Wheat

Here again wheat was the great and important crop.

The advantages gained for the wheat are so great that the temptation for planting it cannot be resisted. None of the above combinations can, we consider, be exact, as experience has taught that rye is better to precede the beet, as the quantity of manure required for its cultivation is less than for wheat. The portions of the manure still remaining in the ground after the harvesting will have less effect upon the beet crops that immediately follow.

We do not recommend any particular rotation, as before stated. This must greatly vary, but, suffice it to say, that many small crops, such as colza, flax, barley, etc., should be utilized, as their elements enter into direct consumption in the feeding of the animals of the farm, and should consequently be planted proportionally to their demand.[1]

In the United States Indian corn is grown to so great an extent, and forms so profitable a crop, that it also should take a prominent part in the rotation.

[1] If N be the number of animals and C the consumption of a given element, the total consumed will be $C \times N$. If A is the yield in pounds or bushels to the acre, $\dfrac{C}{A} \times N$ would represent the number of acres of each crop to be planted.

PART IV.

CHAPTER I.

GENERAL CONSIDERATIONS ON ECONOMICAL TRANSPORTATION—DECAUVILLE, PROVIN, LINARD, ETC.

IN consequence of the bad condition of the roads when the beet harvest commences, caused either by excessive rain or snow, and the importance of gathering the entire crop with the shortest possible loss of time, and thereby avoiding the frost; and, as the responsibility and expense interest principally the manufacturer, various plans have been proposed for its accomplishment. By such means as these, economy over the ordinary wagon drawn by oxen or horses is obtained, and we will pass the most important of them in review. Evidently, the idea of replacing animal traction by steam—road locomotives—was soon thought of, and Duffriné Brothers, sugar manufacturers, were the first to utilize road locomotives for this purpose. They estimated the cost at about 0.18 franc ($0.03) per kilometric ton. Then Corbin brought to notice his so-called "wagon locomotive," which was able to carry eighteen tons of beets, and having a velocity of four kilometres per hour. This machine was an expansion engine, the detent taking place at half stroke of the piston, and the latter having a diameter of 18 centimetres (6.48). The main shaft had a velocity of 160 revolutions per minute, and to every three revolutions of this corresponded one of the driving wheel.

According to various calculations made, it has been estimated that the cost per kilometric ton was only $0.02.[1] This evidently was a great progress realized, but the inconvenience was the same as before mentioned, that is to say, it necessitated roads in a perfect condition, and even under the most favorable circumstances these would soon become broken up in consequence of the continual passage over them of the machine.

This plan was necessarily abandoned by Corbin for another called *"porteur universelle"* (porteur or small car); this being far better, has since received many improvements.

1. *Mr. Corbin's Idea.*—This was not exactly original, as it had previously been adopted in Belgium. This system may be divided into two parts: first the *portable track* and second the "porteur." The first has a length of 5.30 m. (17.39 feet) per section which weighs about 21 kil. (46.2 lbs.); is composed of two "travées" of

---

[1] The ordinary transportation is estimated at 20 cents per ton; in the above evidently many items have been neglected.

wood, which are united by transversal portions, the object of which is to keep the gauge constant. On these travées a flat iron forms the track in immediate contact with the wheels of the porteur. These so-called travées can be united end to end, thus permitting the passage over any soil without special preparation, such as ballasting and general earthworks. Curves are also made in the same manner. The train of porteurs is composed of a series of small cars having each a capacity of 50 kilog. (110 lbs.) to 100 kilog. (220 lbs.); the first of these has four wheels and the others only two; the weight thus supported by the track is distributed over a great length. The number of these cars varies with the general condition of the soil over which they pass, but on a perfect horizontal 10,000 kilog. (22,000 lbs.) can be drawn by a horse. It is estimated that a man can push 1000 kilog. (2200 lbs.) to 1500 kilog. (3,300 lbs.). For many years this system has been employed at Lizy, on the river Ourcq, and also at several other sugar factories in France and Belgium. Corbin estimated that this plan was four times as cheap as the ordinary method of transportation, that is to say, cost about $0.05 per kilometric ton; this evidently is an exaggeration.

The facility with which the track can be placed at a given spot, and then removed and the moderate capital required gives this method many advantages over the old system; but, on the other hand, the travées are composed of wood, these being exposed to the variations of temperature and humidity, will soon alter and will not then support the weight calculated upon. Another objection is, that the porteurs having but two wheels are liable to run off the track too easily, and thus cause a loss of time.

2. *Mr. Decauville's Idea.*—Mr. Decauville who had for many years been in search of some practical solution of economical transportation, and, having in 1875 9,000,000 kilog. (19,800,000 lbs.) of beets to gather in the field, the soil of which being damp, it would have been impossible for any wagon to enter and gather them, it was during this period that he brought to notice his porteur. We made this gentleman a visit at his factory and farm at Petit-Bourg, and consider the information obtained highly satisfactory and important. The principle of the distribution of the load over a considerable length is the same as the one we have just mentioned. This is also a portable track, but the inconveniences of Corbin's are not to be found here. Mr. Decauville had the excellent idea of giving his rail the same form as the original Vignol (which is now generally employed by railroad companies the world over), every portion of which being reduced he thus obtained a resistance corresponding to the maximum charge iron or steel can be submitted to. The rails, sleepers, and fish-plates form one piece. The gauge is only 0.40 m. (1.30 feet), which is considered to give better results than when greater, as the minimum material is here employed it becomes of greater

interest. The rails have a length of 5.00 m. (16.40 feet), and are bolted on the sleepers, which are placed about every metre (3.28 feet); the total travée, which is composed of two rails 5.00 m. (16.40 feet) each, and five sleepers, two fish-plates, united on the end, weighs but 47 kilog. (103.4 lbs.), which can be easily carried by a man standing in the middle with a rail in each hand. It is only in very exceptional cases where it would be necessary to use wooden sleepers in addition to the above. These can be fastened by small bolts passing through holes that are placed by way of precaution. On many soils this would become important.

In many cases where a horse cannot enter the field on account of the mud, the tracks will not sink even when the porteur passes full. This track can be made permanent, and even then the wooden sleepers are not, as a general thing, necessary. To unite the sections one to the end of the other the fish-plates are riveted cold—these are of soft iron. As for the curves, they have radii of 8 metres (26.24 feet), 6 metres (19.68 feet), or even 4 metres (13.12 feet), and generally form one piece; curve to the right and to the left or in one direction only. Frequently the factory is established on the other side of the main road, then a "*passage à niveau*" is at our disposal. This is also portable. When it becomes necessary to change the direction of the track the movement of the switch is accomplished by a kick with the foot. The turn-tables are here also

220   THE SUGAR BEET.

very complete. We have at our disposal two models. They differ only in size from those adopted by the railway companies; one of these is simply composed of two thin plates of iron, one over the other; at their centre is a pivot. These weigh but 90 kilog. (198 lbs.), and at each side a handle is placed which enables two men to carry them with ease.

We will now say a few words concerning the "porteur" (see fig. 42), which is extremely simple in construction.

Fig. 42.

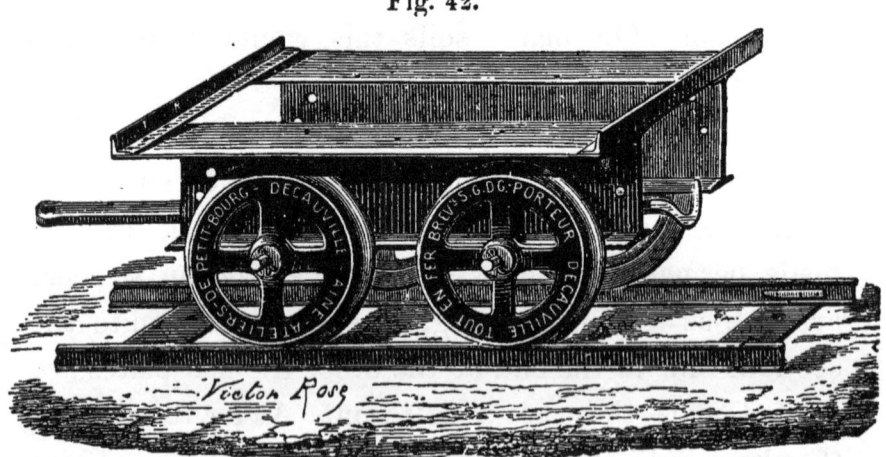

Porteur Decauville.

This is composed of two **T**-irons 0.10 m. (0.32 feet) in height, which are fastened to the axles which become fixed. On their upper portion are riveted two plates of iron three-quarter inch in thickness. At each end of these is riveted an ⌐-iron. Between the plates is an open space; this has the advantage of preventing an accumulation of dirt on the platform.

These porteurs weigh 47 kilog. (103.4 lbs.), and are the ones most generally adopted on the farms. The beets are gathered in the civieres (fig. 43), which are constructed of flat and rounded irons, and great solidity

"Civieres" for transportation of beets.

is thus obtained, while they weigh but 18 kilog. (39.6 lbs.) including the handles, which are of wood. Their shape is conical; the upper portion is 0.68 c. m. (2.23 feet) in width and the lower 0.44 c. m. (1.44 feet), height 55 c. m. (1.80 feet), capacity is about 130 kilog. (286 lbs.), and can be carried for a short distance full of beets by two men.

Having at our disposal one or more solutions of an economical and portable track will not alone be sufficient to give good results, for if these are not made use of in a rational manner it will require as much time to gather the beets on the field and take them to the silos as with the ordinary wagon, leaving aside the bad condition of the weather. Another problem now presents itself: What is the minimum material and labor required to obtain the maximum results? We ourselves had a general organization in view, which generally agreed with Mr. Decauville's idea, with which we have now become familiar; he having had some twenty years' experience in the planting of beets. We will give his plan, and make no mention of our own: The material necessary is 300 to 400 metres of rails, a switch, a few curves, some of which turn to the right and others to the left, two trains, composed each of 15 porteurs, to go with these 45 civieres. Besides the above we must in all cases suppose that there exists a permanent track, which is in direct communication with the factory, farm, or distillery.

The problem will in this case be to establish our silos along the main track, or, again, to heap the beets in piles when they are to be immediately utilized. The general disposition of the movable track in both cases is the same, the sidings alone differing. When the first case presents itself the curves in communication with this movable track and siding should be both turning to the left, and in the second case one to the right and the other to the left. The rails being on the ground, the next problem is, what number of workmen are necessary? Two men to fill the civieres and to place them on the porteurs, a boy to help to fill these, and one to lead the horse, and two men to place the beets in the silos. (Fig. 44 shows the arrangement.)

Fig. 44.

Building of a silo near the main track. System Decauville.

We will suppose that each train is at its siding, the first will be called *A* and the second *B*. The boy attaches his horse to the train *A*, which is composed of 15 porteurs and 30 civieres; 15 of the latter are immediately filled with beets, after which the train is hauled in the direction of the silos. During their absence the 15 remaining civieres are being prepared for the train *B*, which returns immediately whilst *A* is being unloaded by the two men at the silos; in this manner no time is lost. But 15 minutes are required to place the 300 yards of this movable track, 30 yards further to one side than it had previously been.

What is most remarkable in this system is the economy of the first cost and the rapidity with which the work can be executed. Mr. Decauville says from his experience he is able to gather 40,000 kilog. of beets in 10 hours, place these in silos for the moderate sum of 0.50 franc $0.10 per 1000 kilog. The above material is sold for about $1000 a kilometre; as for the porteurs, they are worth $7.00, and each civiere $3.00. As shown, with a small outlay, marvellous results can be obtained.

3. *Linard's Idea.*—At the sugar factory of Goumand, Linard & Co., at Origny, St. Benoit, the fuel, etc., utilized in the establishment arrives by a canal, which is situated some three kilometres from the centre. A permanent ballasted track has here been established, on which is a small locomotive; the curves on which this can turn have a radius of 8.00 m. (26 feet); the gauge is 0.75 m. (2.46 feet), and the rail here also is a Vignol, weighing $6\frac{1}{2}$ to 7 kilog. (15.4 lbs.) the linear metre. The first cost of this track was $9000, with

material. About nine tons can be carried each trip, and one hour is required to go and come, consequently in ten hours ninety tons. The expense of running the machine is nearly $8.00 per day, without the interest of first cost and sinking fund, the loading and unloading.

We cannot recommend the adoption of this method, even in the most extraordinary cases, on account of the first expenditure. Evidently there are many circumstances under which it is impossible to establish a track, to carry to the factory the roots that farmers would be willing to raise for any reasonable sum, as the general formation of the surrounding country, hills, rivers, etc., varies.

An ingenious plan was soon thought of, which consisted in having a wire rope suspended in the air.

Aerial Transportation.—Two methods have been adopted, in the first the movement is given to the rope, while in the second the rope is stationary.

1. *Hodgson's Idea.* This will give perfect satisfaction at distances as great as six, eight, or even more miles. At the factory of Bazin, Letrilliart & Co. the rope has a length of over six miles. The first cost, including drums, supports, various machines, etc., may be estimated at $2000 per kilometre. The movement is given by the engine (10 H. P.) to the main drum (which is horizontal); this is transmitted to the two ropes, each of these moving in opposite directions. The supports on which they pass have small

wooden pulleys; their arms are horizontal. These supports are placed at distances varying from 60 m. (196.8 feet) to 80 m. (262 feet). The buckets conveying the beets have a half cylindrical shape, and a capacity of about 50 kilog. (110 lbs.). Their movement is due to the adherence to the wire rope. The placing of these buckets on the latter is accomplished by hand, and when in contact with the pulleys on the support they pass over them in consequence of their momentum. When at their destination they leave the end drum, passing on a small track, which is at a tangent to the same. The acquired velocity is sufficient for the movement to continue for a short distance. About 7500 kilog. (16,500 lbs.) can thus be carried per hour, and in ten hours 165,000 lbs. The pulp is returned from the factory to the farms in a given direction in the same manner. All calculations made $0.06 will represent the cost for hauling per kilometric ton. This sum does not include the placing in silos or gathering of the roots.

2. *Provin's Idea.*—Here the rope is fixed at both ends. The baskets move by gravity on a slant of 21 mm. per metre. This idea in many respects is most excellent. The rope is supported in the air by an ingenious apparatus, as shown in fig. 45. Evidently if some precautions were not taken it would be likely to break in consequence of repeated shocks received at the point of intersection of the rope and support at the passage of each basket. To avoid this, to the arm

A, is affixed a weight, which gives way at the dangerous moment and returns afterwards to its normal position, it

Support for the wire in Provin's idea.

exerting a leverage, which is important, as the momentum to be overcome varies with the position the support

228 THE SUGAR BEET.

occupies on the rope, and the height from the ground varies according to circumstances.

Fig. 46.

Gathering the beets upon the field.

The fig. 46 gives an idea of the manner in which the beets are gathered in the field. These being placed, as shown in fig. 47, on the rope, pass directly under a

ECONOMICAL TRANSPORTATION. 229

trestle. Seen at a distance, here they are hoisted with a windlass to a certain height, as the case may be

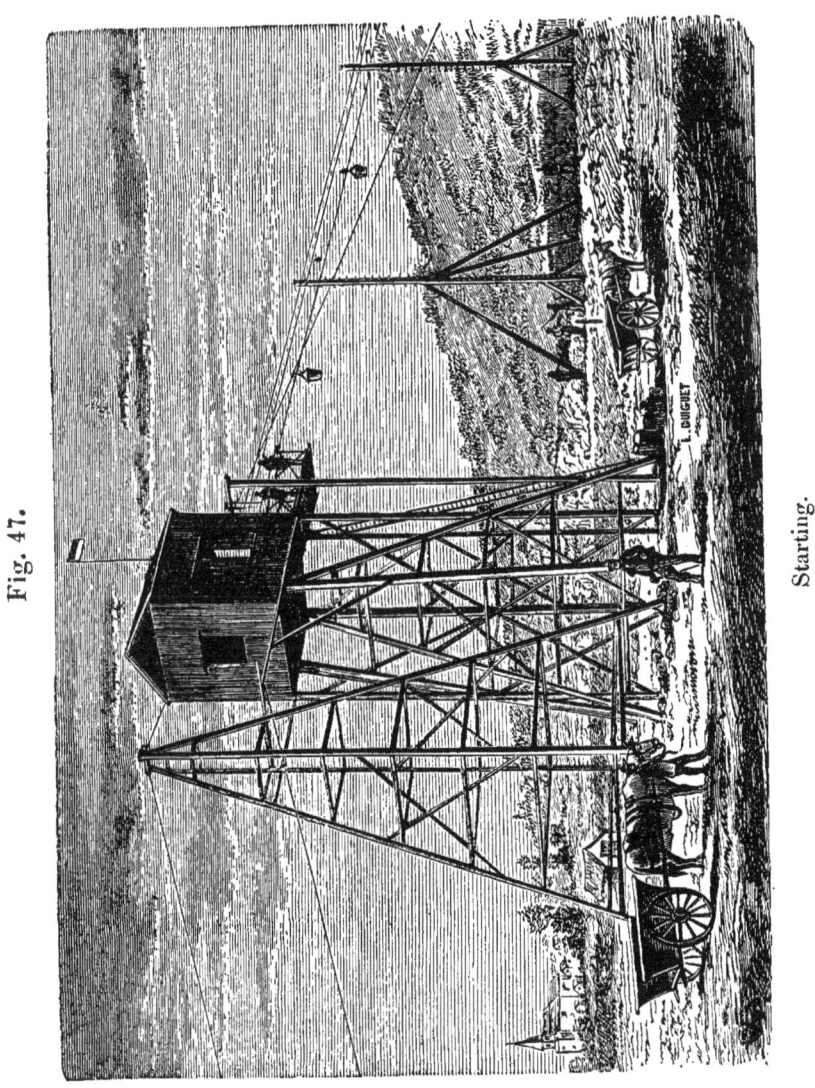

Fig. 47.

(see fig. 48), to obtain the given start; for example, for a distance of 100 m. (328 feet) this would be 2.10 metres (6.8 feet). These arrive in a perfect state at the factory. The empty baskets return by a second rope, which has a smaller section, having less to support.

Fig. 48.

Arrival of the beets.

The slant here is the contrary of that of the first mentioned cable.

The first cost of this may be estimated at $900 per

mile. Evidently this sum is not mathematical, as it increases inversely with the distance, that is to say, if the first mile would cost $900 the second would be much less.

This system can be worked by two men and a boy, but, if with a greater number of hands, as many as 100,000 kilog. (220,000 lbs.) can be sent to the factory daily. This idea in Europe is considered most excellent, but for short distances only. But it strikes us that there are thousands of cases, if applied as it should be, even at a distance of several miles, where most satisfactory results could be obtained. Cases we have up to the present examined have been for factories working under comparatively favorable circumstances, that is to say, within a short distance of limestone that is required, near a railway station or a canal facilitating the arrival and departure of the fuel consumed or sugar manufactured daily; or, again, within a few kilometres of the farm which furnishes the beets that are required.

We will now, on the contrary, suppose these conditions changed, and a factory working 100,000,000 to 150,000,000 of kilogrammes per annum, and situated ten or more miles from land yielding beets; this location having been chosen not on account of the special quality of the soil, but principally for commercial considerations. The above plans of transportation have been most excellent when the factory was comparatively small, but, when on a scale as we now suppose, the problem would be far too complicated, and cause too much general confusion by the arrival and weighing of the roots.

Underground Pipes, Linard's Idea.—In 1867 Mr. Linard, at his establishment at Montcourt, where we had the honor of being received, was the first to give a practical solution to this difficult problem, which example has been followed by some fifty other factories in France and Belgium, and has in all cases given entire satisfaction. The idea consists in having small pipes, through which the juice flows; this having been previously pressed at the farms in small buildings called "raperies." Leaving aside the first cost of these pipes, this transportation is reduced to a minimum or nearly so. If a slight difference between the elevation of the raperies and the factory should exist, this difference of level would be sufficient to permit the juice to flow with ease. If, on the contrary, the factory be more elevated than the raperie, an engine of one or two horse power is sufficient to overcome the friction of the juice in the pipes. At the factory at Nezapoin this difference is one hundred yards, and here evidently more power is needed. The juice before leaving the raperies is united with 5 per cent. in volume of lime, having a normal density of 23° B. The importance of this is very great, as it prevents all fermentation, which would otherwise occur. The velocity is 25 m. (82 feet) to 50 m. (164 feet) per second, the first figure gives better results than the second.

These pipes are of cast iron, and are manufactured with every possible care, and are submitted to a pressure of fifteen atmospheres with water before the juice is permitted to enter. The length of each is 30 m. (98.4 feet). The joint should be perfect, and precaution is taken to give an internal and external coating of tar. Their diameter varies with the circumstances, from 65 mm. to 120 mm. Their price per mile is 5000 francs ($1000) to 7000 francs ($1400). They are placed in the soil to a depth of 80 c. m. (2.6 feet), this being, in Europe, sufficient to prevent the action of the frost, which depth in America would not be sufficient, but 1.00 m. (3.28 feet) we consider would give good results. These pipes follow the general undulations of the country over which they pass, and the place generally chosen is the roadside. If the least escape occurs this will be noticed on the surface, as a froth will soon show itself. A superintendent is generally walking to and for, who gives the alarm. Nothing prevents, and it is advisable to have an apparatus at each end giving the pressure in the interior of the pipe. If this, at a given moment, should indicate a great decrease, an accident is to be suspected, but these are of rare occurrence. The principal causes are an accumulation of pulp frequently carried with the juice, or, again, by the lime which has not yet combined with the liquid.

Generally certain precautions are taken to prevent these accidents by filtering the juice through chopped straw. Mr. Maumené considers that the juice should be left for twenty-four hours before being pumped through the pipes. In this manner the solid portions are soon deposited at the bottom. Another precaution, which we think important, is to thoroughly clean these pipes by means of a rapid circulation of water before and after the juice is to be, or has been, circulated through them. If these points be attended to the above accidents are not to be feared. The raperies are generally in communication with the central factory by a telegraphic wire, with the assistance of which in a moment's notice the movement of the liquid can be stopped. It might be well to state that air is frequently carried with the juice; this is gotten rid of by an apparatus which is placed over the most elevated portion of the pipe. The first cost of these raperies may be estimated at $6.00 per 1000 lbs. of beets to be pressed. From what has been said, we may conclude that there exist many advantages in the establishing of these raperies when it is necessary to work on a large scale, not, however, from economy in working the beets, as in this case it is more costly to press the roots to extract the juice than when these operations take place at the factory itself, as the steam generated in a boiler to work the rasp is utilized but once. But these losses are greatly compensated by the transportation, the cost being reduced to 4.5 per cent. of what it would otherwise have been, the beets containing but 80 per cent. of their weight in juice. Another item of economy is that the pulp is not carried from the factory to the farm, and thereby diminished in value, by being as it frequently is, exposed to the air for several days, during which time it may have lost much of its nourishing properties, by being submitted to excessive rains, etc. When, at the raperie, on the contrary, the farmer has fresh pulp directly from the beets he has furnished without loss of time or of quality. How frequently it occurs that given crops are poor from want of water, owing to the excessive dryness of the season. These dangers are not to be dreaded on the farms in the direct neighborhood of the raperies, as water can be furnished when required through the pipes which are in direct communication with the factory. It has also been proposed to irrigate with the distiller's wash resulting from the distillation of molasses, this containing the foreign elements of the primitive beets; in this manner we would return to the soil to a great extent what had been previously extracted.

Conclusions.—From all that has been said we may conclude that the various plans of economical transportation vary with circumstances, that is to say:—

1. If we have at our disposal within four miles the land required to supply an ordinary sugar factory with beets, by all means adopt Mr. Decauville's porteur.

2. If there exist several yards difference in the elevation of the farm and factory, which is in the direct vicinity (that is one mile) adopt *Provin's* idea.

3. If the beets are grown on the other side of a stream over which there exists no permanent bridge, this being placed some three miles from the factory, then adopt the Hodgson system.

4. If, on the contrary, the factory is working on a very large scale, and it becomes necessary to grow beets distances from the factory of twenty to thirty miles to supply the demands, then we have Linard's idea, where the number of raperies may vary with the work going on, and the above incumbrances of the daily arrival of large volumes of roots are no longer to be dreaded.

CHAPTER II.

CONSERVATION OF THE SUGAR BEET.

History.—The importance of keeping roots in a perfect condition during the entire or a portion of the year is not new, and was well understood by the ancients, and even at the present day there are but few countries in Europe, Asia, or Africa where some device of this description is not in existence.

The conservation takes place in a so-called *silo*, from the Spanish, meaning an underground cellar.

The Egyptians had their *silos* made of granite, which were of various dimensions, and entirely beneath the surface of the ground.

The Romans and Arabians and others frequently made excavations in solid rocks which served as *silos*, and even the Chinese have had their *silos* for thousands of years.

The system at present adopted in Europe is generally above the ground—Russia being an exception.

General Considerations.—There is no problem more difficult to solve, and yet easy in appearance, than the conservation of the sugar beet, and its importance cannot be overrated, and, if badly done, will result in a loss to all interested.

We know of no silos that completely fulfil the conditions demanded, and these are to keep beets for many months without loss of *sugar* or *weight*.

There is no country in Europe where less attention is given to this important subject than in Germany. The reason of this is that their beets are rich in sugar, and from observations made from time to time these will keep with greater ease than others, such as those grown in Belgium. A few experiments which we made some years ago may be of interest.

In September the beets were placed in a silo of ordinary dimensions; these beets had an average of 14 per cent. of sugar:—

In October there was	14.03 per cent.
" November "	14.20 "
" December "	14.10 "
" January "	13.90 "
" February "	13.02 "

The above shows that 1 per. cent. has been lost. The results obtained from beets having 8 per cent. were a loss of over 2 per cent. in the same time, which goes to prove the foregoing theory.

The loss of weight is also an important item—more to the farmer than to the manufacturer. We consider that if a mass of beets measuring one cubic metre and weighing 550 kilog. (1210 lbs.) be placed in the silos for six months their weight would then be 485 kilog. (1067 lbs.), thus representing a loss of 65 kilog. (143 lbs.). If a considerable crop be on hand the difference is worthy of notice.

Many manufacturers (Compte, Bombrisky, and others) contend with reason that if this loss of weight takes place within certain limits there is an advantage to be derived; it prevents a second growth. If in excess, will cause an alteration of the total mass. Mr. Walkhoff fixes this limit at 10 per cent. of its normal quantity of water; beets which have lost their weight and are withered give much difficulty to the manufacturer.

Causes of the Loss of Sugar.—These causes are numerous, and may be divided under two heads: 1st. Before being placed in the silos;[1] 2d. Whilst in the silos.

The loss of sugar whilst in the silos is to be attributed to two causes:—

(α) The second growth.

(β) Fermentation; three causes { Temperature { 1. Heat. 2. Cold. } Want of ventilation. }

(α) The second growth taking place it will absorb the greater amount of the oxygen in the silos, replacing the same by carbonic acid. From an analysis of these sprouts made by Barbet it can be seen exactly what this loss is:—

Water	90.70 per cent.
Ashes	0.44 "
Sugar	0.95 "
Grape sugar	2.25 "
Nitric elements	1.80 "
Organic elements	3.86

[1] See "Harvesting."

(β) 1. *Heat.*—Caused by the conditions of the outer atmosphere or by the excessive height of the piles of beets which crush the lower layers by their weight, thus causing a certain fermentation, resulting from an elevation of temperature, during which period the sugar is being exhausted.

2. *Cold.*—Beets when exposed to a temperature of 27° F. freeze, a thaw then takes place, when fermentation will set in, having the same effect as before mentioned.

Want of Ventilation.[1]—The importance of ventilation was observed by Pasteur,[2] who noticed that when beets were placed in an atmosphere of carbonic acid they were rapidly attacked by a fermentation, wasting a portion of the sugar of the beet, that remaining being transformed into grape sugar. Some few lines above we mentioned the fact that beets rich in sugar were more easily kept than those having but a small percentage. The cause of this difference we attribute to the excess of nitric elements in the beets having little sugar, which will activate a decomposition, but others believe it is owing to the difference of the physical constitution of the tissue.[3]

Prevention of this Loss.—Various ideas have been proposed to prevent the above loss of sugar caused by

---

[1] In Mr. Grant's book on beet-root sugar he says: "I have seen such vast quantities kept in such fine condition, etc., *we doubt its necessity.*"

[2] See Pasteur's "Theorie des Ferments."

[3] Champignon and Pellet.

second growth, etc.; as a principal it is of great importance to keep out all light and dampness.

Mr. Ballon two years ago made some experiments in public to show how these young sprouts might be destroyed. These consisted in causing a current of sulphurous acid to circulate through the entire mass of the *silos;* this will have for effect not only the above, but will prevent a similar growth in the future. This chemical is forced through pipes placed in different portions of the silos; the latter are perforated with small holes.

Another important operation is to strongly ventilate in order to get rid of CO_2, replacing this by an equivalent volume of air. The fermentation is the most difficult of all things to prevent.

If beets that are not in a good condition be placed with others that are perfectly healthy the disease soon spreads; hence the importance of dividing the silos into several compartments. In this manner whatever occurs it will be local. The height of the piles of beets should not exceed six feet without special precaution, and that is to activate a ventilation by communicating with the exterior. These openings should be one-fourteenth of a square metre to every cubic metre of beets in the silos; in this manner an excess of heat is not to be dreaded. When a given temperature is obtained it should, if possible, be kept constant. One of the best non-conductors is earth, which will keep the mass from the spontaneous changes that so frequently take place in the outer atmosphere.

The method of preventing cold air penetrating in excess is similar to the above; if the ambient air be 29° F. the circulation should be at once stopped.

It is important not to make use of straw, as when this becomes wet, which it is sure to do, and, when in close contact with beets, it will rot, and, after a short time, the entire silos will be in the same wet condition.

Causes of the Loss of Weight.—This may, as a general thing, be attributed to the evaporation which takes place while the beets are in the interior of the silos or before being placed therein.[1] If this evaporation has not been of a too long duration, the normal weight may be restored by sprinkling the mass with water. This method is frequently adopted in France. If the above continues the tissues will be composed of small holes, which will soon become filled with air, and thus cause a fermentation, spreading itself through the entire mass. This malady[2] is called by Baron Liebig "deremacausie." In regard to this evaporation, if it can be obtained in a rapid manner by ventilation, the result will be a general fall in the temperature. In a new country like the United States, where beets rich in sugar cannot at first be expected, and where a loss, however small, will be of more importance than in Europe, we consider it of great importance to dwell in a very extended manner upon this subject.

[1] See "Harvesting."
[2] See "Diseases of the Beet."

Silos.—Their situation should, when possible, be in the immediate proximity to the factory, but, as a general thing, more efforts are made to place them near the roadside, as during the winter, in consequence of the rain, mud, snow, etc., the farmers are anxious to deliver as many as possible before these last-mentioned difficulties present themselves, and for that reason also the beets are frequently placed on the soil within a few feet from where they have been grown. We think in many cases this is the best plan, as it is impossible to carry beets any distance without injury, the consequence resulting, as before stated, is a general fermentation. On various farms that we visited near Magdeburg all without exception adopted this plan. These silos should be in a direction north to south, as the heat of the sun is less to be dreaded than if placed from east to west. When the time, etc., permit we would advise the establishment of the silos on a soil neither too wet nor too dry, and on an elevated portion of the land. The inundations are then less to be dreaded. The soil gives the best results when it has a slight slant; the drainage becoming more easy. Beets that are placed in a valley lose a greater amount of water than those situated on a hill.

In the early portion of this century Chaptal[1] gave a description of his idea of preserving beets. The results obtained by him he considered very satisfactory, but

---

[1] Chaptal, "Culture de la bettrave."

facts of the present day have changed, as we look for greater yields than were ever thought of years ago. He advises leaving the beets for the longest possible time in the field, thus permitting the maximum evaporation before being placed in the silos. The disadvantage of this plan we have already called attention to.[1] The beets were then to be gathered and stored in an ordinary stone building, the precaution having been taken of placing against the walls a certain quantity of straw, against which the beets were to be thrown, the general height being 2.50 m. (8.20 feet); the outer portion, as shown in the fig. 49, was also covered with

Fig. 49.

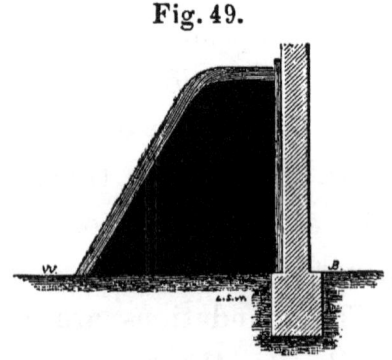

Sectional view of Chaptal's idea of a *silo*, straw being placed over the roots and between the wall and them.

straw. Evidently, if beets are to remain but for a short time (one month) the objections to this plan are few, and we have no doubt that good results could be obtained, but when for six months the conditions change, the evaporation would then take place, thus causing

[1] See "Harvesting."

the straw to become wet. The temperature will rise, and decomposition will soon find its way through every portion of the silo. In order to ascertain the exact condition of the beets, Chaptal's idea was to open the centre of the silo. If the beets were in a good condition in the centre he concluded the entire mass was the same; but here was an error, the portions he should have most watched were those in direct contact with the straw. We cannot repeat too often the importance of rejecting this covering, as we are certain that nothing like the results can be obtained with it as by the simple use of earth—when they are to remain for any length of time.

When beets are to be used within a few days, the most simple method is to pile them on the ground, forming a sort of triangular prism, covering it with

Fig. 50.

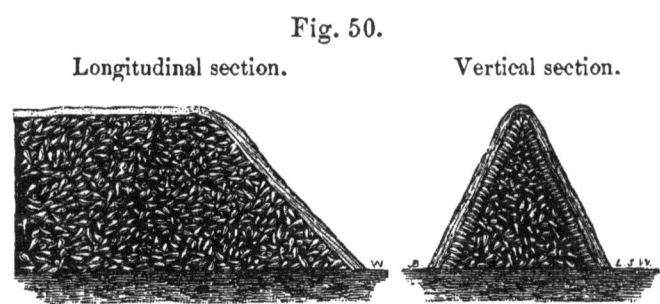

Longitudinal section. Vertical section.

Roots to be utilized shortly, piled on the ground with a slight covering of straw.

straw, the thickness augmenting with the fall in the exterior temperature. The fig. 50 shows a silo of this description; the height is 1 m. (3.28 feet) and length variable; the beets as they are required from one hour to another are taken from the ends, the precaution being taken to cover the same immediately with straw.

A system adopted in the Palatinate, where the beets are planted with the idea of feeding cattle, gives satisfaction. A trench is dug having 1 m. (3.28 feet) in depth and 1.50 m. (4.92 feet) at the bottom, and 2 m. (6.56 feet) at the top; the roots are thrown in until within a few inches of the surface, and it is then filled with earth. Here we have no ventilation, the evaporation is great, and the resulting vapors condense at the bottom; the beets in immediate contact with this soon decompose, but the consequence is not of very great importance. (See fig. 51.) One of the first ideas for

Fig. 51.

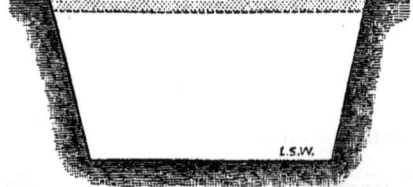

Silo where beets are placed in the Palatinate.

ventilating silos above ground consisted in building a cone about 3 m. (9.8 feet) in height. (See fig. 52.) A stick is placed in the ground in a vertical position, the roots are placed around the same, each layer being a fraction smaller than its precedent; when near the top this centre is extracted; thus leaving a chimney where the gases can escape; this is covered with a small quantity of straw when the exterior temperature is

CONSERVATION OF THE SUGAR BEET. 247

such that the beets would be in danger. The outer portions are also protected by a certain quantity of earth, the thickness of which is variable. Another type of silo, adopted some thirty years ago, was a first

Fig. 52.
Vertical section.

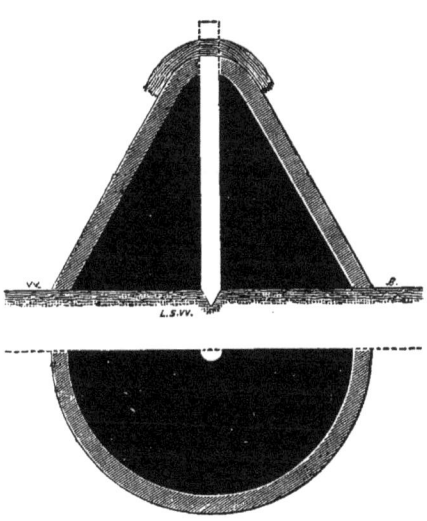

Half horizontal section.
Conical silo, in the centre of which is a sort of chimney, can be closed with straw.

step towards improvement. A ditch was dug having about 1.20 m. (3.93 feet) in depth and 10 m. (32.80 feet) in length, into which the beets were thrown, the whole being then covered with earth. (See fig. 53.) The shape given was that of a roof, the idea of which was to cause the water resulting from rain to pass beyond the silo. The results were negative. The principles of ventilation were only partly understood. Near each extremity a certain quantity of straw was placed, through which the resulting gases could make their escape; but where was the new supply of fresh air to come from? The resulting consequences were as ex-

Fig. 53.
Longitudinal section.

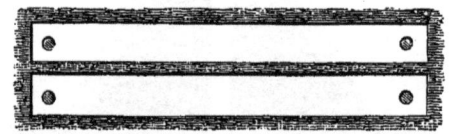

Horizontal section.

Silos permitting gases to make their escape only.

plained a few lines above. The roots were thrown in the silos without the previous precaution having been taken, preventing the direct contact of the beets and soil forming the bottom of the silos. The resulting evaporation not only from the ground but also from the beets was considerable.

These silos had a capacity of ten tons, and were separated from their neighbors by a wall, the thickness of which was 0.25 m. (0.82 foot).

A plan frequently adopted to make sure of good drainage consists in placing the silos on a slant, the water from rains, etc., flowing into a small gutter. (See fig. 54.) The dimensions given to a silo of this description 2.00 m. (6.56 feet) for its largest horizontal width and 1.00 m. (3.28 feet) for its height; the length is variable.

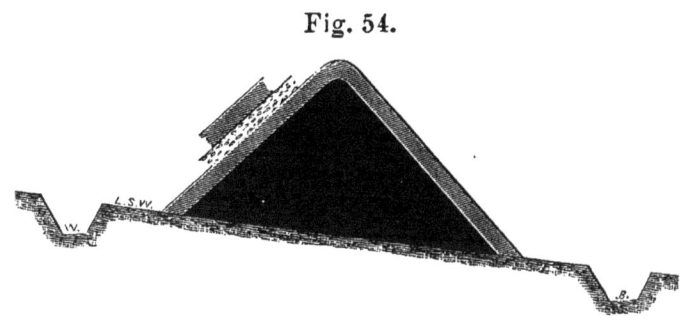

Fig. 54.

Silo on a slant, preventing a deposit of water.

The English were the first to understand the importance of underground drainage. We will give Pailly's idea. (See fig. 55.) It consisted in having

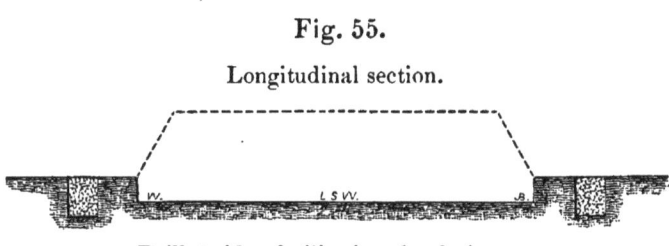

Fig. 55.

Longitudinal section.

Pailly's idea facilitating the drainage.

the silos penetrate the soil only 0.30 m. (0.98 foot); two ditches were dug having 0.50 m. (1.64 foot) or 0.20 m. (0.65 foot) in excess of the lowest portion of the silos; these were filled with stones, the water filtering through the lower portion would be carried away by this plan of drainage.

These silos were covered with earth in the usual manner, and had one great objection, which was that of being wanting in ventilation. The disasters before spoken of were much to be dreaded.

A type of silo frequently employed (see fig. 56) possesses but one advantage, and that is preventing

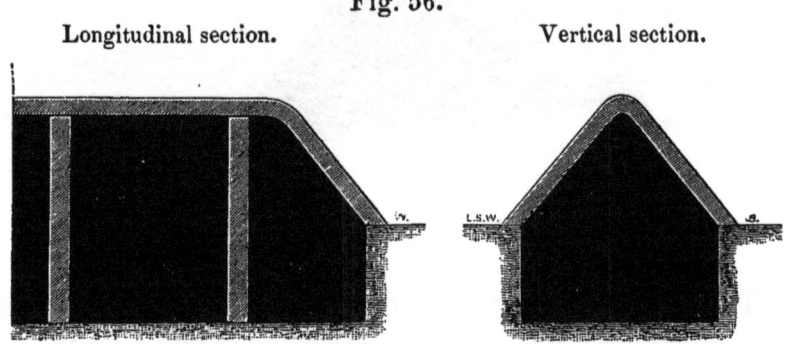

Fig. 56.

Longitudinal section.   Vertical section.

Walls of earth preventing the disease from spreading.

the disease from passing through the entire mass when one portion is attacked, this being accomplished by

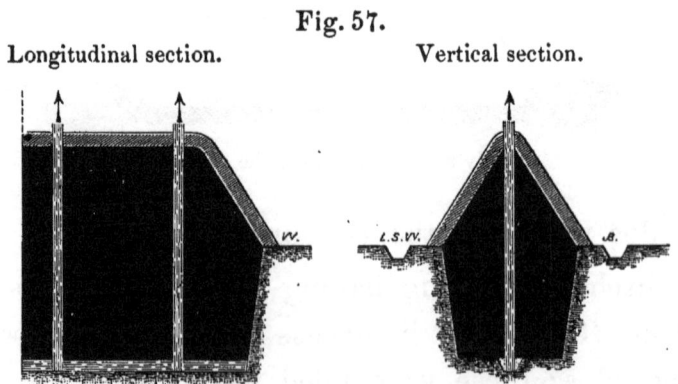

Fig. 57.

Longitudinal section.   Vertical section.

Type of silo permitting the water resulting from evaporation to settle.

walls of a certain thickness. As shown above, a slant is given to facilitate the flow of water, etc. Here we have no attempt to ventilate, but in the next (fig. 57) the system of construction is very similar, but precautions have been taken which are of a considerable importance. In the first place on each side we have a gutter to carry off the water that has fallen from the roof of silo. In the above case the water frequently filters through and gains the mass by the lower portion. The plan of ventilation consists in having at the bottom a certain number of sticks; perpendicular to these, others are placed, which enable the gases to make their escape between the same. But there is no possibility of renewing the air. A precaution taken here, worthy of notice, is to have a gutter at the bottom where the water resulting from the evaporation can collect.

In Saxony we are told that their silos hold several hundred tons of beets. (See fig. 58.) These, as can be

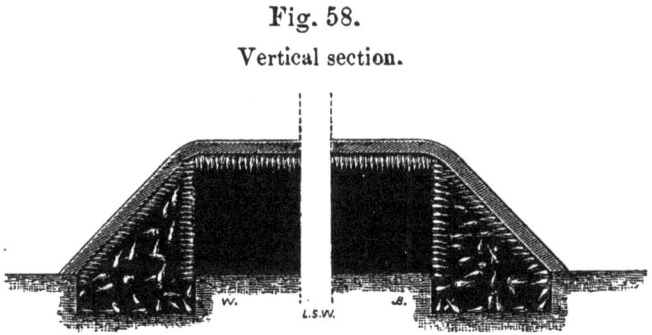

Fig. 58.
Vertical section.

Type of silo employed in Saxony

imagined, are of a size far too great to give good results, and their construction, we should judge, would be costly to the farmer; it consists in the digging of two ditches, the lengths of which are variable, two feet in depth, and six feet in width. The ditches are placed parallel to each other, the distance separating them being forty feet. The beets are placed in a regular manner until they fill the ditch, the inner ones remaining on the vertical. The outer ones are arranged in order to obtain a slant which meets this vertical, four feet from the surface. As can be imagined, we have here forty feet of vacant space between the ditches; the beets are thrown into this centre until it is full, the upper portion being arranged in a regular manner, and covered with earth. The ends of this silo can be constructed in exactly the same manner.

The silo shown in fig. 59 is, we consider, a very economical one, and at the same time has many advan-

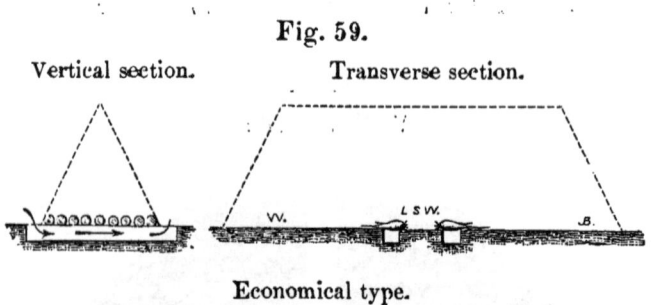

Fig. 59.

Vertical section.   Transverse section.

Economical type.

tages over those that we have just examined. Its construction is most simple, and consists in digging two gutters, the depth of each being at the will of the farmer. As for the width, it should be somewhat less than the average size of a beet. The shape given to these silos does not differ from any other. The length is 10 m. (32.8 feet), and the distance between the gut-

CONSERVATION OF THE SUGAR BEET.

ters is 1.50 m. (4.92 feet); over these the roots are placed with regularity, the longest being chosen for this purpose, the object of which is to prevent immediate contact with the water that results from the evaporation of the silos or that is placed there with an object. If we examine what takes place we see that the current of fresh air can circulate without difficulty, and in this manner the total mass can be kept at any temperature that may be required. During very cold weather it is advisable to close these openings, as we have just mentioned the fact that water was at times placed in the gutters, the object of which is to make sure of a circulation of air, for as it flows from the opposite side a certain volume is carried along. The objection to this silo is that there exists no ventilation from the top.

We now have a type (see fig. 60) which we consider decidedly the best of any we have up to the present

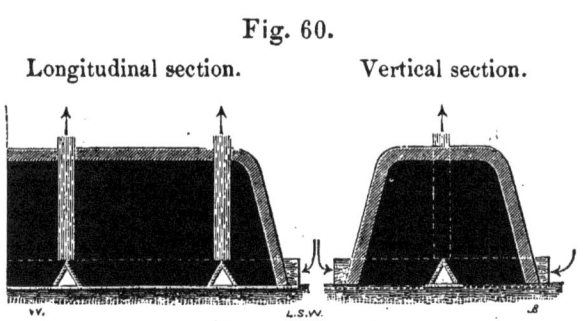

Fig. 60.

Longitudinal section.   Vertical section.

Good type of silo, ventilation being well understood.

time examined, that is fulfilling more nearly the requirement that the beet shall be delivered after a certain number of months in the same condition as when taken from the ground. A plank is placed on the soil; this must have a slight slant, and represents the exact centre of the silo; perpendicular to same others are placed also in the horizontal plane. The distance between each should be about 4.00 m. (13.12 feet), the total length being variable. Two slanting boards form an equilateral triangle, each side of which is equal to the width of the plank. A similar arrangement is adopted for the lateral planks (above mentioned), and we thus have two passages through which the air can circulate. At the intersection of these are placed in a vertical position several sticks, permitting the gases to make their escape, and the drainage is as nearly perfect as possible, and the ventilation may be made as rapid as desired. The only objection that can here be urged is the excessive evaporation resulting, thus causing a loss of weight; but nothing prevents the injection of a certain quantity of water.

In Russia for some time past the importance of keeping the temperature constant in the silos has been well understood, and within late years Mr. Walkhoff has called public attention to these facts, from which one can conclude the exact condition of the beets. When the thermometer indicates 42° F., which is a maximum, fermentation is to be dreaded, and it is advisable to act in consequence. (Never permit the exterior air to enter when above 42° F. or below 32° F.) Compte de Bombrisky and others make use of silos which are beneath the surface of the ground, having a thermometer in direct communication with the outer atmosphere. As a general thing, as before stated, the problem of preservation is the same in America as in Russia, and for that reason underground houses should be built. The expense of these is considerable, but at the same time they give excellent results.

A method when adopted that will give as a general thing entire satisfaction, consists in having a cellar, the lower portion of which is covered with several

Fig. 61.

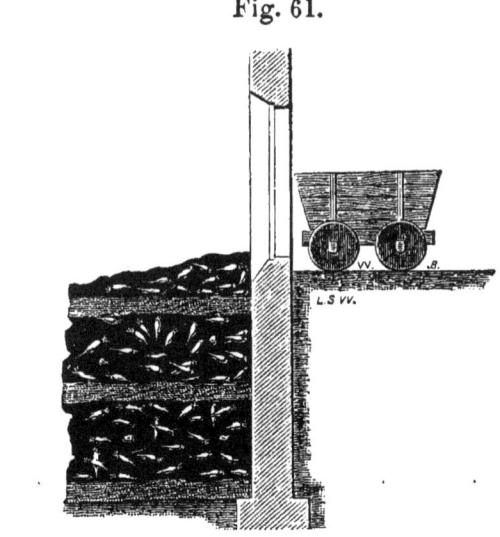

Type of mode of conservation where charcoal is placed between the layers and the bottom.

inches of charcoal or cinders, the beets are thrown in, as shown in the fig. 61, and but little care is required. The expense in this case is very small.

The fig. 62 gives an idea of an underground house

such as we propose for America, which we consider has many advantages over those up to the present time built in Russia, and have been made known to the public. Its capacity depends upon the length, which

Fig. 62.

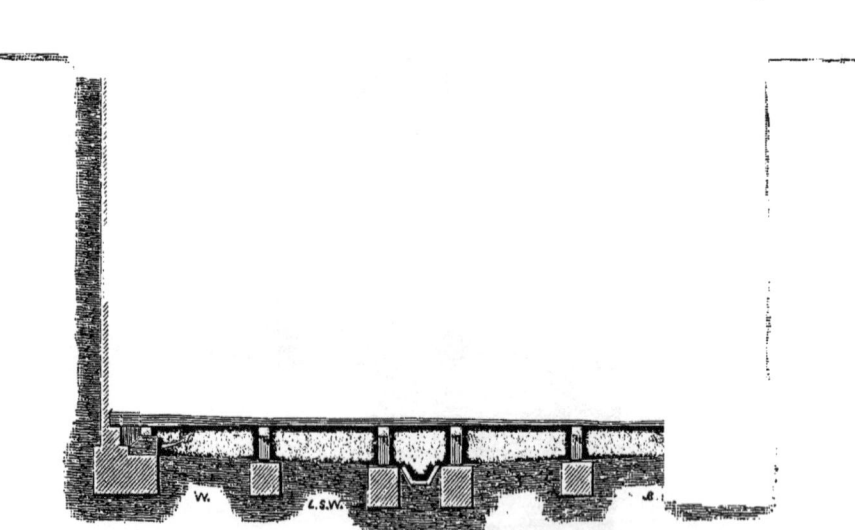

Type of an underground house suitable for conservation in America.

can be variable, but if built as indicated, there is no objection even if this be considerable. (Let it be remembered that one cubic metre contains nearly 700 kilog. of beets.) The walls are of masonry; the bottom has a slight slant, which enables the water resulting from evaporation to collect in a gutter (g). We suppose four stories, the distance between each rafter is 2.00 m. (6.56 feet), and every 3.00 m. (9.84 feet) we have vertical supports, between which, we suppose, basket work; the latter is constructed in a very rough manner during the filling of each compartment (A and B, for example). This has a double advantage: 1st, keeping A separate from B, and at the same time permitting the air to circulate at will. The flooring is constructed in exactly the same manner.

The beets are to be brought in carts and emptied through the door d. As this total height is 32.8 feet, the fall would be considerable, and for that reason we would advise the use of a series of slanting boards, which are taken away as the floors are filled.

To facilitate the carrying of the beets from one portion of the building to the other, we propose a track, on which circulates a car which can be brought to any horizontal by the means of a windlass; this being placed in the upper portion of the roof. As for the ventilation, it is as nearly perfect as can be, the heated air making its escape through C, whilst the cool air can enter by O. If it be required to make a complete change of air in the house, this can be done by kindling a small fire in the chimney. The effect thus produced may be easily understood. The roof, as shown, is covered with earth.

Preservation of the Sugar Beet.

Up to the present time we have only spoken of the different methods proposed and adopted for the keeping of the beets without injury or change in their normal condition. In the following we will give a few ideas concerning the freezing, desiccation, and preservation of the juice.

Freezing.—Many consider this the best method of preservation. It consists in keeping the beets in a room or ice-house where the temperature is about 26° or 27° F. The beets are taken out when required. This idea is wholly theoretical, and even in the coldest country is not practical, and would cost considerable. If the outer temperature alone were depended upon after the first thaw there would be a complete loss of the total crop, if other precautions had not been taken in advance.

Desiccation.—We consider this is one of the best ideas, and is carried on with great success in Germany. It consists in cutting the roots with a *coupe-racine*. These slices are dried either in towers constructed for the express purpose, or in the sun. When it is required to manufacture sugar they are mixed with a certain volume of water, which must be again evaporated. Here is a double expense, and for that reason seems absurd (*evaporation* to remove the water from the root, and *evaporation* to obtain the solid portion in solution, which is the sugar).

Many similar attempts have been made in the same direction for the sugar-cane. The advantage of this method is that it permits the manufacturer to work throughout the entire year; a problem of the highest importance in America.

Preservation of the Juice.—Mr. Maumené has here made several suggestions. He contends that in order to keep the juice in a perfect condition during the greater portion of the year, obtaining after that time a maximum of sugar, various operations are necessary. The roots are first placed in a rasp, and the resulting pulp is submitted to a hydraulic press, the juice is united with lime in the proportion of 2 or 5 per cent., and then placed in cisterns of 20.00 m. (65.6 feet) in length, containing 1200 litres. The great objection to this method is getting rid of the excess of lime. Mr. Walkhoff tells us the idea is interesting, but has no practical application.

Preservation of the Leaves.

From what will be said hereafter,[1] it will be easy to understand the importance of keeping the leaves in a perfect condition during several months of the year.

Various plans have been proposed. We will give first of all the most simple, and one which the ordinary farmer can adopt without any special scientific knowledge.

---

[1] See " Feeding Qualities of the Leaves of Beet."

This idea is to have a silo beneath the surface, its sides being constructed of cement. The angles we made rounded, the object of which is to prevent any accumulation either of air or water resulting from evaporation. The shape is slightly conical, that is to say, the upper portion is a fraction wider than the lower. (See fig. 63.)

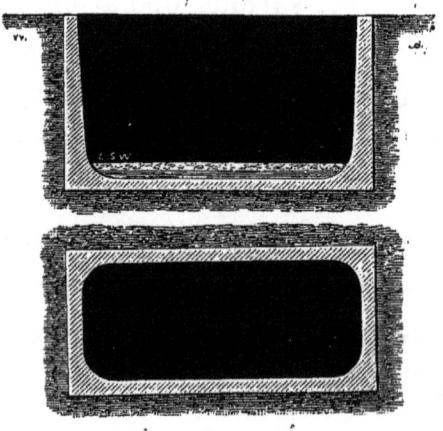

Fig. 63.
Vertical section.

Horizontal section.
Silo for preservation of leaves.

A certain quantity of chopped straw is placed on the bottom, this to a depth of about 12 cm., then the leaves on top, with which are united 4 to 5 kilog. (8 to 11 lbs.) of salt to every 1000 kilog. (2200 lbs.) of leaves. Great precaution should be taken to compress as much as possible each layer of leaves. The thickness is 20 cm. (0.65 feet); when the silo is full the whole is covered with straw. The leaves that are taken from the beet in the morning should be left until the afternoon, the idea being to get rid of a certain quantity of water, for, if left for several days, they change color and give a bad odor. When the silo is opened vertical slices are extracted; in this manner equal portions of the three above elements are obtained. This is eaten with much relish. Mr. Mchay has directed much time to this subject, and he contends that the results obtained by him far surpass anything up to the present time attempted in this direction. His idea is to make use of a certain quantity of hydrochloric acid, marking 3° to 4° B. The leaves are placed in baskets, through which the liquid in excess can filter; this is collected in a reservoir. After a certain number of hours they are taken out and piled on the ground, where they remain for three days, after which time they are ready to be placed in silos similar to the one just described. Mr. Mchay considers that a hole dug in very dry soil will answer the purpose; but when it is considered that a small quantity of air between the layers will cause a general change in the entire mass, too much precaution cannot be taken to prevent the entrance of it. It is estimated that two men and two boys are sufficient to prepare 26,000 lbs. of leaves per day. These leaves greatly diminish in weight in consequence of the vegetable water being extracted. 20,000 lbs. of green represent 10,000 lbs. of dried leaves.

The hydrochloric acid combines with the potassium

and sodium, thus forming chloride of potassium and chloride of sodium.

The resulting liquid can be utilized also for feeding, or again for distillation, the yield in alcohol being from .1 to $1\frac{1}{2}$ per cent.

Frequently the leaves are sliced or cut in pieces to facilitate the fermentation of the acid.

Another series of experiments, made also by Mchay, was to ascertain if any advantage could be gained by boiling, and the conclusions were that equal results are obtained in both cases.

PART V.

ENEMIES OF THE SUGAR BEET.

THE sugar beet, like all other plants, has its enemies, which, by their ravages, cause great destruction and loss both to the manufacturer and farmer. These may be divided into two categories:—

Insects and Diseases.

To give a complete list of all the insects that have up to the present day attacked the beet (causing a loss which is estimated in France at $400,000 yearly), would be impossible, from the fact that there are many in existence[1] that have not thus far been brought before the public; and then, again, it does not imply that because a certain insect or its *larva* should have a preference for this saccharine plant in Europe, that the same case should present itself in the Northern States. But at the same time it is probable that the most important of these will conduct themselves in a manner somewhat similar at all portions of the globe in which they may happen to be. Their entomological

---

[1] Mr. Brame, a French savant, in his treatise on Agriculture, says: "There are but few insects that attack the beet." This is a great error.

classification is given, the object of which is to enable the reader, if desired, to obtain further information. We will not give an anatomical description of these insects, as it would have but little interest, but only an idea of the habits of each, and the method proposed and adopted for their destruction.

Insects.—They all, without exception, belong to one of the three great classes of entomology: *Cleoptera, Diptera,* and *Lepidotera.*

The first mentioned comprises those having a hard substance on their backs, and which are commonly called *beetles.* The habits of these are the best known, and they are the greatest agricultural enemy. The most destructive of all is the *Melolontha vulgaris,* or cock-chafer (belonging to the eighth family—Melonthidæ—of the Petalocera; the last mentioned being the second family of Lamellicornes, which is the second division of Chilognathomorphia, the latter being the third tribe of Pentameria.[1]) These cock-chafers are not of the most beautiful, their color being either dark or light brown, having their bodies covered with minute scales. (See fig. 64.)

Habits.—The Melolontha vulgaris makes its first appearance either about the 1st of April or the 1st of May, according to the weather and temperature.

[1] The above classification is the one adopted by Westwood. In *Blanchard* the new French classification is given which places the above as belonging o the twenty-seventh family (Scarbeii) and third tribe (Melolonthides).

Strange to say, the heat of the day has a most singular effect, causing them to remain in a sort of a trance state. After sundown their activity commences, when they move in swarms, seeming to have

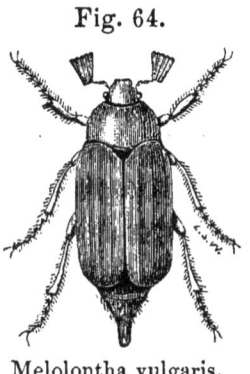

Fig. 64.

Melolontha vulgaris.

but little control over their flying, and will strike any object that happens to be in their way, and which causes them to fall to the ground. After a few hours of darkness they search for food, which is the leaf of a plant or tree. We have noticed that when they have not at their disposal the leaves of the former, they will fly in the direction of the woods. In this case their destruction is impossible. They will remain during the whole day on the leaf they so happen to find themselves on in the morning. After a given number of weeks the male deems it his duty to fulfil his procreative functions, which last from twelve to twenty-four hours, after which he falls to the ground from fatigue or exhaustion, and shortly after dies. The female, on the contrary, seems to be full of life and activity, and digs a hole about five or ten inches in depth, into which some thirty or forty yellow and oval eggs are deposited. The soil preferred seems to be the one corresponding to the greatest agricultural yield. After a short time the female expires. These eggs each give a small white worm, which is the larva of the Melolontha. These worms require three years before their metamorphosis is complete. Their body is white, having a row of spots and composed of twelve rings. The fig. 65 represents the actual size of it. If the young plant be attacked (the point of the root being

Fig. 65.   Fig. 66.

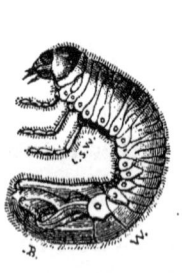 

Larva of the Melolontha.   A young root that has been attacked.

preferred) and has not strength to resist, the leaves droop. (See fig. 66.) The number of months which these spend in eating would probably be for the Northern States—

    1st year, 25th June to 1st November . . . 4
    2d   "   16th April " 1st November . . . 7
    3d   "   16th April " 25th June 3
              Total 14

When these insects are exposed to the action of the sun their color becomes dark.

Destruction of the Melolontha Vulgaris.—There have been many and diverse arguments from time to time in regard to the state (insect or larva) and time this destruction should take place. We consider that there can be no doubt that it is better to destroy the beetle, and not wait until forty eggs are deposited, which are each likely to be the cause of as much harm as the cock-chafer itself. If these beetles be on a tree in the neighborhood, by shaking it they will fall to the ground, as they have but little, if any, control over their actions; they should be gathered and destroyed in the most convenient manner. If on the leaves of the plant, the difficulty in gathering them is greatly decreased. If this destruction is not complete, which it never is, a second effort is then made upon its larva (white worm), which under the ordinary conditions would now have reached a number which it would be impossible to estimate.

In many sections of France and Belgium a heavy fine is imposed upon the farmer if any white-worms are found on his land, thus forcing him to destroy this enemy. The method adopted is for the women and children to follow the plough and pick them up. If the soil be tilled three times in the season, as in many cases, 70,000 have been frequently noticed per acre. Mr. Jules Reiset, an energetic Frenchman, gathered on his farm, in one season, 350,000 lbs. of these worms, each of which weighed 0.07 of an ounce.

Mr. Walkhoff, a German manufacturer, tells us when these are concentrated in a given portion of the field, the best method is to localize them, thus saving the remaining crop. The plan consists in the digging of a trench several feet in depth, filling the same with dried leaves; this will form an obstruction that they can never overcome. This plan is good in Germany, where labor is much less than in America. We consider one of the best methods is to render the soil compact, not sufficiently so to prevent the growth of the root, but yet causing the worm to perish, as it requires more or less space to move. Some farmers have told us from time to time that the use of lime mixed with water will be an advantage to the plant and destroy its enemy. Some authors have also contended that during the great heat of the summer or during heavy rains the greater number of these worms die. We do not consider this a fact, as under these conditions they dig deeper, and are thus sheltered from all atmospheric changes.

Uses of the Melolontha Vulgaris.—It can be easily understood that from time to time the chemist as well as the farmer has made efforts to utilize in some manner the large number of beetles gathered, and the result obtained has been highly satisfactory.

In Hungary the problem was solved some thirty years ago, consisting in the manufacture of an oily substance, utilized for lubricating carriage axles. Then again in France, Mr. Breard made from them a good lamp oil.

In order that this plan should be a success, a good price should be paid for a bushel of these cock-chafers. Unfortunately this industry has made but little progress up to the present day, and various other plans have been proposed and adopted, the most important being the utilization of the nitric substances they contain in the shape of a fertilizer. The quality is said to be nearly equal to the best guano.

To make this practicable, various plans have been suggested, such as to pay a given sum for a given weight, for example, $1.00 for 200 lbs., or $11.20 per ton, which, when prepared, is worth much more. For this manufacture the machines and chemicals to be made use of are most simple, it being sufficient to have a reservoir which is filled with a solution of ammonia[1] (water from gas works answers the purpose). The Melolonthas die in this after seven hours; they are then taken out, placed in layers three inches in depth, then a small quantity of earth, after which a second layer of beetles, etc., until the total height is three feet, the whole being covered with several inches of earth.

Frequently these insects become black and give a fetid odor when they are not dead. If they are utilized as a fertilizer under these circumstances, more harm than good will result. A good plan is to reduce the total to a powder, and then there remains no doubt.

Placed in boiling water, these beetles have frequently

---

[1] A small quantity of sulphuric acid is frequently added to the above.

been known to survive after remaining therein forty-eight hours.

From experiments that we have made from time to time, we consider that the most deadly poisons to man have but little effect upon these insects.

Their analysis, according to Pagnoul, is for 100 in weight destroyed by water:—

Water	73.60
Nitrogen	2.81
Organic substances	22.02
Phosphates	0.40
Other mineral substances	1.17
	100.00

It may be of interest to state that in certain French schools the professors frequently call their scholars' attention to the importance of making money off of the cock-chafer, from neighboring farms, and offer prizes to those gathering the greatest number, and at the same time impose as punishment the accomplishment of this work gratis.

We will now speak of a small insect, not much larger than the end of a needle, which, on account of the number, does nearly as much harm as the one just described, and which easily escapes notice. How frequently it has happened that farmers attribute the total loss of their beet crop to disease, bad drainage, or frost, which in reality was caused by the ravages of this insect called *Atomaria*, causing the young plant to perish as soon as above the ground. The most to be dreaded in this class are the 1st, Atomaria lineris;[1] 2d, Atomaria ferruginea;[2] 3d, Atomaria pygmœa. They all belong to the sixth family (Mecetophagidæ) of the group of Necrophaga, the latter being the second division of Rypophagous pentamera.

The *Atomaria lineris* (see fig. 67) is elongate and depressed, having a black color, on which can be seen

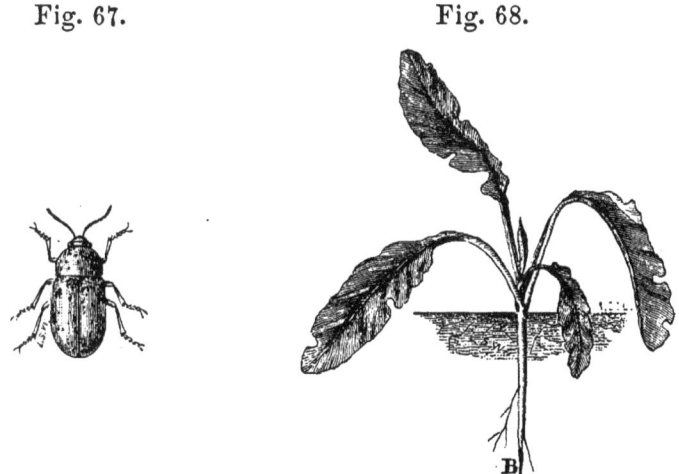

Fig. 67.
Atomaria lineris.

Fig. 68.
Plant having had its leaves and root attacked by the Atomaria—breathing its last.

certain small spots. It makes its first appearance later than the *Melolontha*, sometimes in July; but, unlike

---

[1] The above is Westwood's classification. *Atomaria lineris.* According to Blanchard the French classification is fifth species of (Atomaria) the fourteenth family (Crytophagii).

[2] Atomaria ferruginea. See Erich's Nat. Hist. (18), p. 452; see Sturm, Ins. (18), p. 5, t. 330.

the latter, it greatly enjoys a fine day, and comes above the ground when it can have the advantage of the sun, during which time it attacks the leaves. Many are frequently on the same plant at the same time, some above and others beneath the ground. The fig. 68 represents a young plant that has been able to resist for some time, and finally the whole end (B) has been eaten, and it is now breathing its last.

The great problem is to cause the plant to grow before the enemy has made its appearance; under these conditions it would be sufficiently strong to resist. Utilization of manure has been suggested, but has for direct effect (as before stated) a large yield and but little sugar. Steeping[1] of the seed for about twenty-four hours in a solution of lime water will have the advantage of causing the grain to grow rapidly. The best of all is to make use of a heavy roller, and to compress the soil. It is important that when the seeds are to be planted for the second time (the first having been destroyed), not to act sparingly, as the excess will be eaten by the insect, and there will, in the greater number of cases, remain yet sufficient for a good yield.

Next comes the *Curculilo* or a variety of weevil; the exact species is not as yet known (but, according to the German classification, it belongs to the sixty-second family (Curculiondæ); it is a coleoptera insect.

---

[1] See "Sowing of the Seed."

It has not as yet been noticed in France, but from what we have been told by German farmers it originated in Russia, and is gradually finding its way into the first-named country. This coleoptera, unlike others of its group, is not beautiful in color, this being dark gray, and when the weather is rainy it becomes jet black. It is about half an inch in length. Very little if any harm is done by the Curculilo before it arrives at complete maturity. The time for rest and meals seems to be regulated; the amount eaten is about equal to 0.2 of a square inch of a leaf, after which it penetrates the soil. Sleep takes place during the night and bad weather, and it greatly fears the cold. The animal functions take place from the first day of its appearance until July.

The female is larger than the male, and her method of depositing her eggs differs from the *Melolontha*, from the fact that but a few are placed in each hole; and but three weeks are required before the larvæ are hatched.

The number estimated per acre is 400,000. This insect can only fly a few feet. The method proposed for its destruction is to dig trenches having a width greater than they can get over, they thus fall into this trap whence they cannot escape. As to the climbing of a vertical wall it is quite impossible.

Next comes the *Silpha* (belonging to second family (Silphidæ) of Necrophaga, the last mentioned being the second division of Rypophagous pentamera[1]). The species that attack the beet are: 1st, *Silpha opaca;*[2] 2d, *Silpha thoracia.*[3]

We cannot understand why insects of this variety should ever trouble the sugar beet, as their habits and tastes are unlike any other similar enemy of the root. They have a most fetid odor, which is sufficiently strong to be transmitted to all the neighborhood. The cause of this we imagine to be the food they prefer, which is dead bodies in an advanced state of decomposition. They are distinguishable by the flattened form of their bodies.

The larvæ when deposited by the female are in a very advanced state.

Silpha opaca.—This insect made its "debut" in Sweden and was noticed in France ten years ago. The destruction it causes takes place during the early portion of the spring, and lasts but a short time. It is well to plant (if not too late) the seeds which will come up after the metamorphosis has commenced.

Silpha thoracia (see fig. 69).—Its color is black, with a yellow border.

Altica[4] or *Haltica.* There are a great variety of

---

[1] The above is Westwood's classification. The German classification is the twelfth family (Silphidæ).

[2] *Silpha opaca.* See for further information Guerin, Ann. Fr., 1846, Bull, p. 72.

[3] *Silpha thoracia.* See for further information Linné's Sys. Nat. (2), p. 571. Eschsch, Deg. Cat., 3d, p. 132.

[4] The word Altica is taken from the Greek, which signifies to jump.

these insects. This class belongs to the second subfamily (Falticides) of (Galerucidæ) Pseudotetramera, the last mentioned being the third general section of

Fig. 69.

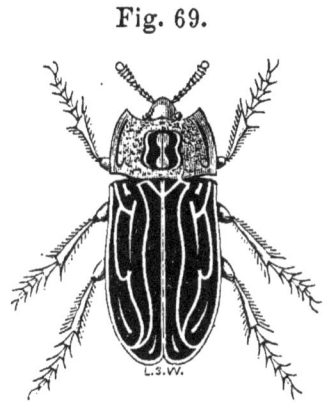

Silpha thoracia.

the Coleoptera.[1] The species that attack the beet are: 1st, Altise, having a gold-like head; 2d, Altica oleraca.[2]

These insects were so numerous at Montpellier some thirty years ago that prayers were offered in all the churches that the assistance of God would come to the help of the people and rid them of them.

The larvæ of these insects eat any vegetable. There exists a great variety of them. In fig. 70 we give the general type, showing the development of the hinder legs.

---

[1] Westwood's classification is the above. The German classification is sixty-eighth family (Chrysomelidæ) of Coleoptera.

[2] *Altica oleraca.* See for further information Cornel's Stett. Zeitt., 1864, p. 98; Oliv. Ext. 6, p. 705.

Altica oleraca.—This insect is of a greenish-blue, and confines itself to leaves.

Fig. 70.   Fig. 71.

Altica.   Cassida.

Cassida.[1]—This insect belongs to the first family (Cassididæ) of the second division (Cyclica) of the Pseudotetramera phytophaga[2]. The species that attack the leaves are: 1st, Cassida nebulosa; 2d, Cassida equestrie (see fig. 71.)

These insects are flat, and of various colors. The method adopted for their destruction is similar to that pursued with the Melolontha; but, in order to save time and labor, between the rows of beets another grain is planted (mustard) which this insect prefers.

Agriote.[3]—This species belongs to the third family (Elateridæ) which belongs to a sub-tribe called Priocerata (serricornes). The species that attack the beet are: 1st, *Agriote sputâleur;* 2d, *Agriote segnitum.*

---

[1] To obtain further information see Syst. Nat. ed. (12), p. 575; Cornel's Stett. Zeitt., 1864, p. 397.

[2] The above is Westwood's classification. The one adopted by Blanchard is the forty-second family (Chrysometii), second sub-family (Chrysomelinis) second tribe (Cassidides), second group (Cassidites).

[3] Westwood's classification.

The larvæ of these insects do much harm, from the fact that they live in a small cavity, which they make in the upper portion of the beet, from which the sweet juice continually flows. The larva of these insects is frequently taken for the white worm, owing to an existing similarity. For their destruction it has been proposed to make use of a certain quantity of vinegar or sour sulphate of copper. Sulphur has been tried, but, from experiments that we have made, we do not consider success possible with it.

We must not forget to mention the *Nematodes* (belonging to thirty-seventh family[1] (Eucnemidæ) of the Coleoptera) which are frequently seen during the damp and wet seasons on the surface of acidulous soils. These are generally found in great numbers. The method of destruction adopted is to plough deeply and as frequently as possible; in this manner they are placed at a depth beyond their power to rise again to the surface. Then, again, a good plan is to plant the beet only after many years on a soil where they have been noticed.

Belonging to the same family we have another insect, which is said to attack this plant, and that is *Heteroderes*. The last of all, but not the least important of the Coleoptera, is the Cryptophagous (belonging to the fourth family (Engidæ) of Necrophagie; the last mentioned being the second division of Rypo-

---

[1] The above is the German classification.

phagous petamera[1]). The name of this insect is *Cryptophagous bettæ;* having been noticed but a few years ago.

We will now speak of insects that belong to another great class of entomology called Lepidotera. The most important, and consequently the most to be dreaded, is the Noctua (belonging to the ninth family (Noctuidæ) of Heterocera, which is the second division of the Lepidotera insects.)[2] Those attacking the sugar beet are: 1st, Noctua segetum; 2d, Noctua oleracia; 3d, Noctua brassicæ; 4th, Noctua promba.

Noctua segetum.—Causes yearly great harm in the northern portions of France. As shown in fig. 72, it

Fig. 72.

Noctua segetum.

has two pair of wings, the outer being reddish-brown, with a black border.

Habits.—The larva of these undergoes a transformation under ground into cocoons, which are composed partly of silk and partly of earth. The Noctua has

---

[1] Blanchard's classification would be third species of fourteenth family of Crytophagii.

[2] The above is Westwood's classification.

but little activity during the day, remaining in the crevices of old walls, etc. Its larva has the same habit, remaining under ground during the day and at night coming to the surface and eating the leaves until morning.

The *Noctua* deposits its eggs in small packages on the leaves of the beet.

Destruction.—This is a most difficult problem to solve on account of their number. We have noticed as many as four hundred per square inch, near every root in the portion of the soil on which they were located. Some farmers advocate the use of lime with hydrochloric acid, but this has but little if any effect. A plan similar to the one before spoken of is to localize the same by digging a ditch and filling it with water. The caterpillar creeping from one portion of the field to the other will fall in and drown; as many as one hundred and fifty pounds per day have been destroyed in this manner. It has been suggested to have these larvæ gathered after ploughing; the cocoons can be gotten rid of in the same manner. In Germany some farmers make use of lighted lamps at night, which are inclosed in boxes made of glass, on the surface of which is a certain quantity of oil, the *Noctua* will fly against the same and there be caught.

As this insect makes its appearance very late in the season, a good plan is to sow the seeds as early as possible, and when the enemy comes the plant is strong enough to resist it. Then, again, a good one is to compress the soil, thus preventing the butterfly from coming to the surface as soon as the metamorphosis is complete. We consider the best plan of all for America, where wood is cheap, is to make large fires on the neighboring hills; the Noctuas for miles will come to the light at once and be burned. The other insects of this class have similar habits, the difference being their color, which becomes more and more beautiful, for those accustomed to fly during a certain portion of the day.

Then, again, these caterpillars' tastes seem to vary, some preferring the top of the beet to the leaves. In this case we consider there is even more harm done than when the latter alone are attacked, as from the crevices made by these insects small roots will grow, thus diminishing the quantity of sugar.

The last insect known to us of the group of Lepidotera is the *Hadena bassicæ*. We are not familiar with its habits, but are informed that it frequently does considerable harm.

We will now speak of a class of insects belonging to the group called *Diptera*. Unfortunately the entomologists have not given sufficient attention to this portion of their science, and consequently but little is known regarding their habits, a knowledge of which is necessary for their destruction.

The most important of these insects, a sort of fly (see fig. 73), having wings which are slightly yellow, and which is called *Phytomyzides*, belonging to the nineteenth family (Scenopinidæ), the latter being the second general division (Brachocera) of the Diptera insects.[1]

Fig. 73.

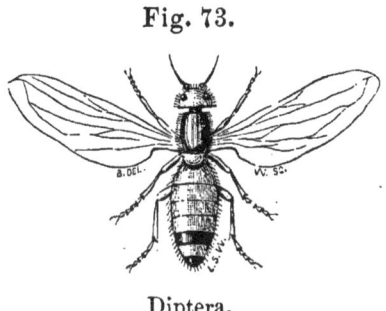

Diptera.

The Phytomyzide deposits its eggs on the leaves of the beet, and the resulting larvæ devour and penetrate the root by the lower portion of the stem, thus causing much harm.

The second insect of this group is the Hylemyie coarcata belonging to the seventh species of the third class of Diptera.[2] Very little is known in regard to this insect.

We conclude from all that has been said regarding the insects already named that the best plan of destruction is to compress the soil with a heavy roller, thus causing these enemies to perish. Such is what man can do, but nature has furnished moles and birds that destroy without trouble the greater number of them.

If the farmers of all countries would only understand

---

[1] The above classification is the one adopted by Westwood.

[2] For those who wish information concerning the Diptera, we advise them to read Maquart, "Diptere exotique."

the importance of the above, and plant a few trees where birds could build their nests and consequently have the comfort they require, and if they were protected from destruction, we are sure they would be more than compensated for it.

We do not wish to convey the idea that all insects would be thus gotten rid of, for such is not the case, as animals, like men, soon tire of the same food.

We will now speak of the second enemy of the beet, which does nothing like the harm of the above, but in a new country like the United States it is beyond human power to foresee which of the two is the most to be dreaded in the cultivation of the beet on a large scale.

Diseases.—Remarkably little has as yet been accomplished towards ascertaining the real causes of diseases that seem to exist not only in the growth of the sugar beet, but in plants in general. And whatever be the theory advanced, there are arguments *pro* and *con*, causing much confusion in the minds of men of science.[1]

Dr. Montague's theory is, that all so-called diseases are caused either by small insects or parasite fungi, and even at the present day it is difficult to convince the farmer that his crop has been destroyed by a disease. Without doubt in many cases these fungi do

---

[1] We desire here to call attention to the interesting array of facts bearing upon this subject, and the deductions from them, contained in a pamphlet entitled "Protection to Home Labor and Home Productions necessary to the Prosperity of the American Farmer." By Henry Carey Baird. New York, 1860.

ENEMIES OF THE SUGAR BEET.

exist, for plants, like human beings, have their parasites, which in most cases are a consequence of neglect.

In general cultivation an excess of nitric elements employed in the fertilizers seems to activate the growth of the above. Then, again, the use of manures containing invisible insects, which are frequently in great number, is the cause of injury.

Fig. 74.

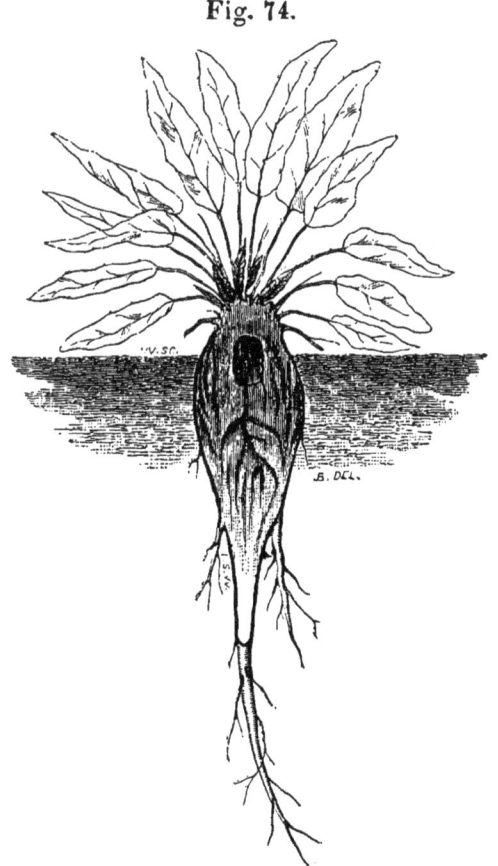

A vertical section of a root attacked by the "brown penetration."

The sugar beet has no special disease; those existing are common to other plants. The most important of all that have been noticed up to the present day is the *brown penetration*, similar to the well-known potato disease. This was noticed for the first time in France in 1846 by numerous farmers. A committee was appointed to investigate the causes of it, and at the same time to make suggestions regarding a method for preventing its renewal; having for presidents Mr. Dumas and Mr. Payen. Their report was published, and, with a few exceptions, we are happy to state, that from time to time we have been able to testify to the truth of the theories therein advanced.

The first external evidences are brownish spots on the lower leaves, which shortly cause them to droop, and, as the malady advances, the entire number have the same fate, and frequently fall to the ground, and are replaced by a second growth.

Often the beet is attacked, while but few external indications are apparent to indicate the existence of the disease. A section should be made through the axis of the root, when this brown penetration is quite visible.[1] The portion most affected seems to be the centre itself, then continuing until it penetrates the entire diameter, after which it seems to extend rapidly to the outer portions. This disease, or one similar, frequently attacks the radicle. In fig. 75 we suppose the radicle in a perfect condition. Above the spongiole may be noticed a certain number of hairs gathered

---

[1] This should be noticed immediately, as, even in a healthy beet, if exposed to the air it will change its color.

around this rudimentary root; the spongiole itself being entirely free.

The fig. 76 represents the radicle when attacked by the disease. As shown, the spongiole has greatly in-

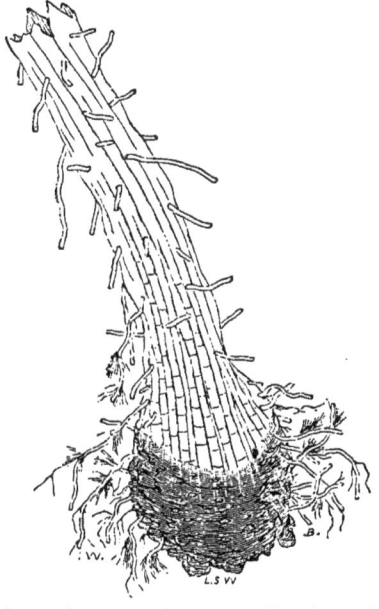

Fig. 75.

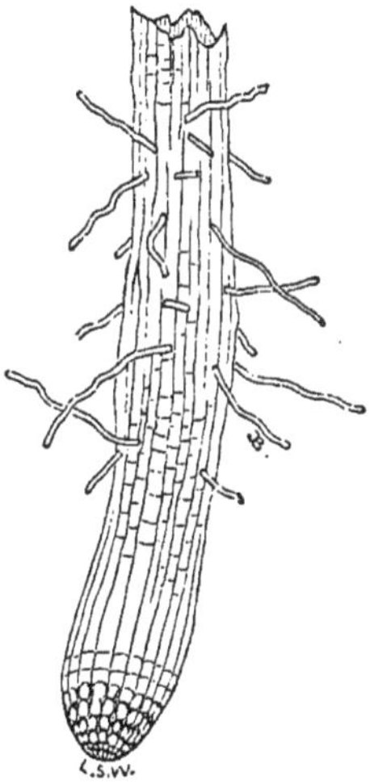

Radicle in a healthy condition. Above the spongiole exists a hairy growth.

Fig. 76.

Spongiole attacked, showing its hairy growth.

creased in size, and has now a considerable number of hairs on its outer surface. The fig. 77 represents a radicle where the malady has penetrated through the same, causing a total loss of the spongiole.

Mr. Payen contends that if the organic substances contained in the diseased spongiole be placed in a weak solution of iodine, this latter will become a brownish orange yellow, similar to the organic substance frequently obstructing the respiratory organs of the sickly leaves of plants.[1]

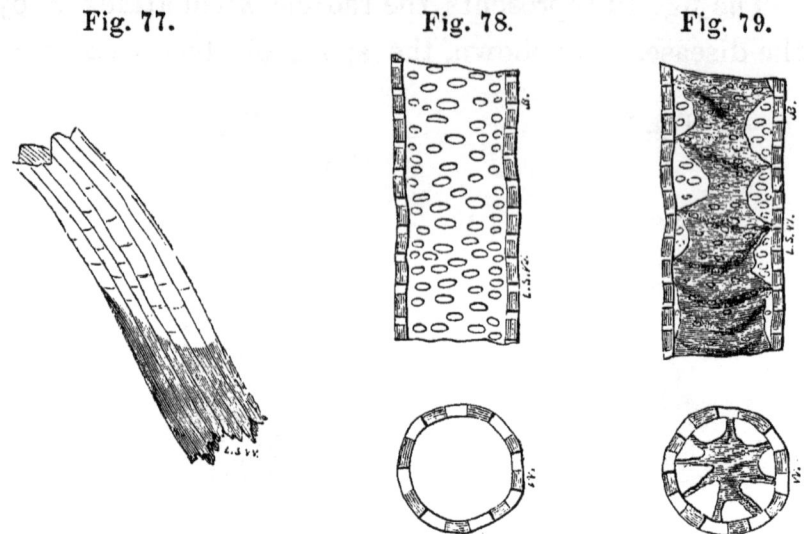

Fig. 77.—The malady has penetrated through the radicle, causing a total loss of the spongiole.
Fig. 78.—One of the vessels of the vascular tissue in perfect health.
Fig. 79.—One the vessels of vascular tissue suffering from disease.

The fig. 78 represents one of the vessels of the vascular tissue in a perfect condition of health. The fig. 79 represents the same when attacked, and, as can be seen, the disease seems to have penetrated by degrees the elliptical openings.

Payen[2] says this brown organic substance resists

---

[1] Our intention had been to make these experiments, but we have not as yet had the leisure.

[2] Mr. Payen and others, in 1851, spoke of methods adopted to prevent the above disease, which are to make use of chemical fertilizers. Fifteen years later he acknowledges that if these be used in excess they may be the direct cause of the disease. The last hypothesis we consider the most rational.

the action of water, and also sulphuric acid nearly concentrated.

The causes of the above may generally be attributed either to the too frequent planting of the beet on the same soil, thus causing an exhaustion of alkaline elements,[1] or the want of a sufficient volume of oxygen. The disease brought about by the first cause is but little to be dreaded in America for the present, as our soil, in the greater number of cases, unlike the foreign, contains too much of the above chemicals, and, as we have before stated, the beet should be planted with caution; preliminary experiments being necessary. The second cause of disease we consider the most to be dreaded in the United States, the want of sufficient oxygen, caused by bad drainage. On the greater number of farms in Europe at the present day, when the circumstances require it, a most excellent system of drainage exists. In America the importance of this does not yet seem to be understood.

The soil most to be dreaded is the one containing fragments of roots, either of beets planted the year previous or of trees.

Different degrees of fermentation take place, absorbing the oxygen from the surrounding air, and replacing it by carbonic acid. The nourishing elements the plant requires no longer exist, and the consequence is it is suffocated and dies.

The fig. 80 shows a beet growing where the end of

---

[1] See "Choice of a Soil."

288   THE SUGAR BEET.

its root has finally penetrated the stratum wanting in oxygen; the disease immediately declares itself in this portion, and, after a very limited time, succeeds in

Fig. 80.

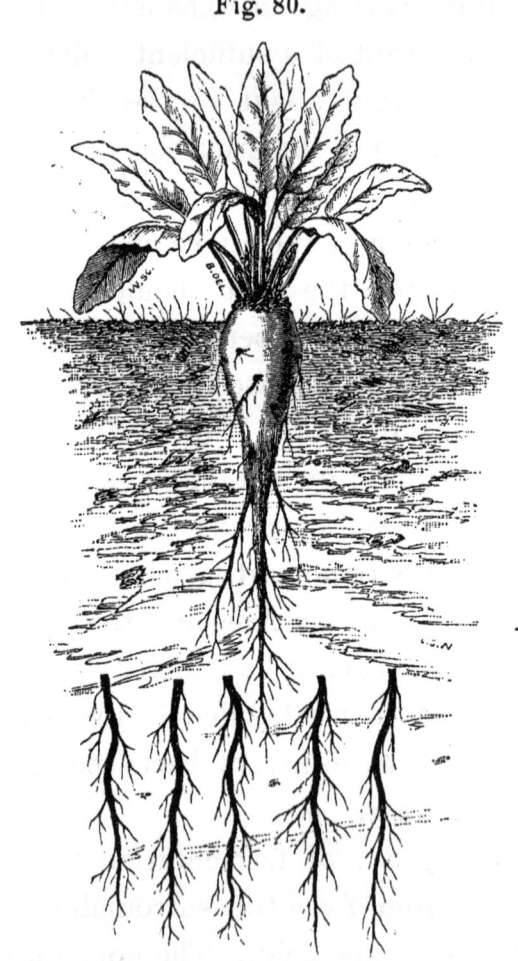

The beet growing, the end of the root penetrating the portion where the ends of previous roots still exist.

attacking the entire beet. At first the leaves have their brown spots, droop, etc., as in the case before mentioned. It has been remarked that if on this same soil a beet be transplanted without the extreme end of its root, and which cannot consequently penetrate the unhealthy soil, it will remain in a perfect condition; this being sufficient proof of the exactitude of the theory advanced.

Remedy.—The second case—the want of oxygen—being of the greatest interest, we would say that there are two methods of preventing it, either of which should be adopted, or, better still, both combined:—

1st. The use of a subsoil plough, penetrating the soil as deeply as possible, and thus bringing the lower portion in contact with the air.

2d. System of drainage before spoken of. The method advocated by Payen and Richard is shown in fig. 81, but we consider that any other plan will answer

Fig. 81.

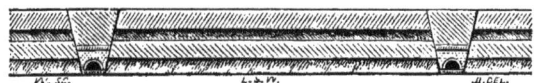

System of drainage.

as well, when the drain pipes are placed at a sufficient depth. The object of this is to carry off the excess of water, the oxygen[1] being absorbed through the stratum from the surface.

The sugar beet, like other plants, grown on poor

---

[1] When water passes through a porous substance the oxygen of the atmosphere penetrates by suction.

soil is occasionally attacked by a disease called *piedchaud*; its ravages take place before the plant has six leaves.

The *rachitis* as a general thing attacks young plants that have been badly transplanted; but it is not of sufficient importance to speak more fully upon.

A disease, if it can be so called, which is to be greatly dreaded in America, and the exact cause of which we can give no exact explanation, consists in a

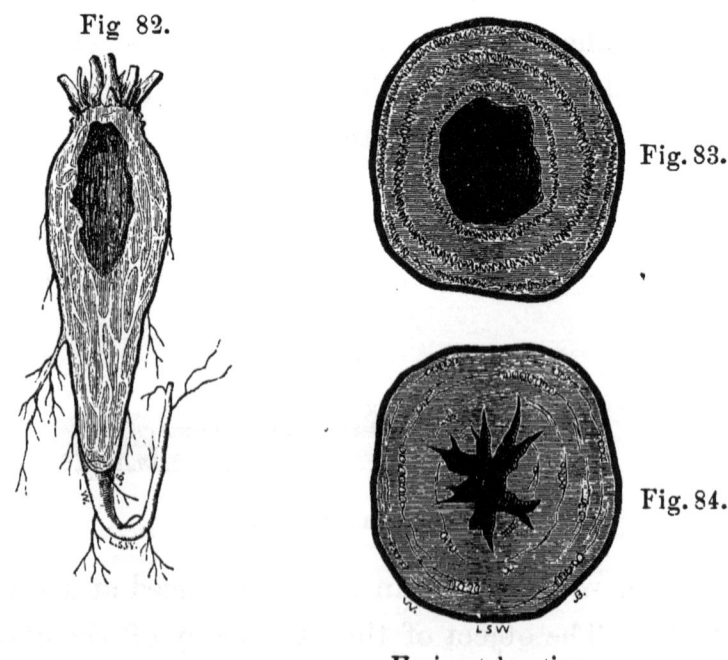

Fig 82.

Fig. 83.

Fig. 84.

Horizontal section.

hollowness (see figs. 82, 83, 84), which generally commences near the upper portion of the root, and continues frequently through the entire mass. This we have noticed on beets that were planted on a sandy-loam in New Jersey, and where the temperature of the summer was much greater than the plant had been accustomed to, causing, as we consider, a sort of an internal dryness, having for effect the absorption of the medullary portion. As the parenchyma seemed to be in a perfect condition, it is probable that an expansion of the same had taken place, thus permitting the entrance of rain water, and causing a general internal decomposition.

If these diseases are of frequent occurrence in a crop, we consider it advisable to feed the roots attacked to cattle rather than to attempt uniting them with others to be reduced to a pulp for the manufacture of sugar. In all cases of brown penetration, the beets should be used when the first indications are visible. If this precaution be not taken, no sugar can be extracted from them. In addition to all we have said upon this subject, we must not forget mentioning those enemies, such as rain, frost, wind, etc., to counteract the effects of which man can do but little.

PART VI.

Feeding qualities of the beet.
1. The Beet.
2. The Pulp.
   (α) Made directly from the Beet.
   (β) Residue from Beet Sugar Factory.
   (γ) Residue from Distillery.

1. *Feeding Qualities of the Beet.*

As a general thing it may be said that many advantages are obtained by uniting roots with ordinary forage, as animals' stomachs in winter soon tire of the dry elements alone, after which they are liable to become constipated. Roots given in excess will have a contrary effect; and those that have made the experiment will agree with us that an ox or a cow much prefers the beet to the potato, turnip, carrot, etc.

In consequence of several experiments made at the "Ecole de Gringnon," we arrive at the conclusion that in feeding cows with beets—

1st. There will be an improvement in the quality of the milk.

2d. Augmentation in the quantity of milk.

3d. Augmentation in the weight of the animal.

This is in direct opposition to Schwertz's idea, he contending that if a cow be fed on food containing any proportion of beets, these will be sufficient to cause a decrease in the quantity of milk after a few days, and for this reason beets have not been grown in Alsace.

Baron Crud says that in certain portions of the Palatinate horses are fed during the entire winter on beets, and remain in a perfect condition, having, on the other hand to sustain the fatigue of constant hard work. In direct opposition to this, Groguier contends that horses eat them with little relish, and those that have this food soon become feeble and lazy; then, again, others argue that the meat of animals after having been fed upon roots soon becomes white and flabby, and that the animals do not, as a general thing, care much for beets, in consequence of the large quantity of water they contain, and that they should be given in moderation in winter, otherwise various diseases are to be dreaded. As shown, opinions greatly differ; as for the exact nourishing qualities of the beet we cannot say, but consider the average given below is not far from the truth.

Boussingault contends that 540 kilog. (1188 lbs.) of roots are about equal to 100 kilog. (220 lbs.) of hay; this represents fewer nourishing properties than the greater number of well-known agriculturists are willing to admit, as will be seen by the following estimates of various authorities:—

Black	366k.	
Baron Crud	225	
Pabst	275	
Meyer	250	
Flotou	300	=100 kil. of hay.
Royer	250	
Schwertz	330	
Thaer	460	
Boussingault	540	
Average	333	

As for the quantity of roots to be furnished to an animal daily, it depends upon circumstances, such as age, climate, etc.

We do not advise the use of roots alone, for it is better to unite them with a given quantity of hay or straw, or any other substance of the same sort.

We give in fig. 85 an idea of a stable as it exists in different portions of Belgium. As shown, the beets are stored under the passage way, and are taken out when required; a small quantity of hay is thrown into the manger when these are to be fed to the cow. The resulting manures are thrown against the wall, a practice we cannot recommend.

In 1836 Dr. Schwertzer, of Saxony, made, during a long period of years, many efforts to utilize a small quantity of straw of different sorts for feeding without the assistance of hay, but was not successful. He then tried uniting this with a small quantity of sliced roots, leaving the mass to ferment. Perfect satisfaction was thus obtained; the importance of giving fermented food to animals had then long been understood in Germany.

Fig. 85.

Belgium manner of storing the beets when they are to be used for feeding purposes.

Remarks.—There can be no doubt that every advantage is to be gained by the utilization of colza straw instead of the ordinary straw from wheat, etc., which should form a bed for the animal, and if used for forage, would in the greater number of cases, not leave sufficient for that purpose.

The following analyses are of interest in this connection:—

	Straw from Wheat.		Straw from Colza.
Organic and volatile substances	80.320	78.672	74.761
Ashes	4.013	3.921	6.885
Nitrogen	0.499	0.522	0.702
Water	15.168	16.885	17.652
	100.000	100.000	100.000

As shown in the above, the nourishing elements are in favor of the colza. When it is remembered that the yield per acre is the same as hay, we see that we have here a new fodder, which for years has not been sufficiently appreciated.

The animals do not eat as much of the fermented food as of the dry, and for that reason it is much more economical.

2. (a) *Feeding Qualities of the Pulp made directly from the Beet.*

It has been for a long time thought impossible to raise beets with profit for feeding purposes alone. The following interesting methods prove to the contrary. It is an invention of Mr. Leduc, who contends that he is able to obtain better results with fifty acres of land planted with beets than with one hundred and fifty in ordinary forage. The fig. 86 gives an exact idea of this system. Steam is the principal agent. As shown, there exist six compartments, separated by a wall of 22 c. m. (8.5 inches), these being disposed three on one side and the same number on the other. Between these is a pit, at the bottom of which is placed the main steam pipe, having, by means of smaller pipes communication with each compartment. The pit is covered with boards, permitting the workmen to fill or empty the compartments, as the case may be.

298   THE SUGAR BEET.

After the roots have been sliced into "cossettes," they are thrown into these compartments, after which

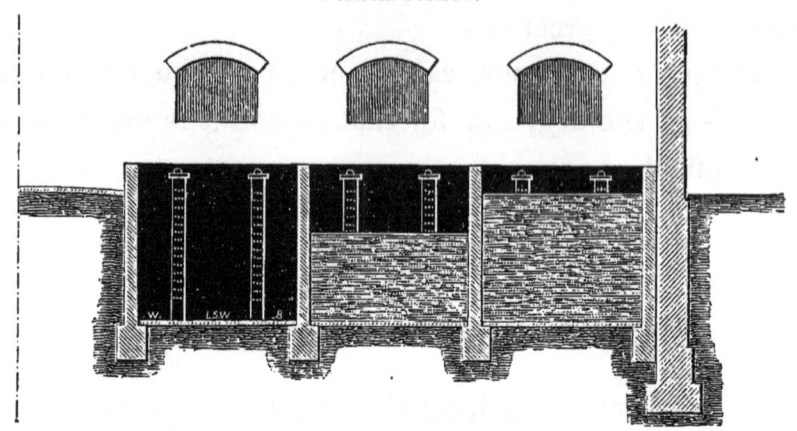

Fig. 86.
Vertical section.

Horizontal section.

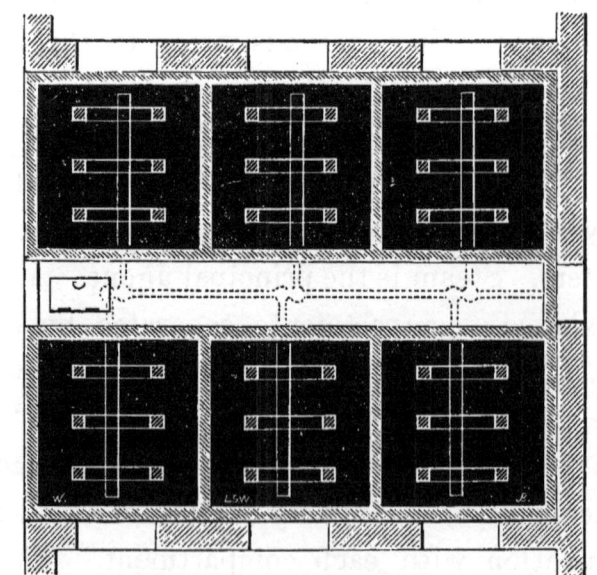

Leduc's method of reducing the beet to a pulp by steam.

the chopped straw is added. The bottom of each compartment is well paved; the smaller pipe (before mentioned) has here six arms, at the extremity of each the steam can make its escape, it passing up through a chimney (see fig. 87), the orifice of which slants downward so as to make sure that the total mass will be well saturated. These chimneys are only placed in position

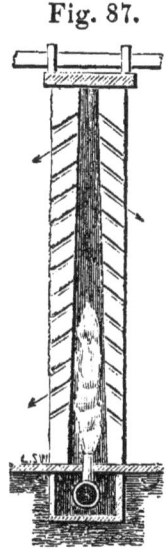

Fig. 87.

Detail of a chimney. Leduc's method.

when the pits are being filled. The capacity of each compartment is twenty cubic metres, and they are emptied one day and filled the next. The steaming lasts about half an hour at a time, and, after the lapse of twelve hours, the whole commences to ferment, and is here left for the remaining portion of the day. This fermented mass is then fed to sheep, to each is given 5 kilog. (11 lbs.); with this 250 grammes (0.55 lb.) of oil cake per day. The time required to fatten greatly depends upon circumstances, this varying from seventy to one hundred and ten days, giving an average of ninety, during which time the amount of pulp furnished would be 450 kilog. (990 lbs.). In all calculations the quantity of manure resulting should not be neglected. For a sheep this is about equal to 500 kilog. (1100 lbs.) to every kilog. (2.2 lbs.) of wool furnished.

Remark.—We are informed that it is of common occurrence with this food to obtain an increase in an ox's weight of 160 kilog. (352 lbs.), 180 kilog. (396 lbs.), and even 190 kilog. (418 lbs.) in ninety-one days. Now, supposing 160 kilog., or about 352 lbs., the augmentation in weight of meat, if this is selling at $0.07, this would represent a profit of $24.64; to this, if we add the resulting manure, which is sufficient for one hectare (two and a half acres) of land, and subtract the first cost and attendance, etc., there will still remain an enormous profit. We will not, for the present, make any calculations, but we consider that this is of much interest to Americans; as for unknown reasons they are not willing to plant the beet on a sufficiently large scale to test the possibility of success of the beet sugar industry.

Our farmers contend that the carrot, turnip, etc., can be planted with much more profit for feeding purposes than the beet. Never was an error greater than this, and even if this idea were correct, no future profit can be derived from the growth of the first-mentioned roots; but, on the contrary, if the sugar beet is planted it will enable our chemists to study the soils, and consequently the manures that may be required to make the success of a new and great industry certain.

In answer to the above, we know many will say that thousands of farmers do plant the beet with this idea in view. There may be some few, but we have not been fortunate enough to meet with them either in Pennsylvania or New Jersey, where what is grown are roots wrongly called *beets*, and containing little or no sugar, and having but little practical value.

β. *Pulp from the Sugar Factories.*

The beets as before stated, are grown in Europe by the neighboring farmers, who have a right to claim 20 per cent. in pulp of the roots supplied, for which is paid about 16 francs ($3.20) per ton; this they feed to their cattle, who furnish the manure, which is utilized on the same soil on which the roots were grown. In this manner nearly the same elements are returned, when this fertilizer is in sufficient quantities, as had been extracted by this supposed exhausting plant, which in reality furnishes more fertilizing principles than any other crop.

Evidently, the composition of this pulp varies with the factories and the method of extracting. The following analysis was made by ourselves of pulp from the northern part of France:—

Water	74.316
Sugar	4.192
Fatty substances	0.721
Cellulose	9.562
Nitric elements	2.434
Mineral substances	1.426
Pectose, etc.	7.349
	100.000

This pulp is given to animals in various proportions, and with it are generally combined chopped straw, etc. There is no general rule or formula for this combination, but it is estimated that an ox or a cow eats about 4 to 5 per cent. of its weight of hay daily. If this rule be correct, an ox weighing 1100 lbs. would eat 44 to 55 lbs. of hay, or about 145 lbs. to 181 lbs. of pulp.[1] At the farm of Mr. Decombecque, at Lens, he gives an ox each day—

Chopped straw .	3	kilog.	(6.6 lbs.)
Hay . . .	2	"	(4.4 ")
Oil cake from flax	1	"	(2.2 ")
Salt . . .	0.80	"	(1.7 ")
Pulp . . .	40	"	(88 ")

We consider the above as most excellent. At some few farms near Lille are given—

Pulp . . .	50	kilog.	(110 lbs.)
Mash from brewery	3	"	(6.6 ")
Chopped straw .	4	"	(8.8 ")
Oil cake . .	2	"	(4.4 ")

It is well to permit the whole to ferment for some twenty-four hours, after which time a small quantity of

---

[1] The above calculation supposes the average given on page 295.

fresh pulp may be added. We would advise in all cases the use of the chopped colza straw and oil cake.

(γ) *Pulp from the Distilleries.*

In Europe many of the beet sugar factories have been transformed into distilleries in consequence of the great competition and the low yield of the roots. While in many cases these distilleries were specially built, the resulting alcohol was of but secondary importance, and, under the most unfavorable circumstances, when this was selling at a very low figure, or even at cost, the remaining pulp would consequently furnish food for nothing, and the increase of weight in the animals would then be a net profit. The most important of these farms existing in France belongs to Cail & Co., is called "Ferme de la Briche," and is situated near Langeis, Department of Indre-et-Loire.

We have thought that a general view of the buildings and grounds would be of interest.[1] As shown, there exist three long structures 60.00 × 20.00 m. (196.80 × 65.60 feet), which are separated from each other by an open space 12.00 m. (39.36 feet) in width. These are stables, each of which will hold two hundred head of cattle. It is seldom one sees a better arrangement of these; we give, in fig. 88, a section of the same. The cattle are arranged in four rows, separated by a passage way—between each pair of rows—1.25 m.

---

[1] See Frontispiece.

(4.11 feet) in width. Here is placed a track on which a car runs containing the pulp. n regard to the ventilation, we may state that it is perfect. The other buildings shown represent the distillery and the sheepfold, where the 4000 sheep are fed.

Fig. 88.

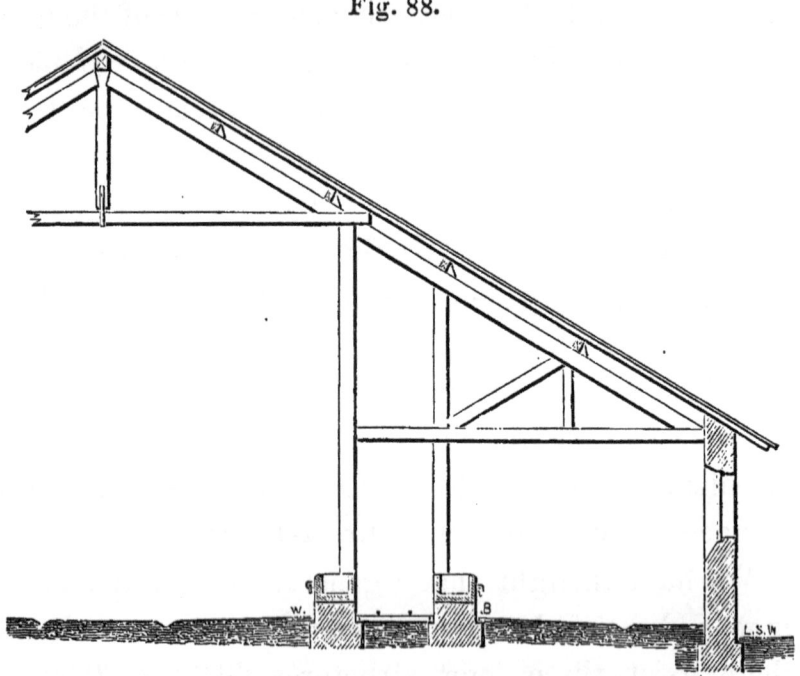

Half section of building of Cail & Co. where cattle are fed on the distillery refuse.

There are two methods which are most generally adopted for the distillation of the beet, the first of which, by far the most important, is the System Champonnois, and the second the System Leplay. We will not for the present give the reader even an idea of the principle on which this distillation is based, as it would carry us away from the subject we wish to discuss.

Mr. Basset some years ago contended that all acidulated pulp was a poor food for animals; the sulphuric acid utilized in the "System Champonnois," acting as an astringent upon the mucus of the stomach, and thus having an irritating effect and that there would also exist a certain quantity of sulphate of potassa and lime; and that animals tired of this fodder sooner than of any other. Now we do not wish in any way to contradict the assertion of this chemist, but can answer to this, that we have consulted farmers that have used this pulp for years, and only good effects have resulted. We consider it most absurd even to suppose that the health of cattle is in any way affected by this small quantity of acid.

In the System Leplay the pulp is nearly reduced to a mush by the action of a jet of steam at a pressure of two atmospheres. After leaving the distilling columns it is washed, and the albumen and soluble salts are extracted. This operation alone renders all comparison between the two pulps impossible.

The pulp from the distillery contains more water than that of the sugar factory, but the quantity of nitric elements in the latter is greater; it being estimated that 100 lbs. are about equal to 135 lbs. of the Champonnois; but when it is considered that the yield from the sugar factory is 20 per cent. of the total, and that from the distillery 88 per cent., evidently more meat and consequently more manure and future crops can be obtained from a distilling establishment. We are informed that the butchers prefer cattle that are fattened with this latter.

We give the analysis of this pulp, and, judging from it alone, one may easily see that it forms a most excellent food:—

```
Water . . . . . . . 87.55
Sugar . . . . . . . .  3.02
Nitric elements  ⎫
Mineral salts, etc. ⎭ . . . . 9.43
                              ─────
                              100.00
```

Here, again, no general rule concerning the quantity of pulp, etc., to be fed daily to a cow can be laid down, as this varies with circumstances. The following is about an average:—

```
Pulp (Champonnois) . . 70 kilog.   (154 lbs.)
Oil cake . . . .  . 5   "          ( 11  " )
Hay . . . . . .  . 4   "           ( 8.8 " )
```

Remark.—Dr. Menrin some years ago prepared a table giving the comparative values of all the pulps mentioned above; we consider this of great interest. It is as follows:—

100 lbs.	Water.	Dry elements.	Nitrogen per cent. in the normal pulp.	Nourishing equivalent standard 100 lbs. hay.
Pulp from the factory .	68.7	31.3	0.3997	287.7
Pulp, Champonnois . .	88.6	11.4	0.2899	396.6
Pulp, Leplay	91.15	8.85	0.2106	546.0
Pulp directly from the beet	83.5	16.5	0.2307	500.0

As shown, everything is in favor of the Champonnois pulp.

3. *Preservation of the Pulp.*

In cases where the manufacturer wishes himself to utilize the resulting pulp, it becomes necessary to adopt some plan for the preservation of the same, as if allowed to remain in contact with the air the fermentation would continue and decomposition would follow, leaving the mass in a condition which, under no circumstances, could be used for feeding purposes, even in small quantities.

Sugar factories can only work with profit when on a large scale. The volume of this pulp is far in excess of the consumption, as it would be sufficient to feed several hundred head of cattle; this number being a greater encumbrance and responsibility than one person is willing to have. Leaving out these circumstances, it should be remembered that the total crop of roots is worked up in one hundred days, hardly sufficient time to have good fattening results; for that reason the pulp must be kept for several months after the campaign is at an end.

Many argue that the pulp from the distillery, System Leplay, is far easier to keep than any other, as it has been submitted to a temperature sufficiently high to render the remaining albumen insoluble. We will not for the present discuss to what extent this theory can be relied upon, but can say that the results obtained in the preservation of the ordinary pulps are quite sufficient to satisfy the present demands.

We saw in the Paris Exhibition of 1878 some that had been on hand for several years; and the owner

Fig. 89.

Vertical section.

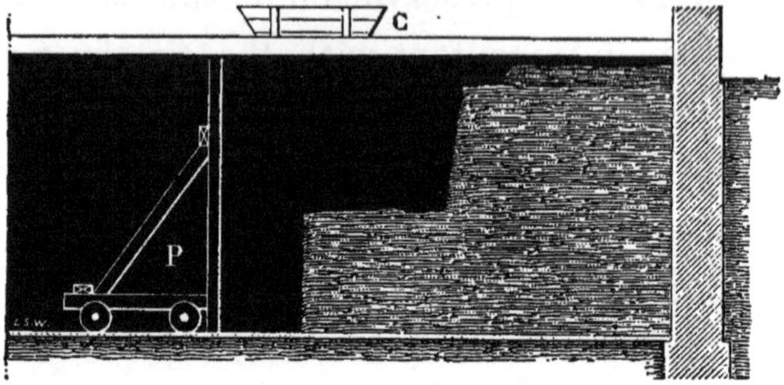

Plan and horizontal section.

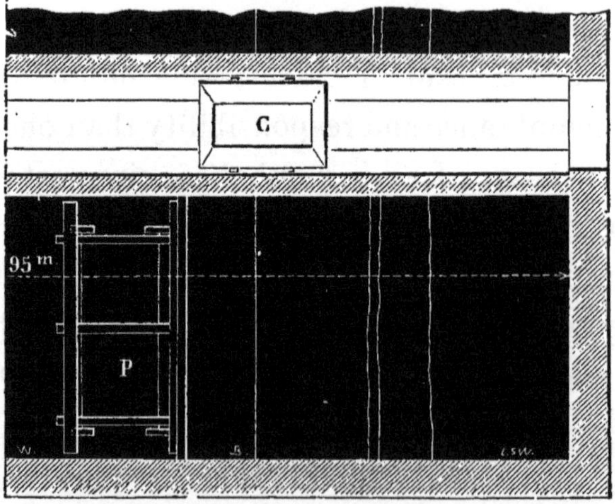

Showing the method of preserving the pulp at Ferme de la Briche.

contended that its feeding qualities had in no way diminished. We fear when as aged as this the volatile acids would be in too great abundance.

This preservation takes place in silos; these are not very varied in form, being most generally ditches dug in a soil as dry as possible, and having for this reason, in the greater number of cases, but little interest for the reader. The most important that we have seen are at the "Ferme de la Briche" fig. 89. The dimensions are 95.00 m. (311 feet) in length and 3.50 m. (11.48 feet) in depth, and only 6.00 m. (19.68 feet) in breadth, giving a total capacity for the two of nearly 4000 cubic metres. The pulp when taken from the mash tubs is placed in cars, in which are united the chopped straw, hay, etc.; this is then brought between the silos at C and here emptied; a second fermentation would follow before these were full, in consequence of their enormous volume. Now here is a point to which we wish to call attention, and where, we consider, great ingenuity has been displayed. The idea consists in having a movable partition P, the section of which is 6.00 m. × 3.50 m. (or 19.68 feet × 11.48 feet) exactly the same as the silos), mounted on wheels, and is placed within a few metres of the end wall; between this space the mixture is thrown and packed as tightly as possible, in order that the fermentation may be regular, and, when nearly full, a layer of earth of 30 cm. (0.98 foot) is placed on the top. This partition is then moved backwards several metres, and the same operations are again repeated, until full. Here the pulp can be kept the greater part of the year.

Mr. Leduc, after a series of experiments concerning

the possibility of keeping the pulp for a longer period, arrived at results which are of interest to all. The objection to his steam process was that the beets must remain in the silos until required, and it was impossible to keep them more than six months, when the food came to an end. The new idea had not this Inconvenience to contend with. The process consisted simply in the slicing of the roots into "cosettes" as small as possible, and uniting them with chopped colza straw, in the proportion of 9.00 lbs. of the first to 1.00 lb. of the second, and placing the same in a silo. This is compressed as before, after which a layer of earth is placed on top, preventing the entrance of the air. After the lapse of several days the fermentation commences, in consequence of a small quantity of air still remaining in the chopped straw. After this air is absorbed the fermentation will continue but for a short time. The atmosphere of carbonic acid in which the mass finds itself prevents all putrid fermentation, and it remains in this condition for a considerable time. The resulting vapors of alcohol have penetrated the pulp, thus rendering it more palatable for the animals. Here arises a question of considerable importance. Is it better for the farmer to sell his beets or to utilize them himself? To this we answer, it depends upon the number of acres of land he has at his disposal. If few, we are convinced there is more profit in preparing them as shown above, and using the fermented mass when required; if many, to sell the root to the distiller or to the beet sugar factory.

Before bringing this important question to an end we wish to call attention to some curious facts that took place on Mr. Leduc's farm. At one period he had several sheep which were about to have young; he fed them with the fermented mixture, and they remained in perfect health. The lambs were born, and he still continued to give the same food; after six months these were sold in a perfect condition. Those which had been fed with the ordinary pulp also after a short time had their young and became sick and died. He repeated this several times, and in each case the results were fatal. Now, as shown, we have here food that all animals will eat, and is at the disposal of the most limited purse and suits the most delicate stomach.

4. *Feeding Qualities of the Leaves.*

The use of leaves as fodder is not new, and at one period the beet was cultivated[1] for its leaves alone. Evidently, at that time the elements constituting the nourishing properties of food could not have been well understood, as it is now a well-known fact that if the root had been utilized in various proportions combined with the leaves, the results obtained would have been éven more satisfactory. The utilization of the beet for sugar manufacture soon brought to public notice principles until then overlooked and unknown.

At the present day these leaves are used in large

---

[1] See "Mémoire de la Societé d'Agriculture de Paris, 1789."

quantities yearly, thus permitting the farmer to have for his cattle fresh green food during the dryest months of the year.

Mathieu de Dombasle, Boussingault and others condemned their use, as they considered them not only a poor food, but exhausting to the soil and ruinous to the crop.[1]

From a series of practical experiments made by Mr. Dumas, he concluded that they formed a most excellent food for young asses, and a very good nourishment for pigs.

We have not made any experiments upon this subject, but we are informed that if given in too large quantities they act as a purge. There can be no doubt that if used in a moderate manner, combined with chopped straw, etc., they will augment the quantity of milk, but this is more watery, and consequently not so good for the manufacture of butter. If their chemical composition be examined it can easily be seen that they evidently contain elements that constitute good food, and we can only say in conclusion, that the farmers would reject them in various parts of Europe if some advantage could not be gained.

---

[1] See "Leaves of the Sugar Beet."

INDEX.

Ad valorum principle in the purchase of sugar in the beet, 202
Advantages, apparent, of barnyard manure, 124
 gained by cultivation in hills, 119, 120
 of harvesting after Ware's idea, 195
 of planting seed in lozenges, 166
 of the beet sugar industry to the farmer, 58
Aerial transportation, 225-232
Age of seed that will not germinate, 155
Agricultural Department U S , 43
 produce, annual yield for the United States, 56
 products of Valenciennes, France, 61
Agriculture, need of a scientific, in the United States, 123
Agriote, 276
Air in germinating, 157
Albumen, 81
 of seed, 165
Albuminoids, 132
Alcohol, first suggestions as to, in the beet, 25
 from beets, 61
Alsace, 294
Altica, 276
Alumina, soils of, 107
Alvarado Company, 42
American soils adapted to beet culture, 101
America, underground house suitable for preservation of the beets in, 256
Ammonia, phosphate of, experiments with, 161
 solution for the destruction of Melolonthas, 269
 sulphate of, 135
Amount of humidity before germination, 159
Analysis of French soils, 104
 of leaves, 93
 of Prussian soils, 102-3
 of root of the beet, 92-93
 of the beet, 83

Analysis—
 of various straws, 296
Analyzing the crop, advantage of, 124
Animal phosphate, advantages of, 137
Annales de Chemie, 26
Arabian silos, 237
Archard, early suggestions and writings of, in regard to the beet, 26, 27, 35, 37
 honorable conduct of, 26, 37
Argillo-calcareous soils, 108
Argout, Comte d', proposals for taxation of beet sugar in France, 29
 sandy soils, 108
Arsenate of potassa, 161
Ash of the beet, 142, 144
Ashes of the beet and saccharine elements, 144
Asparagine, 81
Atomaria lineris, 271, 272
Austria, beet sugar in, 37-38
 factory in, in 1802, 37
 France, Germany, and Russia, sugar beet industry in, xv
 taxation of sugar in, 38
Author's preparation for this work, xi, xiii
Average mean, 163

Baird, Henry Carey, 282
Ballon, M., on sprouts of the beet, 241
Barbet, M , analysis of sprouts, 239
Barnyard manure, xviii, 124, 127
 and chemical fertilizers, comparative results of, 140
Barruel, 27, 28
Basic phosphate of lime, 136
Basset, M , 74
Basset's theory of germination, 158
Beach, Tyler, 42
Beet, analysis of, 83, 84, 86
 and beet sugar, books on, in French and German, xii
 as food for animals, 63
 as food for man, 63
 ash of, 142-144
 book of Abbé Commerel on, 26

Beet—
- chemical examination of, 80–84
- conservation of, 237–262
- culture, greatest difficulty in introducing in America, 59
- Dervaux, 73
- distance in planting the roots of, 165–168
- effects of guano on the, 131
- examination of, xvi, 74–90
- feeding qualities of, 293–312
- first suggestions as to yielding alcohol, 25
- flowers of, 185, 186
- for manufacture of sugar, 63
- Franco-Allemande, 73
- fruit of, 186, 187
- Imperiale, 67, 68
- Improved Carter, 73
- Improved Vilmorin, 70, 71
- leaves of, 91–99
- Magdeburg, 67, 72
- matured, 193
- red, 63
- root sugar, work on, by Professor Crookes, xii
- root, work on, by E. B. Grant, xii, 191, 192, 240
- saccharine changes in, 185
- seed of, 152
- shape of, 87–90
- soil required by, 106
- structure of, 74–90
- sugar can compete with sugar of Cuba, 60
- sugar, education in the manufacture of, in France in 1812, 28
- sugar factory, early, near Steinau, 26
- sugar factories in France, where located, 34
- sugar in, 84–87
  - in Austria, 37–38
  - in Belgium, 38
  - in Germany, 35–37
  - in Holland, 39
  - in Russia, 39
- sugar industry, attempts to introduce, in the United States, 41–44
  - in Europe, 25–40
- sugar industry, results which would follow from its introduction into the United States, 53–62
- sugar, production and consumption of, in Europe, 1877–8, 40
- sugar, production of, in France, 1826–78, 32–33

Beet—
- sugar, production of, in Zollverein, 1836–65, 37
- sugar, taxation of, in France, 29, 30, 31
- taken to Bohemia by the Barbarians, 25
- Tollet, 73
- varieties of, 63–73
- White Silesian, 67, 68
  - Green-top, 69
  - Rose-top, 70
- White Sugar, Grayish-top, 70, 71
- Yellow, 63
- zone and leaves of, 77

Beets, advantages of raising, 57
- arrival of, Porvin's idea, 230
- density of, 179–180
- gathering, 228
- mother, S. Legrand on, 183
- profitable way for manufacturer to pay for, 202
- starting, Provin's idea, 229
- types of, created by Simon Legrand, 73
- value of, 202–206
- various types of, xvi

Belgium, beet sugar in, 38
- farmers of, 161
- France, and Germany visited by the author, xiii
- principles proposed in, for paying for beets, 203
- stable in, 295–296
- taxation of sugar in, 38

Betaine, 81
Bettrave dit Dervaux, 73
  dit Tollet, 73
Black Hawk, Wisconsin, 42
Blanche de Pologne, 68
Blandain, Belgium, spontaneous combustion at, 134
Bohemia, beets taken to, by Barbarians, 25
Boiling the leaves, 262
Bonestel and Otto, 42
Books in French and German on beet sugar, xii
Boussingault, M., on the use of leaves for food, 312
  on the value of beets as food for animals, 294–295
"Bouteuse" sugar beet, 76
Bresleau sugar beet, 68
Bretschneider, M., 77
Broadcast, sowing, 169
Brombrisky, Compte de, 254
Brown penetration, 283–289
  remedy for, 289

INDEX. 315

Cail & Co., xxii, 303
Calcareous fertilizers, xix, 138
    precaution before using, 139
  soils, 107
  soils, reactions of, 134
California, beet sugar in, 42, 43
Cambrai, cost of cultivation in, 199
    France, agricultural statistics of, 34
Cane-mills, the amount of sugar that can be extracted by, 50
Capital utilized for sugar industry in the United States, 45
Carter sugar beet, 73
Cassida, 276
Castlenaudary, Red, 63
  Yellow, 63
Cattle fed on pulp, increase of weight of, 300
Causes of loss of sugar, 239–240
  of loss of weight of beets, 242
Cellulose, 80
Cellular tissue, 87
Champignon and Pellet, analysis of the beet, 86
    analysis of the seed of the beet, 152–153
    experiments of, 77, 82, 86, 92, 144
    on effects of nitric elements in the beet, 132
    on the effects of rain on beets, 175
Champonnois, M., 179
  on cultivation in hills, 117
  system of distillation, 304–305
Changes during vegetation, 173
Chappelet, 28
Chaptal, 27, 28, 243
Chaptal's idea of a silo, 244, 245
Charcoal, use of, in silos, 255
Chatsworth, Illinois, 41
Cheapness not obtained by the brutalization of man, xvii
Chemical examination of the beet, 80–84
  fertilizers, xviii, xix
    and barnyard manure, comparative results of, 140
  test, disadvantages of, 182
Child, David Lee, 41
Chinese system in the cultivation of bi-annual plants, 185
Chloride, 83
  of lime to accelerate germination, 160
  of potassium, 83
    in the ash, 145
  of sodium, 83
Chlorophyl, 80

Civieres for transportation of beets, 221
Classification of sugars, 50
Clay, Henry, 44
  soils of, 107
Clover, disadvantage of, in rotation, 210
Coignet, M., fertilizer, 150–151
Cold in silos, 240
Coleoptera, 264
Color of soils, 102
Colza, 213
  straw, utilization of, 213
Commerel, Abbé, book of, on the beet, 26
Comparative results of chemical fertilizers and barnyard manure, 140
Complete fertilizer, 127
  beneath the surface, 141
  upon the surface, 141
  Ville's, 149
  manure, 146
Composition of a complete manure, 146
  of the mines of Strassfurth, 137
Conservation of the sugar beet, 237–262
Consumption of sugar in England, 46
  in the United States, 1860–76, 46
Corbin's portable track and porteur, 216–218
  wagon locomotive, 215
Corenwinder, M., 93, 98, 134
Corenwinder's experiments, 144–145
  in planting beets on various soils, 137–138
  with fertilizers, 150
Corn stalks, sugar from, 48
Cost of cultivation, xxi
  of cultivation and yield, 196–206
  in America has nothing to do with Europe, 197
  influenced by methods of sowing, 197
Crespel, 27
Crops, rotation of, 207–213
  used for green manures, 129
  which exhaust the soil, 57
Crud, Baron, 294
Cryptophagous, 278
Cultivation in drills, 111–117
  in hills, 117–122
Curculio, 272

Darwin, 176
Davy, Sir Humphry, on beet sugar, 27
Decaisne, experiments of, 77
Decaisne, M., 74, 79, 82
Decauville's idea of transportation, 218–224
Decombecque, M., estimate of food for an ox, 302

Deherain's experiments with manures, 145
Delahayes, 171
Delaware Beet Sugar Co., 43
Delessat, beet sugar made by, in France in 1812, 28
Delesse, 27
Demi-bouteuse sugar beet, 70
Density as a guide for the selection of seed, 154
Deprez & Co. the largest seed growers in France, 181
Deprez et Fils, agricultural laboratory of, 72
Deprez, improved, 72
Depth for sowing, 164
Deremacausie, 242
Dervaux beet, 73
Dervaux, M., method based on density, 180
Desiccation of the beet, 258
Dextro-glucose, 51
Difficulty of introducing the beet sugar industry in the United States, 62
of selection of seed, 154
Diptera, 264, 280, 281
Disease, 282
and insects, 263-291
of spongiole, 285
Distance for the roots, 165-168
Distillation from the beet, advantages of, 61
systems of, 304-305
Distilleries, pulp from, 303-307
Dombasle, Mathieu, 67, 167
on the use of leaves as food, 312
Drainage, Payen and Richard's method of, 289
Drills, cultivation in, 111-117
Dubrumfaut, M., 82, 86, 83
theory of, the sugar in the beet, 86
Duffriné Brothers, road locomotive, 215
Dumas, M , xi
on "brown penetration" in the beet, 284
on the use of leaves for food, 312
Dutch standard, 50

Early organization of the factories for the purchase of the beets in Germany, 35
East Indies yield of cane sugar per acre, 50
Ecole Centrale des Arts, Agriculture et Manufactures, xi
Economical transportation, 215-236
type of silo, 252
Egyptian silos, 237

Electorale sugar beet, 68
Elements of the soil taken up by one hectare of beets, 95
Elwood, N. J., 42
Embryo of seed, 163
Enemies of the sugar beet, xxiii, 263-291
England, consumption of sugar in, 46
Engrais, M. Joulie's, 151
Europe, beet sugar industry in, 25-40
labor bestowed on the soil in, 58
production of beet sugar in, 1877, 8, 40
Evaporation of water in the beet for desiccation, 258
Examination of the beet, 74-90
Exhaustion of American soils, 207
of the soil, 123
Experiments of Corenwinder, 98
of Petterman, 167
External qualities of the beet, 87-90
Extraction of sugar from the cane with cane-mills, 50

Factories in Germany, where situated, 36
number of, in Holland, 39
Farmers, advantage of the beet sugar industry to, 58
of Belgium, 161
Farms near Magdeburg, 200
Feeding of diseased beets to cattle, 291
qualities of the beet, 293-312
early book on, 26
of the leaves, 311-312
of the pulp, 297-307
Ferme de la Briche, xxii, 303, 304
preservation of the pulp at, 308-309
Fertilizer, complete, 127
beneath the surface, 141
upon the surface, 141
Corenwinder's experiments with, 150
from the mines of Strassfurth, 137
M. Coiguet's, 150-151
M. Joulie's, 151
mineral, 131-140
molasses as a, 139
nitric, 131
phosphoric, 135
potassic, 137
Fertilizers, xviii, xix
calcareous, 138
Fertilization of flowers of the beet, 187
Final results from bad cultivation, 59
Flax, 213

Florida, 48
Flowers, fertilization of, 187
   of the beet, 185, 186
Fluctuation of the beet sugar industry in Europe, 25-40
Fond du Lac, Wisconsin, 42
Food for cattle, the Yellow Globe Mangel Wurzel, excellent, 65
Forces of nature, cheapness had by command over, xvii
Fossier, 171
Franco-Allemande beet, 73
France, beet sugar made in, in 1812-13, 28
   decline of the beet sugar industry in, during the Restoration, 28, 29
   early history of the beet sugar industry in, 27
   estimates of cost of cultivation in, 199
   Germany and Belgium visited by the author, xiii
   Germany, Austria, and Russia, sugar beet in, xv
   production of beet sugar in, 1826-78, 32-33
   systems of rotation of crops in, 212, 213
   time for sowing in, 163
Frauds on the revenue, 50
Frederick the Great encourages Archard in his investigations in regard to the beet, 26
Freeport, Illinois, 42
Freezing of the beets, 258
French soils, analysis of, 104
Fruit of the beet, 186, 187
Future crops that follow the beet, 58

Gallicia, factory at, of Schuetzenback, 36
Gasparin, M., 169
Gasparin's idea of harvesting, 190
Gathering the beets upon the field, 228
Gennert Brothers, 41
German Beet Sugar Co., 41
   method in selecting of the mother beet, 177
   Red Mangel Wurzel, 64
Germany and France, cost of cultivation in, xxi
   beet sugar in, 35-37
   estimates of cost of cultivation in, 200
   France, and Belgium, visited by the author, xiii
   France, Austria, and Russia, sugar beet industry in, xv

Germany—
   principle for estimating value of beets in, 202
Germination, xx, 155, 161
   activated by chloride of lime, 160
   by oxalic acid, 161
   air necessary, 157
   heat necessary, 157
   light necessary, 157
   number of degrees of heat necessary, 159
Germinate, percentage that will not, 155
Globe jaune the best beet for transplanting, 170
   Mangel Wurzel, 65
Glucose, 48
Glucose, dextro-, 51
Grant, E. B., xii, 191, 192, 240
Green manures, xviii, 129
Green-top, 69
Grignon, Ecole de, experiments at, on the feeding qualities of the beet, 293-294
Groguier, M., 294
Groven, M., experiments on depth for sowing, 164
Guano, xviii, 130
   and bones, mixture of, 130
   effects of, 131

Hadena bassicæ, 280
Harrow in cultivation in drills, 112
Harvesting, 189-195
   care, 191
   frequently done by contract, 200
   Gasparin's idea, 190
   manner of, hand and machinery, 191
   of beets, xxii
   qualities of colza-straw, 297
   separating the necks from the roots, 192
   Ware's idea, 194
Heat in germination, 157, 159-160, 175
   in silos, 240
   total required, 175
Heavy rains, 121
Hereditary principles in plants and animals, 176
Heteroderes, 277
Hill, shape of, 119
Hills, cultivation in, 117-122
   distance apart, 118
   inclination of, 118
History of the fluctuations in the beet sugar industry in Europe, 25-40
Hodgson's idea for transportation, 225, 226
Hoe, mechanical, 121

INDEX.

Hoeing, 112
  effect produced by, 115
  when seeds are in lines, 114
Hoffmann's analysis of the beet, 84
Holland, beet sugar in, 39
  number of factories in, 39
  taxation of sugar in, 39
Hollowness in beets, 290
Horses fed on beets in the Palatinate, 294
Humboldt, 161
Humidity, 156, 159
  amount of, necessary before germination, 159
Hydrochloric acid for the preservation of leaves, 201

Imperiale, 67, 68
Improved Deprez, 72
  Vilmorin, 70, 71
Improvement of the seed of the beet, 176-188
Indian corn, 213
Insects, analysis of, 270
  and diseases, 263-291
  destruction of, with lime water, 268
Isnard, 27

Joulie, M., engrais, 151
  experiments of, on phosphoric fertilizers, 136
Juice in pipes, 232-235
  preservation of, 259

Knauer, M., 67, 177
  machine for subdividing the roots into piles, 178
Kœchlin's experiments in transplanting, 170

Lancaster County, Pa., crops of tobacco, 56
Large seed, effect produced by, 152
Leaves, author's experiments in stripping, 96
  boiling of, 262
  feeding qualities of, 311-312
  Mehay's method of preparing, 267
  of the beet, analysis, 93
  of the beet, functions of, 91
  of the sugar beet, xxi, 91-99
  preservation of the, 259
  prevent the soil from receiving light, heat, and air, 120
  pulling the, 193
  silos for the preservation of, 260
  stripping of, 94-99

Leduc's experiments on keeping pulp, 309-311
  method for reducing the beet to a pulp, 297-300
Legrand, Simon, types of beets created by, 73
  upon mother beets, 183
Lepidoptera, 264
Leplay, M., 177
  pulp from the distillery of, this system, 307
  researches of, 107
  system of distillation, 304, 305, 307
Lettson, Dr., 64
Levees of sugar lands, 49
  taxation for the building of, 49
Liebig, Baron von, xix
  errors in regard to manures, 125
  name for a malady of the beet, 242
Light in germination, 158
Lille, food given to cattle at, 302
Lime mixed with water for destruction of insects, 268
  plants, 211
  phosphate, basic, 136
  soluble phosphate, 137
  superphosphate, 136
Linard's idea for transportation, 224-225
Livingston Co., Illinois, Company formed in, 41
Locality for a factory, 62
Locomotive, road, 215
Long, White, Green-top Mangel Wurzel, 64
  Red-top Mangel Wurzel, 65
  Yellow Mangel Wurzel, 65
Loss of sugar and weight of beets, 238
  by stripping, 99
  causes of, 239-240
  prevention of, 240-242
Louisiana, 48, 49
  sugar in, xv
Lozenge, seeds planted in, 166

Macarez, E., report of, on sugar factories of Cambrai, 34
Magdeburg beet, 67, 72
  selecting the mother beets at, 177
Maine, encouragement to beet sugar industry, 43
  experiments made in, 202
"Maladie du guano," 130
Malic acid, 81
Mangel Wurzel, 64, 65
Manner of planting the mothers, 184

INDEX.

Manure between hills, the advantage of, 122
 choice of, 145-151
 complete, 146
Manures, xviii, xix, 123-151
 Deherain's experiments with, 145
 green, 129
Maple sugar, 47
Margaff, early suggestions as to extraction of alcohol from the beet, 25, 26
Mathieu, M., 169
Maumené, M., on juice in pulp, 234
 theory for the preservation of juice, 259
Mauritius, yield of cane sugar per acre, 50
Mechanical devices for cultivation, 113
 for farming, xvii
 for sowing, 171, 172
 hoe, 121
Mehay, M., experiments on the density of the roots and of the juice, 180
 method of preparing the leaves, 261
Melolontha, 264-271
 destruction of, 267, 269
 uses of, 268
Menrin, Dr., table of comparative values of pulps, 306
Methods of sowing influence the cost of cultivation, 197
 of sowing the seed, 168
Microscope, examination of the beet with, 74-80
Microscopic vegetable parasite, 130
Mineral fertilizers, xviii, 131, 140
 phosphate, 137
 substances in the beet, 82
Molasses as fertilizer, 139
 from beets, 61
Montague, Dr., 282
Montpellier attacked by Altise insects, 275
Mother beet selecting, 177
Mothers, amount of seed furnished by, 188
 manner of harvesting, 184

Napoleon, 26, 27, 28
Neglect of American farmers, 59
Nematodes, 277
New Jersey and Pennsylvania, yield in, 201
 hollowness of beets grown in, 290-291
 Legislature of, encouragement to beet sugar industry, 43
Nitrate of potassa, the disadvantage of using, 137

Nitrate of potassa—
 results in using, in large quantities, 145
 of soda, 133, 160
Nitric fertilizer, xviii, 131
Nitrogen, manner of absorption by the root, 133
Noctua, destruction of, 279
 segetum, 278
Northampton Beet Sugar Co., 41
Number of acres of land necessary to supply the United States with beets, 53
 of factories in Holland, 39
 of hands employed at Waghaeusel, 36
 of seed in one kilog., 168

Oil cake, xviii, 129
Organic manures, xviii, 127-131
Oxalic acid, 81
 to activate germination, 161

Pagnoul, M., 132
 analysis of insects, 270
 experiments with manures, 140-144, 148, 149
Pailly's silo facilitating drainage, 249
Palatinate, horses fed on beets in, 294
 silo used in the, 246
Paris Exposition of 1878, xiii
 pulp at, 308
Parmentier, 27
Payen, M, xi, 81, 82, 86, 96
 analysis of the beet, 83
 estimate of, of cost for a hectare, 198
 on "brown penetration," in the beet, 284, 285, 286
 theory of the sugar in the beet, 84, 86
Paying for roots according to their saccharine value, 177
Pectic acid, 81
Pectine, 81
Pectose, 81
Pellet and Champignon, experiments of, 77
Pellot-Schunz, 171
Pelouze, M, investigations of, in regard to beet sugar, 29
Pennsylvania and New Jersey, yield in, 201
Percentage of seed that will not germinate, 155
 of sugar in the different zones, 86
 of the total consumption of sugar grown in the United States, 48

Peterman, Dr., experiments on distance for seeds, 166
Phenic acid, 161
Philadelphia, attempt to form a beet sugar company in, 1830, 41
Phosphate, mineral, 137
 of ammonia, experiments with, 161
 of lime, basic, 136
 of lime, percentage, 136
 uniting of, with manure, 137
Phosphates, 83
Phosphoric acid, xix, 128
 fertilizer, 135
Phytomyzides, 280
Pied-chaud, 290
Pierre, J. I., experiments of, 93, 97
Plant, appearance of, when the leaves have attained full growth, 116
 when thinning out can commence, 116
Planting, xx
Plants, composition of, 126
Ploughs, xvii
 in cultivation in drills, 112
Polariscope, 51
 manner of using, for beet analysis, 204
Portable track and porteur of Corbin, 216-218
Porteur, Decauville, 220
Portland, Maine, beet sugar factory at, 43
Position of seeds that are planted, 165
Potash plants, 211
Potassa in beets planted in Italy, 138
Potassic fertilizers, xix, 137
Precautions in harvesting, 191
Precipitated phosphate of lime, 136
Preparation of the soil, 110-122
Preservation of the juice, 259
 of the leaves, 259
 of the pulp, 307-311
 of the sugar beet, 258
Prevention of loss of sugar, 240-242
Prices for beets, 167
Production and improvement of the sugar beet, 176-188
 per capita in Belgium, 38
Proportional area to be planted in a rotation, 213
Provin's idea for transportation, 226-232
Prussians, interest of, in the beet sugar industry, 35
Prussian soils, analysis of, 102-103
Pulp, analysis of, 306
 at Paris Exposition, 308
 composition of, 301-302

Pulp—
 directly from the beet, feeding qualities of, 297-301
 feeding qualities of, 297
 from distilleries, 303-307
  of the system Leplay, 307
 from the sugar factories, 301-303
 Leduc's method for reducing the beet to, 297-300
 method of preserving, at Ferme de la Briche, 308, 309
 preservation of, 307-311
 use of for feeding purposes, xxii
Pulps, comparative values of, 306

Qualities of beets in Russia, 39
Quotient de pureté in the estimation of the value of the beet, 205

Rachitis, 290
Rain, effects of, 174
Red Beet, or Red Castelnaudary, 63
 Castelnaudary, 63
 Globe Mangel Wurzel, 65
 Mangel Wurzel, 64
 Oval Mangel Wurzel, 65
Resemblance of the seed of mangel wurzel to sugar beet, 154
Results of using in large quantities phosphate of soda, 145
 which would be produced by the introduction of the sugar beet industry in the United States, 53-62
 with barnyard manure, 141
Revenue from sugar in the United States, 61
Road locomotive, 215
Roller used, 115-118
Rollers, when to be used in sowing, 171
Rolling of seed, 158
 in plaster, 160
Roman Empire, 123
 silos, 237
Ronaldson, James, 41
Root, appearance of, when the leaves have attained full growth, 116
Roots, analysis of, 92, 93
 manner of growth, 120
Rose-top, 69, 70
Rotation of crops, xx, 207-213
 in United States, 267
 system of, adopted for a given soil, 209
Rubidium, 83
Russia, beet sugar in, 39
 France, Austria, and Germany, beet sugar industry in, xv

INDEX. 321

Russia—
    importance of constant temperature in the silos understood, 254
    quality of beets in, 39
    taxation of sugar in, 39
    time for sowing in, 162
Russian soils, 106
Ruta-baga, 66

Sablo-calcareous, 107
Saccharine changes in the beet, 185
    qualities and ashes of beet, 144
Sacks, M., 80
Saltpetre, 82, 161
Sandy soils, 106
San José, California, 42
Santa Clara Valley Agricultural Society, 42
Saxony, silo used in, 251
Scharcht, M., 77
Schubart, 35
Schuetzenback, 36
Schwartz, M., 90, 294
Schwertze, Dr., of Saxony, on food for cattle, 295
Scientific agriculture, need of, in the United States, 123
Seed, albumen contained in, 163
    amount of water they are capable of absorbing, 156
    embryo, 163
    furnished, amount of, by each mother, 188
    of the beet, 152
        analysis of, 152-154
        effects of the size of, 154
        importance of, 154
    selection of, according to density, 154
    sprinkling, with water before sowing, 160
    their age tested by boiling, 159
Seeds and sowing, 152-175
    large and small, xix
    method of sowing, 168
    number of, in one kilog., 168
    planted in lozenges, 160
    planted in rectangle, advantage of, 166
    rolling of, 158
    various positions of, when planted, 165
Selection of seed according to density, 154
Separation of the necks from the roots in harvesting, 192
Serres, Oliver de, 25
Shape of the beet, 87-90

Sicily, exhaustion of the soil of, 123
Silesian, White, 67,
Silo for America, 256
    for the preservation of the leaves, 260
Silos, xxiii, 223, 237, 243, 257
Silpha, 273-275
Situation of the sugar lands in America, 49
Soda, nitrate of, 133
    substitution of, for potassa, 138
Soil, elements of, taken up by one hectare of beets, 95
    exhaustion of, 123
    for beets, xvi
    the preparation of, 110-122
Soils, American, adapted to beet culture, 101
    analysis of French, 104
        of Prussian, 102-3
    color of, 102
    experiments on, with manures, 146, 149
    general considerations, 101-109
    poor, 137
    required by the beet, 106
    Russian, 106
Soluble phosphate of lime, 137
Sorghum, 47
Sowing and seed, 152, 175
    broadcast, 169
    depth for, 164
    mechanical devices for, 171, 172
    time for, 161, 162
Sowing of the seed in large quantities, for insects, 272
Spanish silos, 237
Spermoderm, 156
Spongiole, disease of, 285
Spontaneous combustion at Blandain, Belgium, 134
Spring ploughing, 112
Sprinkling the seed with urine before sowing, 160
Sprinkling the seed with water before sowing, 160
Steinau, early beet sugar factory near, 26
Stephenson Co., Illinois, company in, 41
Strassfurth, 137
    fertilizer from the mines of, 137
Striking increase of the production of beet sugar in Austria, 38
Structure of the beet, 74-90
Suberine, 81
Subsoil ploughing, xvii
    the importance of, in America, 59

Substitution of soda for potassa, 138
Sugar and saline elements, 181
    annual import of, into the United States, xv, 53
    beet, conservation of, 237-262
    of to-day, 25
    consumption of, in the United States, 1860-76, 46
    countries from which imported into the United States, 47
    factories in France turned into distilleries, 30
    pulp from, 301-303
    frauds on the revenue, 50
    from corn-stalks, 48
    high percentage of, 66
    industry in the United States, 45-62
    in the beet, 84-87, 128
    in the roots, paying for, xxi
    land levees, 69
    lands of the United States, where they are mainly situated, 49
    value of, in the United States, 49
    large imports of, into the United States, 45
    maple, 47
    of beets, loss of, 238-240
    percentage of, in different beets, 64-73
    production of, in the United States, 47, 50
Sugars, classification of, 50
Sulphate of ammonia, 135, 145
Sulphate of zinc, 161
Sulphates, 82
Superphosphate of lime, 136
    to activate germination, 160

Tannin, 81
    use in beet estimation, 265
Taxation for the building of levees, 49
    of beet sugar in Austria, 38
    in Belgium, 38
    in France, 29, 30, 31
    in Germany, 36
    in Holland, 39
    in Russia, 39
Taxes on sugar in the United States, 61
Temperature in degrees necessary for germination, 159
    freezing, in preservation of the beet, 258
Test, chemical, disadvantages of, 182
    for the age of seed by boiling, 159
Texas, 48
Thiers, M., services of, in saving the beet sugar industry of France, 30

Thinning out, 113
    device for, 117
Tillage, 110-122
Tobacco crop in Lancaster County, Pa., 56
Tollet beet, 73
Transparent zones in the beet, 84
Transplanting, 169, 170
    Kœchlin's experiments, 170
Transportation, aerial, 225-232
    advantages of different plans of, 235, 236
    Corbin's portable track and porteur, 216-218
    wagon locomotive, 215
    Decauville's idea, 218-224
    Duffriné Brothers, road locomotive, 215
    economical, 215-236
    Hodgson's idea for, 225, 226
    Linard's idea for, 224-225, 232-235
    Provin's idea for, 226-232

Underground pipes for juice, 232-235
United States, annual imports of sugar into, xv
    attempts to introduce in, beet sugar industry, 41-44
    consumption of sugar in, 1860-76, 46
    results which would follow from the introduction of the beet sugar industry, 53-62
    rotation in, 213
    soil of, adapted to the beet culture, xxiv
    sugar industry in, xv, 45-62
Urine, sprinkling the seed with, before sowing, 160
Utilization of the waste products of the factory, 139

Valenciennes, France, agricultural products of, 61
Value of beets, 202-206
    of cane sugar lands in the United States, 49
Variation in the cost of cultivation, 197
Varieties of the beet, 63-73
Vascular tissue, 286
Vaughn, John, 41
Vegetation, changes during, 173
Ventilation, good, in silo, 253
    want of, 240
Ventzke method for estimating the qualities of beets, 204
Ville, George, analysis of barnyard manure, 127

Ville, George—
    complete fertilizer of, 149
    experiments on comparative results of chemical fertilizers and barnyard manure, 140
    investigations of, 125
    on the effects of nitric elements on the beet, 132
Villiant, Sebastian, 186
Vilmorin, M., 64, 67, 68, 69, 70
    experiments to test the density of beets, 179
    improved beet, 71, 75
Violette, M , Charles, 72, 84
    on the form of the beet, 181, 182
    test of the sugar in the beet, 181, 182
    theory of the location of the sugar, 181
Vivien, M., on the effects of nitrates in the beet, 133
    upon manuring soils, 149

Waghaeusel, factory, 86
Walkhoff, M., 77, 103, 130
    advice on the mixture of guano, 130
    experiments with phosphate of ammonia, 161
    on depth for sowing, 165
    on effects of rain, 174
    on estimating the value of beets, 205
    on improvements in the mother beets, 183
    on Melolontha vulgaris, 268
    on Russian soils, 106, 254
    on sugar and saline elements, 181
    on time for sowing in Russia, 162
Ware, L. S., idea of harvesting the beets, 194
Waste products of beet sugar factories, 130
    utilization of, 139
Water that seeds can absorb at various temperatures, 156
Weeding, xvii
Weight of beets, loss of, 238
West Indies yield of cane sugar per acre, 50
Wharton, Joseph, 42

White Green-top Mangel Wurzel, 64
    Red top Mangel Wurzel, 65
    Silesian, 67, 68, 72
        Green-top, 69
        Rose-top, 69, 70
        Sugar Grayish-top, 70–71

Yellow beet, or Yellow Castelnaudary, 63
    Globe Mangel Wurzel, 65
    Oval Mangel Wurzel, 65
Yield and cost of cultivation, 196–206
    in beets to the acre with German Red Mangel Wurzel, 64
        with Improved Vilmorin, 71
        with Long, White Mangel Wurzel, 64
        with Long, White, Red-top Mangel Wurzel, 65
        with Red Globe Mangel Wurzel, 65
        with the Magdeburg type, 67
        with White Silesian, 67
        with White Silesian Grayish-top, 70
        with White Silesian Green-top, 69
    in cane sugar per acre in East Indies, 50
    in West Indies, 50
    in sugar to the acre with German Red Mangel Wurzel, 64
        with Improved Vilmorin, 71
        with Long, White, Green-top Mangel Wurzel, 64
        with Long, White, Red-top Mangel Wurzel, 65
        with Magdeburg type, 67
        with White Silesian, 67
        with White Silesian Grayish-top, 70
        with White Silesian Green-top, 69
        with White Silesian Rose-top, 70

Zollverein, production of sugar in, 1836–65, 87
Zones, transparent, in the beets, 84

THE DREAM OF A NEW AND IMPORTANT INDUSTRY.

SHORTLY TO APPEAR.

"THE SUGAR BEET."

CATALOGUE

OF

PRACTICAL AND SCIENTIFIC BOOKS,

PUBLISHED BY

HENRY CAREY BAIRD & CO.,

Industrial Publishers and Booksellers,

NO. 810 WALNUT STREET,

PHILADELPHIA.

☞ Any of the Books comprised in this Catalogue will be sent by mail, free of postage, at the publication price.

☞ A Descriptive Catalogue, 96 pages, 8vo., will be sent, free of postage, to any one who will furnish the publisher with his address.

ARLOT.—A Complete Guide for Coach Painters.
Translated from the French of M. ARLOT, Coach Painter; for eleven years Foreman of Painting to M. Eherler, Coach Maker, Paris. By A. A. FESQUET, Chemist and Engineer. To which is added an Appendix, containing Information respecting the Materials and the Practice of Coach and Car Painting and Varnishing in the United States and Great Britain. 12mo. $1.25

ARMENGAUD, AMOROUX, and JOHNSON.—The Practical Draughtsman's Book of Industrial Design, and Machinist's and Engineer's Drawing Companion:
Forming a Complete Course of Mechanical Engineering and Architectural Drawing. From the French of M. Armengaud the elder, Prof. of Design in the Conservatoire of Arts and Industry, Paris, and MM. Armengaud the younger, and Amoroux, Civil Engineers. Rewritten and arranged with additional matter and plates, selections from and examples of the most useful and generally employed mechanism of the day. By WILLIAM JOHNSON, Assoc. Inst. C. E., Editor of "The Practical Mechanic's Journal." Illustrated by 50 folio steel plates, and 50 wood-cuts. A new edition, 4to. $10.00

ARROWSMITH.—Paper-Hanger's Companion:
A Treatise in which the Practical Operations of the Trade are Systematically laid down: with Copious Directions Preparatory to Papering; Preventives against the Effect of Damp on Walls; the Various Cements and Pastes Adapted to the Several Purposes of the Trade; Observations and Directions for the Panelling and Ornamenting of Rooms, etc. By JAMES ARROWSMITH, Author of "Analysis of Drapery," etc. 12mo., cloth. $1.25

ASHTON.—The Theory and Practice of the Art of Designing Fancy Cotton and Woollen Cloths from Sample:
Giving full Instructions for Reducing Drafts. as well as the Methods of Spooling and Making out Harness for Cross Drafts, and Finding any Required Reed, with Calculations and Tables of Yarn. By FREDERICK T. ASHTON, Designer, West Pittsfield, Mass. With 52 Illustrations. One volume, 4to. $10.00

BAIRD.—Letters on the Crisis, the Currency and the Credit System.
By HENRY CAREY BAIRD. Pamphlet. 05

BAIRD.—Protection of Home Labor and Home Productions necessary to the Prosperity of the American Farmer.
By HENRY CAREY BAIRD. 8vo., paper. 10

BAIRD.—Some of the Fallacies of British Free-Trade Revenue Reform.
Two Letters to Arthur Latham Perry, Professor of History and Political Economy in Williams College. By HENRY CAREY BAIRD. Pamphlet. 05

BAIRD.—The Rights of American Producers, and the Wrongs of British Free-Trade Revenue Reform.
By HENRY CAREY BAIRD. Pamphlet. 05

BAIRD.—Standard Wages Computing Tables:
An Improvement in all former Methods of Computation, so arranged that wages for days, hours, or fractions of hours, at a specified rate per day or hour, may be ascertained at a glance. By T. SPANGLER BAIRD. Oblong folio. $5.00

BAIRD.—The American Cotton Spinner, and Manager's and Carder's Guide:
A Practical Treatise on Cotton Spinning; giving the Dimensions and Speed of Machinery, Draught and Twist Calculations, etc.; with notices of recent Improvements: together with Rules and Examples for making changes in the sizes and numbers of Roving and Yarn. Compiled from the papers of the late ROBERT H. BAIRD. 12mo. $1.50

BAKER.—Long-Span Railway Bridges:
Comprising Investigations of the Comparative Theoretical and Practical Advantages of the various Adopted or Proposed Type Systems of Construction; with numerous Formulæ and Tables. By B. BAKER. 12mo. $2.00

BAUERMAN.—A Treatise on the Metallurgy of Iron:
Containing Outlines of the History of Iron Manufacture, Methods of Assay, and Analysis of Iron Ores, Processes of Manufacture of Iron and Steel, etc., etc. By H. BAUERMAN, F. G. S., Associate of the Royal School of Mines. First American Edition, Revised and Enlarged. With an Appendix on the Martin Process for Making Steel, from the Report of ABRAM S. HEWITT, U. S. Commissioner to the Universal Exposition at Paris, 1867. Illustrated. 12mo. . $2.00

BEANS.—A Treatise on Railway Curves and the Location of Railways.
By E. W. BEANS, C. E. Illustrated. 12mo. Tucks. . . $1.50

BELL.—Carpentry Made Easy:
Or, The Science and Art of Framing on a New and Improved System. With Specific Instructions for Building Balloon Frames, Barn Frames, Mill Frames, Warehouses, Church Spires, etc. Comprising also a System of Bridge Building, with Bills, Estimates of Cost, and valuable Tables. Illustrated by 38 plates, comprising nearly 200 figures. By WILLIAM E. BELL, Architect and Practical Builder. 8vo. . $5.00

BELL.—Chemical Phenomena of Iron Smelting:
An Experimental and Practical Examination of the Circumstances which determine the Capacity of the Blast Furnace, the Temperature of the Air, and the proper Condition of the Materials to be operated upon. By I. LOWTHIAN BELL. Illustrated. 8vo. . . $6.00

BEMROSE.—Manual of Wood Carving:
With Practical Illustrations for Learners of the Art, and Original and Selected Designs. By WILLIAM BEMROSE, Jr. With an Introduction by LLEWELLYN JEWITT, F. S. A., etc. With 128 Illustrations. 4to., cloth. $3.00

BICKNELL.—Village Builder, and Supplement:
Elevations and Plans for Cottages, Villas, Suburban Residences, Farm Houses, Stables and Carriage Houses. Store Fronts, School Houses, Churches, Court Houses, and a model Jail; also, Exterior and Interior details for Public and Private Buildings, with approved Forms of Contracts and Specifications, including Prices of Building Materials and Labor at Boston, Mass., and St. Louis, Mo. Containing 75 plates drawn to scale; showing the style and cost of building in different sections of the country, being an original work comprising the designs of twenty leading architects, representing the New England, Middle, Western, and Southwestern States. 4to. . $10.00

BLENKARN.—Practical Specifications of Works executed in Architecture, Civil and Mechanical Engineering, and in Road Making and Sewering:
To which are added a series of practically useful Agreements and Reports. By JOHN BLENKARN. Illustrated by 15 large folding plates. 8vo. $9.00

BLINN.—A Practical Workshop Companion for Tin, Sheet-Iron, and Copperplate Workers:
Containing Rules for describing various kinds of Patterns used by Tin, Sheet-Iron, and Copper-plate Workers; Practical Geometry; Mensuration of Surfaces and Solids; Tables of the Weights of Metals, Lead Pipe, etc.; Tables of Areas and Circumferences of Circles; Japan, Varnishes, Lackers, Cements, Compositions, etc., etc. By LEROY J. BLINN, Master Mechanic. With over 100 Illustrations. 12mo. $2.50

BOOTH.—Marble Worker's Manual:
Containing Practical Information respecting Marbles in general, their Cutting, Working, and Polishing; Veneering of Marble; Mosaics; Composition and Use of Artificial Marble, Stuccos, Cements, Receipts, Secrets, etc., etc. Translated from the French by M. L. BOOTH. With an Appendix concerning American Marbles. 12mo., cloth. $1.50

BOOTH AND MORFIT.—The Encyclopedia of Chemistry, Practical and Theoretical:
Embracing its application to the Arts, Metallurgy, Mineralogy, Geology, Medicine, and Pharmacy. By JAMES C. BOOTH, Melter and Refiner in the United States Mint, Professor of Applied Chemistry in the Franklin Institute, etc., assisted by CAMPBELL MORFIT, author of "Chemical Manipulations," etc. Seventh edition. Royal 8vo., 978 pages, with numerous wood-cuts and other illustrations. . $5.00

BOX.—A Practical Treatise on Heat:
As applied to the Useful Arts; for the Use of Engineers, Architects, etc. By THOMAS BOX, author of "Practical Hydraulics." Illustrated by 14 plates containing 114 figures. 12mo. $5.00

BOX.—Practical Hydraulics:
A Series of Rules and Tables for the use of Engineers, etc. By THOMAS BOX. 12mo. $2.50

BROWN.—Five Hundred and Seven Mechanical Movements:
Embracing all those which are most important in Dynamics, Hydraulics, Hydrostatics, Pneumatics, Steam Engines, Mill and other Gearing, Presses, Horology, and Miscellaneous Machinery; and including many movements never before published, and several of which have only recently come into use. By HENRY T. BROWN, Editor of the "American Artisan." In one volume, 12mo. . . . $1.00

BUCKMASTER.—The Elements of Mechanical Physics:
By J. C. BUCKMASTER, late Student in the Government School of Mines; Certified Teacher of Science by the Department of Science and Art; Examiner in Chemistry and Physics in the Royal College of Preceptors; and late Lecturer in Chemistry and Physics of the Royal Polytechnic Institute. Illustrated with numerous engravings. In one volume, 12mo. $1.50

BULLOCK.—The American Cottage Builder:
A Series of Designs, Plans, and Specifications, from $200 to $20,000, for Homes for the People; together with Warming, Ventilation, Drainage, Painting, and Landscape Gardening. By JOHN BULLOCK, Architect, Civil Engineer, Mechanician, and Editor of "The Rudiments of Architecture and Building," etc., etc. Illustrated by 75 engravings. In one volume, 8vo. $3.50

BULLOCK.—The Rudiments of Architecture and Building:
For the use of Architects, Builders, Draughtsmen, Machinists, Engineers, and Mechanics. Edited by JOHN BULLOCK, author of "The American Cottage Builder." Illustrated by 250 engravings. In one volume, 8vo. $3.50

BURGH.—Practical Illustrations of Land and Marine Engines:
Showing in detail the Modern Improvements of High and Low Pressure, Surface Condensation, and Super-heating, together with Land and Marine Boilers. By N. P. BURGH, Engineer. Illustrated by 20 plates, double elephant folio, with text. . . . $21.00

BURGH.—Practical Rules for the Proportions of Modern Engines and Boilers for Land and Marine Purposes.
By N. P. BURGH, Engineer. 12mo. $1.50

BURGH.—The Slide-Valve Practically Considered.
By N. P. BURGH, Engineer. Completely illustrated. 12mo. $2.00

BYLES.—Sophisms of Free Trade and Popular Political Economy Examined.
By a BARRISTER (Sir JOHN BARNARD BYLES, Judge of Common Pleas). First American from the Ninth English Edition, as published by the Manchester Reciprocity Association. In one volume, 12mo. Paper, 75 cts. Cloth $1.25

BYRN.—The Complete Practical Brewer:
Or Plain, Accurate, and Thorough Instructions in the Art of Brewing Beer, Ale, Porter, including the Process of making Bavarian Beer, all the Small Beers, such as Root-beer, Ginger-pop, Sarsaparilla-beer, Mead, Spruce Beer, etc., etc. Adapted to the use of Public Brewers and Private Families. By M. LA FAYETTE BYRN, M D. With illustrations. 12mo. $1.25

BYRN.—The Complete Practical Distiller:
Comprising the most perfect and exact Theoretical and Practical Description of the Art of Distillation and Rectification; including all of the most recent improvements in distilling apparatus; instructions for preparing spirits from the numerous vegetables, fruits, etc.; directions for the distillation and preparation of all kinds of brandies and other spirits, spirituous and other compounds, etc., etc. By M. LA FAYETTE BYRN, M. D. Eighth Edition. To which are added, Practical Directions for Distilling, from the French of Th. Fling, Brewer and Distiller. 12mo. $1.50

BYRNE.—Handbook for the Artisan, Mechanic, and Engineer:
Comprising the Grinding and Sharpening of Cutting Tools, Abrasive Processes, Lapidary Work, Gem and Glass Engraving, Varnishing and Lackering, Apparatus, Materials and Processes for Grinding and Polishing, etc. By OLIVER BYRNE. Illustrated by 185 wood engravings. In one volume, 8vo. $5.00

BYRNE.—Pocket Book for Railroad and Civil Engineers:
Containing New, Exact, and Concise Methods for Laying out Railroad Curves, Switches, Frog Angles, and Crossings; the Staking out of work; Levelling; the Calculation of Cuttings; Embankments; Earth-work, etc. By OLIVER BYRNE. 18mo., full bound, pocket-book form. $1.75

BYRNE.—The Practical Model Calculator:
For the Engineer, Mechanic, Manufacturer of Engine Work, Naval Architect, Miner, and Millwright. By OLIVER BYRNE. 1 volume, 8vo., nearly 600 pages $4.50

BYRNE.—The Practical Metal-Worker's Assistant:
Comprising Metallurgic Chemistry; the Arts of Working all Metals and Alloys; Forging of Iron and Steel; Hardening and Tempering; Melting and Mixing; Casting and Founding; Works in Sheet Metal; The Processes Dependent on the Ductility of the Metals; Soldering; and the most Improved Processes and Tools employed by Metal-Workers. With the Application of the Art of Electro-Metallurgy to Manufacturing Processes; collected from Original Sources, and from the Works of Holtzapffel, Bergeron, Leupold, Plumier, Napier, Scoffern, Clay, Fairbairn, and others. By OLIVER BYRNE. A new, revised, and improved edition, to which is added An Appendix, containing THE MANUFACTURE OF RUSSIAN SHEET-IRON. By JOHN PERCY, M. D., F.R.S. THE MANUFACTURE OF MALLEABLE IRON CASTINGS, and IMPROVEMENTS IN BESSEMER STEEL. By A. A. FESQUET, Chemist and Engineer. With over 600 Engravings, illustrating every Branch of the Subject. 8vo. $7.00

Cabinet Maker's Album of Furniture:
Comprising a Collection of Designs for Furniture. Illustrated by 48 Large and Beautifully Engraved Plates. In one vol., oblong $3.50

CALLINGHAM.—Sign Writing and Glass Embossing:
A Complete Practical Illustrated Manual of the Art. By JAMES CALLINGHAM. In one volume, 12mo. $1.50

CAMPIN.—A Practical Treatise on Mechanical Engineering:
Comprising Metallurgy, Moulding, Casting, Forging, Tools, Workshop Machinery, Mechanical Manipulation, Manufacture of Steam-engines, etc., etc. With an Appendix on the Analysis of Iron and Iron Ores. By FRANCIS CAMPIN, C. E. To which are added, Observations on the Construction of Steam Boilers, and Remarks upon Furnaces used for Smoke Prevention; with a Chapter on Explosions. By R. Armstrong, C. E., and John Bourne. Rules for Calculating the Change Wheels for Screws on a Turning Lathe, and for a Wheel-cutting Machine. By J. LA NICCA. Management of Steel, Including Forging, Hardening, Tempering, Annealing, Shrinking, and Expansion. And the Case-hardening of Iron. By G. EDE. 8vo. Illustrated with 29 plates and 100 wood engravings . . . $6.00

CAMPIN.—The Practice of Hand-Turning in Wood, Ivory, Shell, etc.:
With Instructions for Turning such works in Metal as may be required in the Practice of Turning Wood, Ivory, etc. Also, an Appendix on Ornamental Turning. By FRANCIS CAMPIN; with Numerous Illustrations. 12mo., cloth $3.00

CAREY.—The Works of Henry C. Carey:
FINANCIAL CRISES, their Causes and Effects. 8vo. paper . 25
HARMONY OF INTERESTS: Agricultural, Manufacturing, and Commercial. 8vo., cloth $1.50
MANUAL OF SOCIAL SCIENCE. Condensed from Carey's "Principles of Social Science." By KATE MCKEAN. 1 vol. 12mo. $2.25
MISCELLANEOUS WORKS: comprising "Harmony of Interests," "Money," "Letters to the President," "Financial Crises," "The Way to Outdo England Without Fighting Her," "Resources of the Union," "The Public Debt," "Contraction or Expansion?" "Review of the Decade 1857-'67," "Reconstruction," etc., etc. Two vols., 8vo., cloth . . . .
PAST, PRESENT, AND FUTURE. 8vo. $2.50
PRINCIPLES OF SOCIAL SCIENCE. 3 vols., 8vo., cloth $10.00
THE SLAVE-TRADE, DOMESTIC AND FOREIGN; Why it Exists, and How it may be Extinguished (1853). 8vo., cloth . $2.00
LETTERS ON INTERNATIONAL COPYRIGHT (1867) . 50
THE UNITY OF LAW: As Exhibited in the Relations of Physical, Social, Mental, and Moral Science (1872). In one volume, 8vo., pp. xxiii., 433. Cloth $3.50

CHAPMAN.—A Treatise on Ropemaking:
As Practised in private and public Rope yards, with a Description of the Manufacture, Rules, Tables of Weights, etc., adapted to the Trades, Shipping, Mining, Railways, Builders, etc. By ROBERT CHAPMAN. 24mo. $1.50

COLBURN.—The Locomotive Engine:
Including a Description of its Structure, Rules for Estimating its Capabilities, and Practical Observations on its Construction and Management. By ZERAH COLBURN. Illustrated. A new edition. 12mo. $1.25

CRAIK.—The Practical American Millwright and Miller.
By DAVID CRAIK, Millwright. Illustrated by numerous wood engravings, and two folding plates. 8vo. $5.00

DE GRAFF.—The Geometrical Stair Builders' Guide:
Being a Plain Practical System of Hand-Railing, embracing all its necessary Details, and Geometrically Illustrated by 22 Steel Engravings; together with the use of the most approved principles of Practical Geometry. By SIMON DE GRAFF, Architect. 4to. . $5.00

DE KONINCK.—DIETZ.—A Practical Manual of Chemical Analysis and Assaying:
As applied to the Manufacture of Iron from its Ores, and to Cast Iron, Wrought Iron, and Steel, as found in Commerce. By L. L. DE KONINCK, Dr. Sc., and E. DIETZ, Engineer. Edited with Notes, by ROBERT MALLET, F.R.S., F.S.G., M.I.C.E., etc. American Edition, Edited with Notes and an Appendix on Iron Ores, by A. A. FESQUET, Chemist and Engineer. One volume, 12mo. $2.50

DUNCAN.—Practical Surveyor's Guide:
Containing the necessary information to make any person, of common capacity, a finished land surveyor without the aid of a teacher. By ANDREW DUNCAN. Illustrated. 12mo., cloth. . . . $1.25

DUPLAIS.—A Treatise on the Manufacture and Distillation of Alcoholic Liquors:
Comprising Accurate and Complete Details in Regard to Alcohol from Wine, Molasses, Beets, Grain, Rice, Potatoes, Sorghum, Asphodel, Fruits, etc.; with the Distillation and Rectification of Brandy, Whiskey, Rum, Gin, Swiss Absinthe, etc., the Preparation of Aromatic Waters, Volatile Oils or Essences, Sugars, Syrups, Aromatic Tinctures, Liqueurs, Cordial Wines, Effervescing Wines, etc., the Aging of Brandy and the Improvement of Spirits, with Copious Directions and Tables for Testing and Reducing Spirituous Liquors, etc., etc. Translated and Edited from the French of MM. DUPLAIS, Ainé et Jeune. By M. McKENNIE, M.D. To which are added the United States Internal Revenue Regulations for the Assessment and Collection of Taxes on Distilled Spirits. Illustrated by fourteen folding plates and several wood engravings. 743 pp., 8vo. $10.00

DUSSAUCE.—A General Treatise on the Manufacture of Every Description of Soap:
Comprising the Chemistry of the Art, with Remarks on Alkalies, Saponifiable Fatty Bodies, the apparatus necessary in a Soap Factory, Practical Instructions in the manufacture of the various kinds of Soap, the assay of Soaps, etc., etc. Edited from Notes of Larmé, Fontenelle, Malapayre, Dufour, and others, with large and important additions by Prof. H. DUSSAUCE, Chemist. Illustrated. In one vol., 8vo. . $12.50

DUSSAUCE.—A General Treatise on the Manufacture of Vinegar:
Theoretical and Practical. Comprising the various Methods, by the Slow and the Quick Processes, with Alcohol, Wine, Grain, Malt, Cider, Molasses, and Beets; as well as the Fabrication of Wood Vinegar, etc., etc. By Prof. H. DUSSAUCE. In one volume, 8vo. . . $5.00

DUSSAUCE.—A New and Complete Treatise on the Arts of Tanning, Currying, and Leather Dressing:
Comprising all the Discoveries and Improvements made in France, Great Britain, and the United States. Edited from Notes and Documents of Messrs. Sallerou, Grouvelle, Duval, Dessables, Labarraque, Payen, René, De Fontenelle, Malapeyre, etc., etc. By Prof. H. DUSSAUCE, Chemist. Illustrated by 212 wood engravings. 8vo. $25.00

DUSSAUCE.—A Practical Guide for the Perfumer:
Being a New Treatise on Perfumery, the most favorable to the Beauty without being injurious to the Health, comprising a Description of the substances used in Perfumery, the Formulæ of more than 1000 Preparations, such as Cosmetics, Perfumed Oils, Tooth Powders, Waters, Extracts, Tinctures, Infusions, Spirits, Vinaigres, Essential Oils, Pastels, Creams, Soaps, and many new Hygienic Products not hitherto described. Edited from Notes and Documents of Messrs. Debay, Lunel, etc. With additions by Prof. H. DUSSAUCE, Chemist. 12mo.

DUSSAUCE.—Practical Treatise on the Fabrication of Matches, Gun Cotton, and Fulminating Powders.
By Prof. H. DUSSAUCE. 12mo. $3.00

Dyer and Color-maker's Companion:
Containing upwards of 200 Receipts for making Colors, on the most approved principles, for all the various styles and fabrics now in existence; with the Scouring Process, and plain Directions for Preparing, Washing-off, and Finishing the Goods. In one vol., 12mo. . $1.25

EASTON.—A Practical Treatise on Street or Horse-power Railways.
By ALEXANDER EASTON, C.E. Illustrated by 23 plates. 8vo., cloth. $3.00

ELDER.—Questions of the Day:
Economic and Social. By Dr. WILLIAM ELDER. 8vo. . $3.00

FAIRBAIRN.—The Principles of Mechanism and Machinery of Transmission:
Comprising the Principles of Mechanism, Wheels, and Pulleys, Strength and Proportions of Shafts, Coupling of Shafts, and Engaging and Disengaging Gear. By Sir WILLIAM FAIRBAIRN, C.E., LL.D., F.R.S., F.G.S. Beautifully illustrated by over 150 wood-cuts. In one volume, 12mo. $2.50

FORSYTH.—Book of Designs for Headstones, Mural, and other Monuments:
Containing 78 Designs. By JAMES FORSYTH. With an Introduction by CHARLES BOUTELL, M. A. 4to., cloth. $5.00

GIBSON.—The American Dyer:
A Practical Treatise on the Coloring of Wool, Cotton, Yarn and Cloth, in three parts. Part First gives a descriptive account of the Dye Stuffs; if of vegetable origin, where produced, how cultivated, and how prepared for use; if chemical, their composition, specific gravities, and general adaptability, how adulterated, and how to detect the adulterations, etc. Part Second is devoted to the Coloring of Wool, giving recipes for one hundred and twenty-nine different colors or shades, and is supplied with sixty colored samples of Wool. Part Third is devoted to the Coloring of Raw Cotton or Cotton Waste, for mixing with Wool Colors in the Manufacture of all kinds of Fabrics, gives recipes for thirty-eight different colors or shades, and is supplied with twenty-four colored samples of Cotton Waste. Also, recipes for Coloring Beavers, Doeskins, and Flannels, with remarks upon Anilines, giving recipes for fifteen different colors or shades, and nine samples of Aniline Colors that will stand both the Fulling and Scouring process. Also, recipes for Aniline Colors on Cotton Thread, and recipes for Common Colors on Cotton Yarns. Embracing in all over two hundred recipes for Colors and Shades, and ninety-four samples of Colored Wool and Cotton Waste, etc. By RICHARD H. GIBSON, Practical Dyer and Chemist. In one volume, 8vo. . . $6.00

GILBART.—History and Principles of Banking:
A Practical Treatise. By JAMES W. GILBART, late Manager of the London and Westminster Bank. With additions. In one volume, 8vo., 600 pages, sheep $5.00

Gothic Album for Cabinet Makers:
Comprising a Collection of Designs for Gothic Furniture. Illustrated by 23 large and beautifully engraved plates. Oblong . . $2.00

GRANT.—Beet-root Sugar and Cultivation of the Beet.
By E. B. GRANT. 12mo. $1.25

GREGORY.—Mathematics for Practical Men:
Adapted to the Pursuits of Surveyors, Architects, Mechanics, and Civil Engineers. By OLINTHUS GREGORY. 8vo., plates, cloth $3.00

GRISWOLD.—Railroad Engineer's Pocket Companion for the Field:
Comprising Rules for Calculating Deflection, Distances and Angles, Tangential Distances and Angles, and all Necessary Tables for Engineers; also the art of Levelling from Preliminary Survey to the Construction of Railroads, intended Expressly for the Young Engineer, together with Numerous Valuable Rules and Examples. By W. GRISWOLD. 12mo., tucks $1.75

GRUNER.—Studies of Blast Furnace Phenomena.
By M. L. GRUNER, President of the General Council of Mines of France, and lately Professor of Metallurgy at the Ecole des Mines. Translated, with the Author's sanction, with an Appendix, by L. D. B. Gordon, F. R. S. E., F. G. S. Illustrated. 8vo. . . . $2.50

GUETTIER.—Metallic Alloys:
Being a Practical Guide to their Chemical and Physical Properties, their Preparation, Composition, and Uses. Translated from the French of A. GUETTIER, Engineer and Director of Foundries, author of "La Fouderie en France," etc., etc. By A. A. FESQUET, Chemist and Engineer. In one volume, 12mo. $3.00

HARRIS.—Gas Superintendent's Pocket Companion.
By HARRIS & BROTHER, Gas Meter Manufacturers, 1115 and 1117 Cherry Street, Philadelphia. Full bound in pocket-book form $1.00

Hats and Felting:
A Practical Treatise on their Manufacture. By a Practical Hatter. Illustrated by Drawings of Machinery, etc. 8vo. . . . $1.25

HOFMANN.—A Practical Treatise on the Manufacture of Paper in all its Branches.
By CARL HOFMANN. Late Superintendent of paper mills in Germany and the United States; recently manager of the Public Ledger Paper Mills, near Elkton, Md. Illustrated by 110 wood engravings, and five large folding plates. In one volume, 4to., cloth; 398 pages $15.00

HUGHES.—American Miller and Millwright's Assistant.
By WM. CARTER HUGHES. A new edition. In one vol., 12mo. $1.50

HURST.—A Hand-Book for Architectural Surveyors and others engaged in Building:
Containing Formulæ useful in Designing Builder's work, Table of Weights, of the materials used in Building, Memoranda connected with Builders' work, Mensuration, the Practice of Builders' Measurement, Contracts of Labor, Valuation of Property, Summary of the Practice in Dilapidation, etc., etc. By J. F. HURST, C. E. Second edition, pocket-book form, full bound $2.00

JERVIS.—Railway Property:
A Treatise on the Construction and Management of Railways; designed to afford useful knowledge, in the popular style, to the holders of this class of property; as well as Railway Managers, Officers, and Agents. By JOHN B. JERVIS, late Chief Engineer of the Hudson River Railroad, Croton Aqueduct, etc. In one vol., 12mo., cloth $2.00

JOHNSTON.—Instructions for the Analysis of Soils, Limestones, and Manures.
By J. F. W. JOHNSTON. 12mo. . . . . .

KEENE.—A Hand-Book of Practical Gauging:
For the Use of Beginners, to which is added, A Chapter on Distillation, describing the process in operation at the Custom House for ascertaining the strength of wines. By JAMES B. KEENE, of H. M. Customs. 8vo. $1.25

KELLEY.—Speeches, Addresses, and Letters on Industrial and Financial Questions.
By Hon. WILLIAM D. KELLEY, M. C. In one volume, 544 pages, 8vo. $3.00

KENTISH.—A Treatise on a Box of Instruments,
And the Slide Rule; with the Theory of Trigonometry and Logarithms, including Practical Geometry, Surveying, Measuring of Timber, Cask and Malt Gauging, Heights, and Distances. By THOMAS KENTISH. In one volume. 12mo. $1.25

KOBELL.—ERNI.—Mineralogy Simplified:
A short Method of Determining and Classifying Minerals, by means of simple Chemical Experiments in the Wet Way. Translated from the last German Edition of F. VON KOBELL, with an Introduction to Blow-pipe Analysis and other additions. By HENRI ERNI, M. D., late Chief Chemist, Department of Agriculture, author of "Coal Oil and Petroleum." In one volume, 12mo. $2.50

LANDRIN.—A Treatise on Steel:
Comprising its Theory, Metallurgy, Properties, Practical Working, and Use. By M. H. C. LANDRIN, Jr., Civil Engineer. Translated from the French, with Notes, by A. A. FESQUET, Chemist and Engineer. With an Appendix on the Bessemer and the Martin Processes for Manufacturing Steel, from the Report of Abram S. Hewitt, United States Commissioner to the Universal Exposition, Paris, 1867. In one volume, 12mo. $3.00

LARKIN.—The Practical Brass and Iron Founder's Guide:
A Concise Treatise on Brass Founding, Moulding, the Metals and their Alloys, etc.: to which are added Recent Improvements in the Manufacture of Iron, Steel by the Bessemer Process, etc., etc. By JAMES LARKIN, late Conductor of the Brass Foundry Department in Reany, Neafie & Co's. Penn Works, Philadelphia. Fifth edition, revised, with Extensive additions. In one volume, 12mo. . . $2.25

LEAVITT.—Facts about Peat as an Article of Fuel:
With Remarks upon its Origin and Composition, the Localities in which it is found, the Methods of Preparation and Manufacture, and the various Uses to which it is applicable; together with many other matters of Practical and Scientific Interest. To which is added a chapter on the Utilization of Coal Dust with Peat for the Production of an Excellent Fuel at Moderate Cost, specially adapted for Steam Service. By T. H. LEAVITT. Third edition. 12mo. . . . $1.75

LEROUX, C.—A Practical Treatise on the Manufacture of Worsteds and Carded Yarns:
Comprising Practical Mechanics, with Rules and Calculations applied to Spinning; Sorting, Cleaning, and Scouring Wools; the English and French methods of Combing, Drawing, and Spinning Worsteds and Manufacturing Carded Yarns. Translated from the French of CHARLES LEROUX, Mechanical Engineer, and Superintendent of a Spinning Mill, by HORATIO PAINE, M. D., and A. A. PESQUET, Chemist and Engineer. Illustrated by 12 large Plates. To which is added an Appendix, containing extracts from the Reports of the International Jury, and of the Artisans selected by the Committee appointed by the Council of the Society of Arts, London, on Woollen and Worsted Machinery and Fabrics, as exhibited in the Paris Universal Exposition, 1867. 8vo., cloth. $5.00

LESLIE (Miss).—Complete Cookery:
Directions for Cookery in its Various Branches. By MISS LESLIE. 60th thousand. Thoroughly revised, with the addition of New Receipts. In one volume, 12mo., cloth. $1.50

LESLIE (Miss).—Ladies' House Book:
A Manual of Domestic Economy. 20th revised edition. 12mo., cloth.

LESLIE (Miss).—Two Hundred Receipts in French Cookery.
Cloth, 12mo.

LIEBER.—Assayer's Guide:
Or, Practical Directions to Assayers, Miners, and Smelters, for the Tests and Assays, by Heat and by Wet Processes, for the Ores of all the principal Metals, of Gold and Silver Coins and Alloys, and of Coal, etc. By OSCAR M. LIEBER. 12mo., cloth. . . $1.25

LOTH.—The Practical Stair Builder:
A Complete Treatise on the Art of Building Stairs and Hand-Rails, Designed for Carpenters, Builders, and Stair-Builders. Illustrated with Thirty Original Plates. By C. EDWARD LOTH, Professional Stair-Builder. One large 4to. volume. $10.00

LOVE.—The Art of Dyeing, Cleaning, Scouring, and Finishing, on the Most Approved English and French Methods:
Being Practical Instructions in Dyeing Silks, Woollens, and Cottons, Feathers, Chips, Straw, etc. Scouring and Cleaning Bed and Window Curtains, Carpets, Rugs, etc. French and English Cleaning, any Color or Fabric of Silk, Satin, or Damask. By THOMAS LOVE, a Working Dyer and Scourer. Second American Edition, to which are added General Instructions for the Use of Aniline Colors. In one volume, 8vo., 343 pages. $5.00

MAIN and BROWN.—Questions on Subjects Connected with the Marine Steam-Engine:
And Examination Papers; with Hints for their Solution. By THOMAS J. MAIN, Professor of Mathematics, Royal Naval College, and THOMAS BROWN, Chief Engineer, R. N. 12mo., cloth. . . . $1.50

MAIN and BROWN.—The Indicator and Dynamometer:
With their Practical Applications to the Steam-Engine. By THOMAS J. MAIN, M. A. F. R., Assistant Professor Royal Naval College, Portsmouth, and THOMAS BROWN, Assoc. Inst. C. E., Chief Engineer, R. N., attached to the Royal Naval College. Illustrated. From the Fourth London Edition. 8vo. $1.50

MAIN and BROWN.—The Marine Steam-Engine.
By THOMAS J. MAIN, F. R.; Assistant S. Mathematical Professor at the Royal Naval College, Portsmouth, and THOMAS BROWN, Assoc. Inst. C. E., Chief Engineer R. N. Attached to the Royal Naval College. Authors of "Questions connected with the Marine Steam-Engine," and the "Indicator and Dynamometer." With numerous Illustrations. In one volume, 8vo. $5.00

MARTIN.—Screw-Cutting Tables, for the Use of Mechanical Engineers:
Showing the Proper Arrangement of Wheels for Cutting the Threads of Screws of any required Pitch; with a Table for Making the Universal Gas-Pipe Thread and Taps. By W. A. MARTIN, Engineer. 8vo. 50

Mechanics' (Amateur) Workshop:
A treatise containing plain and concise directions for the manipulation of Wood and Metals, including Casting, Forging, Brazing, Soldering, and Carpentry. By the author of the "Lathe and its Uses." Third edition. Illustrated. 8vo. $3.00

MOLESWORTH.—Pocket-Book of Useful Formulæ and Memoranda for Civil and Mechanical Engineers.
By GUILFORD L. MOLESWORTH, Member of the Institution of Civil Engineers, Chief Resident Engineer of the Ceylon Railway. Second American, from the Tenth London Edition. In one volume, full bound in pocket-book form. $2.00

NAPIER.—A System of Chemistry Applied to Dyeing.
By JAMES NAPIER, F. C. S. A New and Thoroughly Revised Edition. Completely brought up to the present state of the Science, including the Chemistry of Coal Tar Colors, by A. A. FESQUET, Chemist and Engineer. With an Appendix on Dyeing and Calico Printing, as shown at the Universal Exposition, Paris, 1867. Illustrated. In one volume, 8vo., 422 pages. $5.00

NAPIER.—Manual of Electro-Metallurgy:
Including the Application of the Art to Manufacturing Processes. By JAMES NAPIER. Fourth American, from the Fourth London edition, revised and enlarged. Illustrated by engravings. In one vol., 8vo. $2.00

NASON.—Table of Reactions for Qualitative Chemical Analysis.
By HENRY B. NASON, Professor of Chemistry in the Rensselaer Polytechnic Institute, Troy, New York. Illustrated by Colors. . 63

NEWBERY.—Gleanings from Ornamental Art of every style:
Drawn from Examples in the British, South Kensington, Indian, Crystal Palace, and other Museums, the Exhibitions of 1851 and 1862, and the best English and Foreign works. In a series of one hundred exquisitely drawn Plates, containing many hundred examples. By ROBERT NEWBERY. 4to. $12.50

NICHOLSON.—A Manual of the Art of Bookbinding:
Containing full instructions in the different Branches of Forwarding, Gilding, and Finishing. Also, the Art of Marbling Book-edges and Paper. By JAMES B. NICHOLSON. Illustrated. 12mo., cloth. $2.25

NICHOLSON.—The Carpenter's New Guide:
A Complete Book of Lines for Carpenters and Joiners. By PETER NICHOLSON. The whole carefully and thoroughly revised by H. K. DAVIS, and containing numerous new and improved and original Designs for Roofs, Domes, etc. By SAMUEL SLOAN, Architect. Illustrated by 80 plates. 4to. . . . .

NORRIS.—A Hand-book for Locomotive Engineers and Machinists:
Comprising the Proportions and Calculations for Constructing Locomotives; Manner of Setting Valves; Tables of Squares, Cubes, Areas, etc., etc. By SEPTIMUS NORRIS, Civil and Mechanical Engineer. New edition. Illustrated. 12mo, c oth. $1.50

NYSTROM.—On Technological Education, and the Construction of Ships and Screw Propellers:
For Naval and Marine Engineers. By JOHN W. NYSTROM, late Acting Chief Engineer, U. S. N. Second edition, revised with additional matter. Illustrated by seven engravings. 12mo. . . $1.50

O'NEILL.—A Dictionary of Dyeing and Calico Printing:
Containing a brief account of all the Substances and Processes in use in the Art of Dyeing and Printing Textile Fabrics; with Practical Receipts and Scientific Information. By CHARLES O'NEILL, Analytical Chemist; Fellow of the Chemical Society of London; Member of the Literary and Philosophical Society of Manchester; Author of "Chemistry of Calico Printing and Dyeing." To which is added an Essay on Coal Tar Colors and their application to Dyeing and Calico Printing. By A. A. FESQUET, Chemist and Engineer. With an Appendix on Dyeing and Calico Printing, as shown at the Universal Exposition, Paris, 1867. In one volume, 8vo., 491 pages. . $5.00

ORTON.—Underground Treasures:
How and Where to Find Them. A Key for the Ready Determination of all the Useful Minerals within the United States. By JAMES ORTON, A. M. Illustrated, 12mo. $1.50

OSBORN.—American Mines and Mining:
Theoretically and Practically Considered. By Prof. H. S. OSBORN. Illustrated by numerous engravings. 8vo. (*In preparation.*)

OSBORN.—The Metallurgy of Iron and Steel:
Theoretical and Practical in all its Branches; with special reference to American Materials and Processes. By H. S. OSBORN, LL. D., Professor of Mining and Metallurgy in Lafayette College, Easton, Pennsylvania. Illustrated by numerous large folding plates and wood-engravings. 8vo. $15.00

OVERMAN.—The Manufacture of Steel:
Containing the Practice and Principles of Working and Making Steel. A Handbook for Blacksmiths and Workers in Steel and Iron, Wagon Makers, Die Sinkers, Cutlers, and Manufacturers of Files and Hardware, of Steel and Iron, and for Men of Science and Art. By FREDERICK OVERMAN, Mining Engineer, Author of the "Manufacture of Iron," etc. A new, enlarged, and revised Edition. By A. A. FESQUET, Chemist and Engineer. $1.50

OVERMAN.—The Moulder and Founder's Pocket Guide:
A Treatise on Moulding and Founding in Green-sand, Dry-sand, Loam, and Cement; the Moulding of Machine Frames, Mill-gear, Hollow-ware, Ornaments, Trinkets, Bells, and Statues; Description of Moulds for Iron, Bronze, Brass, and other Metals; Plaster of Paris, Sulphur, Wax, and other articles commonly used in Casting; the Construction of Melting Furnaces, the Melting and Founding of Metals; the Composition of Alloys and their Nature. With an Appendix containing Receipts for Alloys, Bronze, Varnishes and Colors for Castings; also, Tables on the Strength and other qualities of Cast Metals. By FREDERICK OVERMAN, Mining Engineer, Author of "The Manufacture of Iron." With 42 Illustrations. 12mo. $1.50

Painter, Gilder, and Varnisher's Companion:
Containing Rules and Regulations in everything relating to the Arts of Painting, Gilding, Varnishing, Glass-Staining, Graining, Marbling, Sign-Writing, Gilding on Glass, and Coach Painting and Varnishing; Tests for the Detection of Adulterations in Oils, Colors, etc.; and a Statement of the Diseases to which Painters are peculiarly liable, with the Simplest and Best Remedies. Sixteenth Edition. Revised, with an Appendix. Containing Colors and Coloring – Theoretical and Practical. Comprising descriptions of a great variety of Additional Pigments, their Qualities and Uses, to which are added, Dryers, and Modes and Operations of Painting, etc. Together with Chevreul's Principles of Harmony and Contrast of Colors. 12mo., cloth. $1.50

PALLETT.—The Miller's, Millwright's, and Engineer's Guide.
By HENRY PALLETT. Illustrated. In one volume, 12mo. $3.00

PERCY.—The Manufacture of Russian Sheet-Iron.
By JOHN PERCY, M.D., F.R.S., Lecturer on Metallurgy at the Royal School of Mines, and to The Advanced Class of Artillery Officers at the Royal Artillery Institution, Woolwich; Author of "Metallurgy." With Illustrations. 8vo., paper. . . . . . . 50 cts.

PERKINS.—Gas and Ventilation.
Practical Treatise on Gas and Ventilation. With Special Relation to Illuminating, Heating, and Cooking by Gas. Including Scientific Helps to Engineer-students and others. With Illustrated Diagrams. By E. E. PERKINS. 12mo., cloth. $1.25

PERKINS and STOWE.—A New Guide to the Sheet-iron and Boiler Plate Roller:
Containing a Series of Tables showing the Weight of Slabs and Piles to produce Boiler Plates, and of the Weight of Piles and the Sizes of Bars to produce Sheet-iron; the Thickness of the Bar Gauge in decimals; the Weight per foot, and the Thickness on the Bar or Wire Gauge of the fractional parts of an inch; the Weight per sheet, and the Thickness on the Wire Gauge of Sheet-iron of various dimensions to weigh 112 lbs. per bundle; and the conversion of Short Weight into Long Weight, and Long Weight into Short. Estimated and collected by G. H. PERKINS and J. G. STOWE. $2.50

PHILLIPS and DARLINGTON.—Records of Mining and Metallurgy;
Or Facts and Memoranda for the use of the Mine Agent and Smelter. By J. ARTHUR PHILLIPS, Mining Engineer, Graduate of the Imperial School of Mines, France, etc., and JOHN DARLINGTON. Illustrated by numerous engravings. In one volume, 12mo. . . $1.50

PROTEAUX.—Practical Guide for the Manufacture of Paper and Boards.
By A. PROTEAUX, Civil Engineer, and Graduate of the School of Arts and Manufactures, and Director of Thiers' Paper Mill, Puy-de-Dôme. With additions, by L. S. LE NORMAND. Translated from the French, with Notes, by HORATIO PAINE, A. B., M. D. To which is added a Chapter on the Manufacture of Paper from Wood in the United States, by HENRY T. BROWN, of the "American Artisan." Illustrated by six plates, containing Drawings of Raw Materials, Machinery, Plans of Paper-Mills, etc., etc. 8vo. $10.00

REGNAULT.—Elements of Chemistry.
By M. V. REGNAULT. Translated from the French by T. FORREST BETTON, M. D., and edited, with Notes, by JAMES C. BOOTH, Melter and Refiner U. S. Mint, and WM. L. FABER, Metallurgist and Mining Engineer. Illustrated by nearly 700 wood engravings. Comprising nearly 1500 pages. In two volumes, 8vo., cloth. . . . $7.50

REID.—A Practical Treatise on the Manufacture of Portland Cement:
By HENRY REID, C. E. To which is added a Translation of M. A. Lipowitz's Work, describing a New Method adopted in Germany for Manufacturing that Cement, by W. F. REID. Illustrated by plates and wood engravings. 8vo. $5.00

RIFFAULT, VERGNAUD, and TOUSSAINT.—A Practical Treatise on the Manufacture of Varnishes.
By MM. RIFFAULT, VERGNAUD, and TOUSSAINT. Revised and Edited by M. F. MALEPEYRE and Dr. EMIL WINCKLER. Illustrated. In one volume, 8vo. (*In preparation.*)

RIFFAULT, VERGNAUD, and TOUSSAINT.—A Practical Treatise on the Manufacture of Colors for Painting:
Containing the best Formulæ and the Processes the Newest and in most General Use. By MM. RIFFAULT, VERGNAUD, and TOUSSAINT. Revised and Edited by M. F. MALEPEYRE and Dr. EMIL WINCKLER. Translated from the French by A. A. FESQUET, Chemist and Engineer. Illustrated by Engravings. In one volume, 650 pages, 8vo. $7.50

ROBINSON.—Explosions of Steam Boilers:
How they are Caused, and how they may be Prevented. By J. R. ROBINSON, Steam Engineer. 12mo. $1.25

ROPER.—A Catechism of High Pressure or Non-Condensing Steam-Engines:
Including the Modelling, Constructing, Running, and Management of Steam Engines and Steam Boilers. With Illustrations. By STEPHEN ROPER, Engineer. Full bound tucks . . . $2.00

ROSELEUR.—Galvanoplastic Manipulations:
A Practical Guide for the Gold and Silver Electro-plater and the Galvanoplastic Operator. Translated from the French of ALFRED ROSELEUR, Chemist, Professor of the Galvanoplastic Art, Manufacturer of Chemicals, Gold and Silver Electro-plater. By A. A. FESQUET, Chemist and Engineer. Illustrated by over 127 Engravings on wood. 8vo., 495 pages. $6.00

☞ *This Treatise is the fullest and by far the best on this subject ever published in the United States.*

SCHINZ.—Researches on the Action of the Blast Furnace.
By CHARLES SCHINZ. Translated from the German with the special permission of the Author by WILLIAM H. MAW and MORITZ MULLER. With an Appendix written by the Author expressly for this edition. Illustrated by seven plates, containing 28 figures. In one volume, 12mo. $4.00

SHAW.—Civil Architecture:
Being a Complete Theoretical and Practical System of Building, containing the Fundamental Principles of the Art. By EDWARD SHAW, Architect. To which is added a Treatise on Gothic Architecture, etc. By THOMAS W. SILLOWAY and GEORGE M. HARDING, Architects. The whole illustrated by One Hundred and Two quarto plates finely engraved on copper. Eleventh Edition. 4to., cloth. . $10.00

SHUNK.—A Practical Treatise on Railway Curves and Location, for Young Engineers.
By WILLIAM F. SHUNK, Civil Engineer. 12mo. . . $2.00

SLOAN.—American Houses:
A variety of Original Designs for Rural Buildings. Illustrated by 26 colored Engravings, with Descriptive References. By SAMUEL SLOAN, Architect, author of the "Model Architect," etc., etc. 8vo. $1.50

SMEATON.—Builder's Pocket Companion:
Containing the Elements of Building, Surveying, and Architecture; with Practical Rules and Instructions connected with the subject. By A. C. SMEATON, Civil Engineer, etc. In one volume, 12mo. $1.50

SMITH.—A Manual of Political Economy.
By E. PESHINE SMITH. A new Edition, to which is added a full Index. 12mo., cloth. $1.25

SMITH.—Parks and Pleasure Grounds:
Or Practical Notes on Country Residences, Villas, Public Parks, and Gardens. By CHARLES H. J. SMITH, Landscape Gardener and Garden Architect, etc., etc. 12mo. $2.25

SMITH.—The Dyer's Instructor:
Comprising Practical Instructions in the Art of Dyeing Silk, Cotton, Wool, and Worsted, and Woollen Goods: containing nearly 800 Receipts. To which is added a Treatise on the Art of Padding; and the Printing of Silk Warps, Skeins, and Handkerchiefs, and the various Mordants and Colors for the different styles of such work. By DAVID SMITH, Pattern Dyer. 12mo., cloth. . . . $3.00

SMITH.—The Dyer's Instructor:
Comprising Practical Instructions in the Art of Dyeing Silk, Cotton, Wool, and Worsted and Woollen Goods. Third Edition, with many additional Receipts for Dyeing the New Alkaline Blues and Night Greens, *with Dyed Patterns affixed*. 12mo., pp. 394, cloth. . $10.50

STEWART,—The American System.
Speeches on the Tariff Question, and on Internal Improvements, principally delivered in the House of Representatives of the United States. By ANDREW STEWART, late M. C. from Pennsylvania. With a Portrait, and a Biographical Sketch. In one volume, 8vo., 407 pages. $3.00

STOKES.—Cabinet-maker's and Upholsterer's Companion:
Comprising the Rudiments and Principles of Cabinet-making and Upholstery, with Familiar Instructions, illustrated by Examples for attaining a Proficiency in the Art of Drawing, as applicable to Cabinet-work; the Processes of Veneering, Inlaying, and Buhl-work; the Art of Dyeing and Staining Wood, Bone, Tortoise Shell, etc. Directions for Lackering, Japanning, and Varnishing; to make French Polish; to prepare the Best Glues, Cements, and Compositions, and a number of Receipts particularly useful for workmen generally. By J. STOKES. In one volume, 12mo. With Illustrations. . $1.25

Strength and other Properties of Metals:
Reports of Experiments on the Strength and other Properties of Metals for Cannon. With a Description of the Machines for testing Metals, and of the Classification of Cannon in service. By Officers of the Ordnance Department U. S. Army. By authority of the Secretary of War. Illustrated by 25 large steel plates. In one volume, 4to. . $10.00

SULLIVAN.—Protection to Native Industry.
By Sir EDWARD SULLIVAN, Baronet, author of "Ten Chapters on Social Reforms." In one volume, 8vo. $1.50

Tables Showing the Weight of Round, Square, and Flat Bar Iron, Steel, etc.,
By Measurement. Cloth. 63

TAYLOR.—Statistics of Coal:
Including Mineral Bituminous Substances employed in Arts and Manufactures; with their Geographical, Geological, and Commercial Distribution and Amount of Production and Consumption on the American Continent. With Incidental Statistics of the Iron Manufacture. By R. C. TAYLOR. Second edition, revised by S. S. HALDEMAN. Illustrated by five Maps and many wood engravings. 8vo., cloth. $10.00

TEMPLETON.—The Practical Examinator on Steam and the Steam-Engine:
With Instructive References relative thereto, arranged for the Use of Engineers, Students, and others. By WM. TEMPLETON, Engineer. 12mo. $1.25

THOMAS.—The Modern Practice of Photography.
By R. W. THOMAS, F. C. S. 8vo., cloth. 75

THOMSON.—Freight Charges Calculator.
By ANDREW THOMSON, Freight Agent. 24mo. . . . $1.25

TURNING: Specimens of Fancy Turning Executed on the Hand or Foot Lathe:
With Geometric, Oval, and Eccentric Chucks, and Elliptical Cutting Frame. By an Amateur. Illustrated by 30 exquisite Photographs. 4to. $3.00

Turner's (The) Companion:
Containing Instructions in Concentric, Elliptic, and Eccentric Turning: also various Plates of Chucks, Tools, and Instruments; and Directions for using the Eccentric Cutter, Drill, Vertical Cutter, and Circular Rest; with Patterns and Instructions for working them. A new edition in one volume, 12mo. $1.50

URBIN.—BRULL.—A Practical Guide for Puddling Iron and Steel.
By ED. URBIN, Engineer of Arts and Manufactures. A Prize Essay read before the Association of Engineers, Graduate of the School of Mines, of Liege, Belgium, at the Meeting of 1865-6. To which is added A COMPARISON OF THE RESISTING PROPERTIES OF IRON AND STEEL. By A. BRULL. Translated from the French by A. A. FESQUET, Chemist and Engineer. In one volume, 8vo. $1.00

VAILE.—Galvanized Iron Cornice-Worker's Manual:
Containing Instructions in Laying out the Different Mitres, and Making Patterns for all kinds of Plain and Circular Work. Also, Tables of Weights, Areas and Circumferences of Circles, and other Matter calculated to Benefit the Trade. By CHARLES A. VAILE, Superintendent "Richmond Cornice Works," Richmond, Indiana. Illustrated by 21 Plates. In one volume, 4to. $5.00

VILLE.—The School of Chemical Manures:
Or, Elementary Principles in the Use of Fertilizing Agents. From the French of M. GEORGE VILLE, by A. A. FESQUET, Chemist and Engineer. With Illustrations. In one volume, 12 mo. . . $1.25

VOGDES.—The Architect's and Builder's Pocket Companion and Price Book:
Consisting of a Short but Comprehensive Epitome of Decimals, Duodecimals, Geometry and Mensuration; with Tables of U. S. Measures, Sizes, Weights, Strengths, etc., of Iron, Wood, Stone, and various other Materials, Quantities of Materials in Given Sizes, and Dimensions of Wood, Brick, and Stone; and a full and complete Bill of Prices for Carpenter's Work; also, Rules for Computing and Valuing Brick and Brick Work, Stone Work, Painting, Plastering, etc. By FRANK W. VOGDES, Architect. Illustrated. Full bound in pocketbook form. $2.00
Bound in cloth. 1.50

WARN.—The Sheet-Metal Worker's Instructor:
For Zinc, Sheet-Iron, Copper, and Tin-Plate Workers, etc. Containing a selection of Geometrical Problems; also, Practical and Simple Rules for describing the various Patterns required in the different branches of the above Trades. By REUBEN H. WARN, Practical Tinplate Worker. To which is added an Appendix, containing Instructions for Boiler Making, Mensuration of Surfaces and Solids, Rules for Calculating the Weights of different Figures of Iron and Steel, Tables of the Weights of Iron, Steel, etc. Illustrated by 32 Plates and 37 Wood Engravings. 8vo. $3.00

WATSON.—A Manual of the Hand-Lathe:
Comprising Concise Directions for working Metals of all kinds, Ivory, Bone and Precious Woods; Dyeing, Coloring, and French Polishing; Inlaying by Veneers, and various methods practised to produce Elaborate work with Dispatch, and at Small Expense. By EGBERT P. WATSON, late of "The Scientific American," Author of "The Modern Practice of American Machinists and Engineers." Illustrated by 78 Engravings. $1.50

WATSON.—The Modern Practice of American Machinists and Engineers:
Including the Construction, Application, and Use of Drills; Lathe Tools, Cutters for Boring Cylinders, and Hollow Work Generally, with the most Economical Speed for the same; the Results verified by Actual Practice at the Lathe, the Vice, and on the Floor. Together with Workshop Management, Economy of Manufacture, the Steam-Engine, Boilers, Gears, Belting, etc., etc. By EGBERT P. WATSON, late of the "Scientific American." Illustrated by 86 Engravings. In one volume, 12mo. $2.50

WATSON.—The Theory and Practice of the Art of Weaving by Hand and Power:
With Calculations and Tables for the use of those connected with the Trade. By JOHN WATSON, Manufacturer and Practical Machine Maker. Illustrated by large Drawings of the best Power Looms. 8vo. $7.50

WEATHERLY.—Treatise on the Art of Boiling Sugar, Crystallizing, Lozenge-making, Comfits, Gum Goods.
12mo. $2.00

WILL.—Tables for Qualitative Chemical Analysis.
By Professor HEINRICH WILL, of Giessen, Germany. Seventh edition. Translated by CHARLES F. HIMES, Ph. D., Professor of Natural Science, Dickinson College, Carlisle, Pa. . . . $1.50

WILLIAMS.—On Heat and Steam:
Embracing New Views of Vaporization, Condensation, and Explosions. By CHARLES WYE WILLIAMS, A. I. C. E. Illustrated. 8vo. $3.50

WOHLER.—A Hand-Book of Mineral Analysis.
By F. WOHLER, Professor of Chemistry in the University of Göttingen. Edited by HENRY B. NASON, Professor of Chemistry in the Rensselaer Polytechnic Institute, Troy, New York. Illustrated. In one volume, 12mo. $3 00

WORSSAM.—On Mechanical Saws:
From the Transactions of the Society of Engineers, 1869. By S. W. WORSSAM, Jr. Illustrated by 18 large plates. 8vo. . . $5.00

RECENT ADDITIONS TO OUR LIST.

AUERBACH.—Anthracen: Its Constitution, Properties, Manufacture, and Derivatives, including Artificial Alizarin, Anthrapurpurin, with their applications in Dyeing and Printing.
By G. AUERBACH. Translated and edited by WM. CROOKES, F. R. S. 8vo. $5.00

BECKETT.—Treatise on Clocks, Watches and Bells.
By SIR EDMUND BECKETT, Bart. Illustrated. 12mo. . $1.75

BARLOW.—The History and Principles of Weaving, by Hand and by Power.
Several Hundred Illustrations. 8vo. $10.00

BOURNE.—Recent Improvements in the Steam Engine.
By JOHN BOURNE, C. E. Illustrated. 16mo. . . . $1.50

CLARK.—Fuel: Its Combustion and Economy.
By D. KINNEAR CLARK, C. E. 144 Engravings. 12mo. . $2.25

CRISTIANI.—Perfumery and Kindred Arts.
By R. S. CRISTIANI. 8vo. $5.00

COLLENS.—The Eden of Labor, or the Christian Utopia.
12mo. Paper, $1.00; Cloth, ... $1.25

CUPPER.—The Universal Stair Builder.
Illustrated by 29 plates. 4to. $5.00

COOLEY.—A Complete Practical Treatise on Perfumery.
By A. J. COOLEY. 12mo. $1.50

DAVIDSON.—A Practical Manual of House Painting, Graining, Marbling and Sign Writing:
With 9 Colored Illustrations of Woods and Marbles, and many Wood Engravings. 12mo. $3.00

EDWARDS.—A Catechism of the Marine Steam Engine.
By EMORY EDWARDS. Illustrated. 12mo. . . . $2.00

HASERICK.—The Secrets of the Art of Dyeing Wool, Cotton, and Linen:
Including Bleaching and Coloring Wool and Cotton Hosiery and Random Yarns. By E. C. HASERICK. Illustrated by 323 Dyed Patterns of the Yarns or Fabrics. 8vo. $25.00

HENRY.—The Early and Later History of Petroleum.
By J. T. HENRY. Illustrated. 8vo. $4.50

KELLOGG.—A New Monetary System.
By Ed. Kellogg. Fifth Edition. Edited by Mary Kellogg Putnam. 12mo. Paper, $1.00; Cloth, ... $1.50

KEMLO.—Watch Repairer's Hand-Book.
Illustrated. 12mo. $1.25

MORRIS.—Easy Rules for the Measurement of Earthworks by means of the Prismoidal Formula.
By Elwood Morris, C. E. 8vo. $1.50

McCULLOCH.—Distillation, Brewing and Malting.
By J. C. McCulloch. 12mo. $1.00

NEVILLE.—Hydraulic Tables, Co-Efficients, and Formulæ for Finding the Discharge of Water from Orifices, Notches, Weirs, Pipes, and Rivers.
Illustrated. 12mo. $5.00

NICOLLS.—The Railway Builder.
A Hand-book for Estimating the Probable Cost of American Railway Construction and Equipment. By Wm. J. Nicolls, C. E. Pocket-book Form. $2.00

NORMANDY.—The Commercial Hand-book of Chemical Analysis.
By H. M. Noad, Ph. D. 12mo. $5.00

PROCTOR.—A Pocket-Book of Useful Tables and Formulæ for Marine Engineers.
By Frank Proctor. Pocket-book Form. . . . $2.00

ROSE.—The Complete Practical Machinist:
Embracing Lathe Work, Vise Work, Drills and Drilling, Taps and Dies, Hardening and Tempering, the Making and Use of Tools, etc., etc. By Joshua Rose. 130 Illustrations. 12mo. . . $2.50

SLOAN.—Homestead Architecture.
By Samuel Sloan, Architect. 200 Engravings. 8vo. . $3.50

SYME.—Outlines of an Industrial Science.
By David Syme. 12mo. $2.00

WARE.—The Coachmaker's Illustrated Hand-Book.
Fully Illustrated. 8vo. $3.00

WIGHTWICK.—Hints to Young Architects.
Numerous Wood Cuts. 12mo. $2.00

WILSON.—First Principles of Political Economy.
12mo. $1.50

WILSON.—A Treatise on Steam Boilers, their Strength, Construction, and Economical Working.
By Robt. Wilson. Illustrated. 12mo. . . . $2.50

Lightning Source UK Ltd.
Milton Keynes UK
UKHW010011050119
334962UK00003B/43/P